THE GREATEST MEDAL OF HONOR
STORIES EVER TOLD

THE GREATEST MEDAL OF HONOR STORIES EVER TOLD

EDITED BY TOM MCCARTHY

Guilford, Connecticut

An imprint of The Rowman & Littlefield Publishing Group, Inc.
4501 Forbes Blvd., Ste. 200
Lanham, MD 20706
www.rowman.com

Distributed by NATIONAL BOOK NETWORK

British Library Cataloguing in Publication Information available

Library of Congress Cataloging-in-Publication Data available

ISBN 978-1-4930-3172-6 (paperback)
ISBN 978-1-4930-3173-3 (e-book)

∞™ The paper used in this publication meets the minimum requirements of American National Standard for Information Sciences—Permanence of Paper for Printed Library Materials, ANSI/NISO Z39.48-1992.

Printed in the United States of America

CONTENTS

Introduction vi

CHAPTER 1.   The Ridge: Michael Murphy. 1
CHAPTER 2.   San Juan Hill: Teddy Roosevelt 29
CHAPTER 3.   Single-Handed: Tibor "Teddy" Rubin. 77
CHAPTER 4.   The Siege of Fort Wagner: William Harvey Carney. . 93
CHAPTER 5.   Above and Beyond: Frank Luke Jr. 113
CHAPTER 6.   Lasting Valor: Vernon J. Baker. 131
CHAPTER 7.   Taking Suribachi: Marines on Iwo Jima. 155
CHAPTER 8.   Mustering the Dead: Clinton Romesha 177
CHAPTER 9.   The Warrior: Roy P. Benavidez 195
CHAPTER 10. "I Could Hardly Stand Up": Dr. Mary E. Walker . .207
CHAPTER 11. Taking Prisoners: Alvin York 219
CHAPTER 12. Stealing the Train: The First Ever Medals 235

Sources 262

INTRODUCTION

THE MEDAL OF HONOR WINNERS YOU WILL MEET IN THESE PAGES DEFY any attempt to neatly categorize them, to tag them as heroes and leave it at that. Make no mistake, they are heroes. But the things they did go far beyond that. Their actions are, first and foremost, stunning—almost incomprehensible, their heroics exceeded by far more common acts of bravery that today deservedly grab headlines and national attention.

That is the essence of winning a Congressional Medal of Honor.

These medal winners were not blessed with an ethereal gift that somehow rendered them fearless. To the contrary, they were as petrified as anyone else would be. Who wouldn't be afraid when outnumbered, outgunned, and alone? Who wouldn't tremble when a simple mistake will cost not only your life but the lives of many others?

These heroes did not simply confront certain death. They got up in its face, smelled its heat, and challenged it to take them. One common trait that everyone in this collection had was an almost casual indifference to personal suffering. They each had responsibilities that trumped their almost certain demise, but they moved ahead nonetheless. Observe the actions of these Medal of Honor winners and you will see that first in their minds was the well-being of their fellows. They were willing to die to save lives. They each wanted to help more than they cared about living.

In all the wars since the first medal was presented in 1861, there have been just a few more than 3,500 acts deemed worthy of this, the most prestigious medal the United States presents to its soldiers—and half that number of medals were bestowed during the Civil War. The winners of a Congressional Medal of Honor are in a rare and stratospheric atmosphere, as well they should be. Most Medal of Honor winners received theirs posthumously—a darkly simple way to gauge what it took to get one. The actions of these extraordinary heroes were, as Abraham Lincoln noted, "the last full measure of devotion."

Take, for example, Michael Murphy, whose story you will read here. A Navy SEAL, Michael Murphy saved his men trapped under heavy and unrelenting Taliban fire on a lonely Afghan mountainside. Already wounded, he crawled into the open to get better communication for those who could provide relief and save his men. He knew he would be a perfect target—that once he was in the open, he would attract the fire of the Taliban. He knew he would die. He also knew that if he didn't make the call, his men would die with him. He was killed, but he got the call off. He did his duty and died for it, so many thousands of miles from home.

The stories in this collection will grip readers, make them take a deep, jolting breath, and then sit back in stunned silence at the selfless acts.

The men—and the one woman to win a Congressional Medal of Honor—who performed such unimaginable acts of bravery had the ability to master fear so they could face the most horrible of deaths, and still move forward. What made them remarkable was that they controlled the fear. They acted as if it didn't matter that they would be suddenly and violently dispatched to Kingdom Come in an instant if things did not work out properly—and things rarely work out properly on the battle-field. Make a mistake in combat and it will be your last.

These Medal winners—all medal winners—confronted their fears and moved into the fray. These remarkable soldiers had in common an unshakable nonchalance about their responsibilities and the heavy consequences they might face. They did not dwell on such vagaries, though. Uncommon valor is an indelible trait that staves off sway from the bloody battlefields of the Civil War through the lonely mountains of Afghanistan. That was their duty. The lives of others meant more to them than their own.

These stories were chosen from hundreds of remarkable, jaw-dropping accounts of heroics, each of which would make any reader with a pulse take a deep breath of appreciation that there are such people alive in our armed forces. Congressional Medal of Honor winners are the best of the best, heroes among heroes.

But there is something else about the winners in this collection. Many of these heroes had fought other, more personal battles before they stepped onto the battlefield. That seems to have made them more resolute, more unflappable in the chaos, better prepared to do their duty.

Vernon Baker, a black lieutenant commanding a segregated platoon on a suicidal mission in World War II, had faced prejudice his entire life. But the values he held dear—his love for his country—superseded any regrets. He moved on. He did his job and got little thanks for it. He would write later, "I was fiercely proud of the fact that my platoon always showed up for the fight. We didn't have that much incentive. A great job hadn't earned black soldiers any special notice. Running away, however, earned infamy. And I made sure everyone knew it."

The Marines on Iwo Jima, many of them veterans of gruesome island assaults in the phenomenally lethal Pacific Island campaign, shrugged off the very high odds that they would not live out the day, and headed in. These Marines had seen what waiting Japanese defenders had done to invading forces, but did their duty anyway. It was pure horror. Said one veteran correspondent: "At Tarawa, Saipan, and Tinian, I saw Marines killed and wounded in a shocking manner, but I saw nothing like the ghastliness that hung over the Iwo beachhead."

Roy Benavidez, part Yaqui Indian, part Mexican orphan, dropped out of school to help his family survive and joined the army. He fought bigotry and found a home in the military. In Vietnam he served with the elite Special Forces and, wounded in battle, still jumped from a hovering helicopter to direct fire away from his platoon.

Tibor Rubin, a Holocaust survivor, was given a surely fatal mission to defend a position by a sergeant who had no time for Jews. Rubin shrugged off the ignorance and single-handedly stopped advancing North Korean troops, manning a machine gun for twenty-four hours straight.

Mary Walker bristled at the thought that she could not do a battle surgeon's job in the Civil War simply because she was a woman. She fought until she was reluctantly granted a commission in the Union Army, and she did her job well. In her spare time she would ride into the countryside, sometimes surrounded by Confederates, to provide medical help to civilians caught in the middle. For her efforts she was captured and held for months in a fetid Confederate prison in Richmond.

Or what about William Harvey Carney of the Massachusetts 54th? He shrugged off the carnage around him as his fellow soldiers moved in on an ill-fated siege and kept the flag from hitting the ground, sustaining serious injuries himself. After, he said it was nothing. "Boys, I only did my duty; the old flag never touched the ground."

But courage was not the purview of only the poor. Teddy Roosevelt, a man born of wealth, loved his country too. And he was willing to put his own privileged life on the line, just like the other heroes in this collection. He wrote of his men, two Rough Riders about to take San Juan Hill during the Spanish-American War: "Capron was going over his plans for the fight when we should meet the Spaniards on the morrow, Fish occasionally asking a question. They were both filled with eager longing to show their mettle, and both were rightly confident that if they lived they would win honorable renown and would rise high in their chosen profession. Within twelve hours they both were dead."

Roosevelt knew what he was up against, and kept going. That's what every Medal of Honor winner has done: They faced death, and they rode on.

CHAPTER ONE

The Ridge: Michael Murphy

Marcus Lutrell

THE GROUND SHOOK. THE VERY FEW TREES SWAYED. THE NOISE WAS worse than any blast all day. . . . This was one gigantic Taliban effort to finish us. We hit the deck . . . to avoid the lethal flying debris, rock fragments, and shrapnel.

Lt. Mike Murphy bellowed out the command, the third time he had done so in the battle. Same mountain. Same command.

"Fall back! Axe and Marcus first!"

He really meant "Fall off!" And so we were all getting real used to it. Axe and I sprinted for the edge, while Murph and Danny, tucked into the rocks, drew fire and covered our escape. I had no idea whether Danny could even move again, with all his wounds.

Lying right along the top of the cliff was a tree trunk with a kind of hollow underneath it, as if it had been washed out by the rains. Axe, who could think quicker on his feet than most people I've ever met, made straight for that hole because the tree trunk would give him cover as he plunged down to whatever the hell was over the goddamned cliff.

The slimly built Axe hit the ground like a javelin, skidded fast into the hollow, shot straight under the log, and out into space. I hit the ground like a Texas longhorn and came to a grinding halt, stuck fast under the log. Couldn't go forward, couldn't go back. Fuck me. Was this a bummer or what?

The Taliban had seen me by now. I was the only one they could see, and I heard a volley of bullets screaming around me. One shot smacked into the tree just to my right. The rest were hitting the dirt and sending up puffs of dust. I heaved at the log. I heaved with all my might, but I could not move that sucker. I was pinned down.

I was trying to look backward, wondering if Mikey had seen me and might try a rescue, when suddenly I saw the stark white smoke trail of an incoming RPG against the mountain. The RPG smashed into the tree trunk right next to me and exploded with a shattering blast as I tried frantically to turn away from it. I can't tell what happened next, but it blew the goddamned trunk clean in half and shot me straight over the cliff.

I guess it was about fifteen feet down to where Axe was moving into firing position, and I landed close. Considering I'd just been blown over the ledge like a freakin' human cannonball, I was pretty lucky to still be standing. And there right next to me on the ground was my rifle, placed there by the Hand of God Himself.

I reached down to pick it up and listened again for His voice. But this time there was no noise, just one brief second of silence in my mind, amid all the chaos and malevolence of this monstrous struggle for supremacy, apparently being conducted on behalf of His Holy Prophet Muhammad.

I was not sure whether either of them would have approved. I don't know much about Muhammad, but, by all that's holy, I don't think my own God wished me to die. If He had been indifferent to my plight, He surely would not have taken such good care of my gun, right? Because how on earth that was still with me, I will never know.

That rifle had so far fought three separate battles in three different places, been ripped out of my grasp twice, been blown over a cliff by a powerful grenade, fallen almost nine hundred feet down a mountain, and was still somehow right next to my outstretched hand. Fluke? Believe what you will. My own faith will remain forever unshaken.

Anyhow, I picked it up and moved back into the rocks where Axe was now picking up fire from the enemy. But he was well positioned and fighting back, blazing away on the left, the flank for which he'd fought so desperately for so long. Actually it had been about forty minutes, but it seemed like ten years, and we were both still going.

4

So, for that matter, were Mikey and Danny, and somehow they had both made the leap down here to the lower level, near the stream, where the Taliban assault was not quite so bad.

Yet.

We looked, by the way, shocking, especially Danny, who was covered head to toe in blood. Axe was okay but badly battered, and Mikey was soaked in blood from that stomach wound; not as bad as Danny, but not very pretty.

When that grenade blew me over the cliff, it probably should have killed me, but the only new injury I had sustained was a broken nose, which I got when I hit the deck, semiconscious. To be honest it hurt like hell, along with my back, and I was bleeding all over my gear. However, I had not been seriously shot, as two of my team had.

Axe was holding the tribesmen off, leaning calmly on a rock, firing up the hill, the very picture of an elite warrior in combat. No panic, rock steady, firing accurately, conserving his ammunition, missing nothing. I was close to him in a similar stance, and we were both hitting them pretty good. One guy suddenly jumped up from nowhere a little above us, and I shot him dead, about thirty yards' range.

But we were trapped again. There were still around eight of these maniacs coming down at us and that's a heck of a lot of enemies. I'm not sure what their casualty rate was, because both Mikey and I estimated Sharmak had thrown 140 minimum into this fight. Whatever, they were still there, and I was not sure how long Danny could keep going.

Mikey worked his way alongside me and said with vintage Murphy humor, "Man, this really sucks."

I turned to face him and told him, "We're gonna fucking die out here—if we're not careful."

"I know," he replied.

And the battle raged on. The massed, wild gunfire of a very determined enemy against our more-accurate, better-trained response, superior concentration, and war-fighting know-how. Once more, hundreds of bullets ricocheting around our rocky surroundings. And once more, the Taliban went to the grenades, blasting the terrain around us to pieces. Jammed between rocks, we kept firing, but Danny was in all kinds of trouble, and I was afraid he might lose consciousness.

That was when they shot him again, right at the base of the neck. I watched in horror as Danny went down, this beautiful guy, husband of Patsy, a friend of mine for four years, a guy who had provided our covering fire until he couldn't stand anymore.

And now he lay on the ground, blood pouring from his five wounds. And I was supposed to be a fucking SEAL medic, and I could not do a damn thing for him without getting us all killed. I dropped my rifle and climbed over the rock, running across open ground to get to him. All right. All right. No hero bullshit. I was crying like a baby.

Danny was saturated in blood, still conscious, still trying to fire his rifle at the enemy. But he was in facedown position. I told him to take it easy while I turned him over.

"C'mon, Dan, we're gonna be all right."

He nodded, and I knew he could not speak and would probably never speak again. What I really remember is, he would not let go of his rifle. I raised him by the shoulders and hauled him into an almost-sitting position. Then, grasping him under the arms, I started to drag him backwards, toward cover. And would you believe, that little iron man opened fire at the enemy once again, almost lying on his back, blasting away up the hill while I kept dragging.

We'd gone about eight yards when everything I dreaded came true. Here I was, just about defenseless, trying to walk backward, both hands full, when a Taliban fighter suddenly loomed up out of the rocks to our right. He was right on top of us, looking down, a smile on his face as he aimed that AK-47 straight at my head.

Neither of us saw him in time to return fire. I just said a quick prayer and stared back at him. Which was precisely when Axe banged two bullets right between his eyes, killed that tribesman stone dead instantly. I didn't have time to thank him, because the grenades were still coming in, and I just kept trying to drag Danny to safety. And like Axe, Danny kept firing.

I got him to the rock face just a few yards from Mikey. And it was clear the enemy had nearly managed to surround us for the fourth time today. We could tell by the direction of the gunfire and occasionally the RPGs. Danny was still alive and willing to fight, and Mikey was now fighting shoulder to shoulder with Axe, and they were inflicting heavy damage.

I still thought we had a chance of getting out, but once more the only option was down, toward that village and onto the flat ground. Fighting uphill, as we had been doing since this battle started, did, in the words of our mission officer, really suck.

I yelled out loudly, "Axe! Moving!" He had time to shout back, "Roger that!" before they shot him in the chest. I watched his rifle fall from his grasp. He slumped forward and slipped down the rock he'd been leaning on, all the way to the ground.

I absolutely froze. This could not be happening. Matt Axelson, a family fixture, Morgan's best friend, a part of our lives. I started calling his name, irrationally, over and over. Privately I thought Danny was dying, and all I could see was a stain of blood gathering in the red dirt where Axe was slumped. For a brief moment I thought I might be losing it.

But then Axe reached for his rifle and got up. He leveled the weapon, got ahold of another magazine, shoved it into the breech, and opened fire again, blood pumping out of his chest. He held his same firing position, leaning against the rock. He showed the same attitude of a solid Navy SEAL know-how, the same formidable steadiness, staring through his scope, those brilliant blue eyes of his scanning the terrain.

When Axe got up, it was the bravest thing I ever saw. Except for Danny. Except for Mikey, still commanding us after taking a bullet through his stomach so early in the battle.

And now Murph was masterminding a way down the escarpment. He had chosen the route and called up to Axe to follow him down. And still the bullets were humming around us as the Taliban started their pursuit. Mikey and Axe were about seventy-five yards in front and I was dragging Danny along while he did everything he could to help, trying to walk, trying to give us covering fire.

"It's okay, Danny," I kept saying. "We just need to catch up with the others. It's gonna be all right."

Right then a bullet caught him full in the upper part of his face. I heard it hit home, I turned to help him, and the blood from his head wound spilled over both of us. I called out to him. But it was too late. He wasn't fighting against the terrible pain anymore. And he couldn't hear me. Danny Dietz died right there in my arms. I don't know how quickly hearts break, but that nearly broke mine.

And the gunfire never abated. I dragged Danny off the open ground maybe five feet, and then I said good-bye to him. I lowered him down, and I had to leave him or else die out here with him. But I knew one thing for certain: I still had my rifle and I was not alone, and neither was Danny, a devout Roman Catholic. I left him with God.

And now I had to get back to help my team. It was the hardest thing I've ever done in my life.

To this day I have nightmares about it, a chilling dream where Danny's still talking to me, and there's blood everywhere, and I have to walk away and I don't even know why. I always wake up in tears, and it will always haunt me, and it's never going to go away.

And now I could hear Murph yelling to me. I grabbed my rifle, ducked down, slipped, and fell off a rock, then started to run toward him and Axe while they provided heavy covering fire nonstop, aimed at the Taliban's rocky redoubt, maybe another forty yards back.

I reached the edge, ran almost blindly into a tree, bounced off, skidded down the slope, which was not very deep, and landed on my head right in the fucking stream. Like any good frogman, I was seriously pissed because my boots got wet. I really hate that.

Finally I caught up with them. Axe was out of ammunition and I gave him a new magazine. Mikey wanted to know where Danny was, and I had to tell him that Danny had died. He was appalled, completely shocked, and so was Axe. Although Mikey would not say it, I knew he wanted to go back for the body. But we both knew there was no time, and no reason. We had nowhere to take the remains of a fallen teammate, and we could not continue this firefight while carrying around a body.

Danny was dead. And strangely, I was the first to pull myself together. I said suddenly, "I'll tell you what. We have to get down this goddamned mountain or we'll all be dead."

And as if to make up our minds for us, the Taliban were again closing in, trying to make that 360-degree movement around us. And they were doing it. Gunfire was coming from underneath us now. We could see the tribesmen still swarming, and I tried to count them as I had been trying to do for almost an hour.

I thought there were now only about fifty, maybe sixty, but the bullets were still flying. The grenades were still coming in, blasting close, sending up dust clouds of smoke and dirt with flying bits of rock. There had never been a lull in the amount of ordnance the enemy was piling down on us.

Right now, again tucked low behind rocks, the three of us could look down and see the village one and a half miles distant, and it remained our objective.

Again I told Mikey, "If we can just make it down there and get some cover, we'll take 'em all out on the flat ground."

I knew we were not in great shape. But we were still SEALs. Nothing can ever take that away. We were still confident. And we were never going to surrender. If it came down to it, we would fight to the death with our knives against their guns.

"Fuck surrender," said Mikey. And he had no need to explain further, either to Axe or to me. Surrender would have been a disgrace to our community, like ringing the bell at the edge of the grinder and putting your helmet in the line. No one who had made it through this far, to this no-man's-land in the Afghan mountains, would have dreamed of giving up.

Remember the philosophy of the US Navy SEALs: "I will never quit.... My Nation expects me to be physically harder and mentally stronger than my enemies. If knocked down, I will get back up, every time. I will draw on every remaining ounce of strength to protect my teammates.... I am never out of the fight."

Those words have sustained many brave men down the years. They were engraved upon the soul of every SEAL. And they were in the minds of all of us.

Mikey suddenly said, above the rage of the battle, "Remember, bro, we're never out of it."

I nodded tersely. "It's only about another thousand yards to flat ground. If we can just get down there, we got a chance."

Trouble was, we couldn't get down there, at least not right then. Because once more we were pinned down. And we faced the same dilemma: The only escape was to go down, but our only defensive strategy was to go up. Once more, we had to get off this ground, away from the ricochets. Back up the left flank.

We were trying to fight the battle our way. But even though we were still going, we were battered half to death. I led the way back up the rocks, blasting away, shooting down anyone I could see. But they caught on to that real quick, and now they really unloaded on us, Russian-made rocket grenades. Coming straight down their right flank, our left.

The ground shook. The very few trees swayed. The noise was worse than any blast all day. Even the walls of this little canyon shook. The stream splashed over its banks. This was one gigantic Taliban effort to finish us. We hit the deck, jamming ourselves into our rocky crevasse, heads down to avoid lethal flying debris, rock fragments, and shrapnel. As before, they did not kill anyone with this type of thunderous bombardment, and as before, they waited till the dust had cleared and then opened fire again.

Above me I could see the tree line. It was not close, but it was nearer than the village.

But the Taliban knew our objective, and as we tried to fight our way forward, they drove us back with sheer weight of fire.

We'd tried, against all the odds, and just could not make it. They'd knocked us back again. And we retreated down, making a long pathetic loop, back the way we'd come. But once more we landed up in a good spot, a sound defensive position, well protected by the rock face on either side. Again we tried to take the fight to them, picking our targets and driving them back, making some new ground toward the village.

They were up and screaming at us, yelling as the battle almost became close quarters. We yelled right back and kept firing. But there were still so many of them, and then they got into better position and shot Mike Murphy through the chest.

He came toward me, asking if I could give him another magazine. And then I saw Axe stumbling toward me, his head pushed out, blood running down his face, bubbling out of the most shocking head wound.

"They shot me, bro," he said. "The bastards shot me. Can you help me, Marcus?"

What could I say? What could I do? I couldn't help except trying to fight off the enemy. And Axe was standing there right in my line of fire.

I tried to help get him down behind a rock. And I turned to Mikey, who was obviously badly hurt now. "Can you move, buddy?" I asked him.

And he groped in his pocket for his mobile phone, the one we hadn't dared to use because it would betray our position. And then Lieutenant Murphy walked into the open ground. He walked until he was more or less in the center, gunfire all around him, and he sat on a small rock and began punching in the numbers to HQ.

I could hear him talking. "My men are taking heavy fire . . . we're getting picked apart. My guys are dying out here . . . we need help."

And right then Mikey took a bullet straight to the back. I saw the blood spurt from his chest. He slumped forward, dropping his phone and rifle. But then he braced himself, grabbed them both, sat upright again, and once more put the phone to his ear.

I heard him speak again. "Roger that, sir. Thank you." Then he stood up and staggered out to our bad position, the one guarding our left, and Mikey started fighting again, firing at the enemy.

He was hitting them, too, having made that one last desperate call to base, the one that might yet save us if they could send help in time, before we were overwhelmed.

Only I knew what Mikey had done. He'd understood we had only one realistic chance, and that was to call in help. He also knew there was only one place from which he could possibly make that cell phone work: out in the open, away from the cliff walls.

Knowing the risk, understanding the danger, in the full knowledge the phone call could cost him his life, Lt. Michael Patrick Murphy, son of Maureen, fiancé of the beautiful Heather, walked out into the firestorm.

His objective was clear: to make one last valiant attempt to save his two teammates. He made the call, made the connection. He reported our approximate position, the strength of our enemy, and how serious our situation was. When they shot him, I thought mortally, he kept talking.

Roger that, sir. Thank you.

Will those words ever dim in my memory, even if I lived to be a hundred? Will I ever forget them? Would you? And was there ever a greater SEAL team commander, an officer who fought to the last and, as perhaps his dying move, risked everything to save his remaining men?

I doubt there was ever anyone better than Mikey, cool under fire, always thinking, fearless about issuing the one-option command even if it was nearly impossible. And then the final, utterly heroic act. Not a gesture. An act of supreme valor. Lieutenant Mikey was a wonderful person and a very, very great SEAL officer. If they build a memorial to him as high as the Empire State Building, it won't ever be high enough for me.

Mikey was still alive, and he carried on, holding the left. I stayed on the right, both of us firing carefully and accurately. I was still trying to reach slightly higher ground. But the depleted army of the Taliban was determined that I should not get it, and every time I tried to advance even a few yards, get even a few feet higher, they drove me back. Mikey too was still trying to climb rock strata above where I was standing. It was a good spot from which to attack, but defensively poor. And I knew this must surely be Mikey's last stand.

Just then, Axe walked right by me in a kind of a daze, making only a marginal attempt at staying in the cover of the rocks. Then I saw the wound, the right side of his head almost blown away.

I shouted, "Axe! Axe! C'mon, old buddy. Get down there, right down there."

I was pointing at the one spot in the rocks we might find protection. And he tried to raise his hand, an act of confirmation that he'd heard me. But he couldn't. And he kept walking slowly, hunched forward, no longer clutching his rifle. He was down to just his pistol, but I knew he could not hold that, aim, and fire. At least he was headed for cover, even though no one could survive a head wound like that. I knew Axe was dying.

Mikey was still firing, but suddenly I heard him scream my name, the most bone-chilling primeval scream: "Help me, Marcus! Please help me!" He was my best friend in all the world, but he was thirty yards up the mountain and I could not climb to him. I could hardly walk, and if I'd move two yards out of my protected position, they would have hit me with a hundred bullets.

Nonetheless, I edged out around the rocks to try to give him covering fire, to force these bastards back, give him a breather until I could find a way to get up there without getting mowed down.

And all the time, he was screaming, calling out my name, begging me to help him live. And there was nothing I could do except die with him. Even then, with only a couple of magazines left, I still believed I could nail these fuckers in the turbans and somehow save him and Axe. I just wanted Mikey to stop screaming, for his agony to end.

But every few seconds, he cried out for me again. And every time it happened, I felt like I'd been stabbed. There were tears welling uncontrollably in my eyes, not for the first time on this day. I would have done anything for Mikey; I'd have laid down my own life for him. But my death here in this outcrop of rocks was not going to save him. If I could save him, it would be by staying alive.

And then, as suddenly as it had begun, the screaming stopped. There was silence for a few seconds, as if even these Taliban warriors understood that Mikey had died. I moved slightly forward and looked up there, in time to see four of them come down and fire several rounds into his fallen body.

The screaming had stopped. For everyone except me. I still hear Mikey, every night. I still hear that scream above all other things, even above the death of Danny Dietz. For several weeks I thought I might be losing my mind, because I could never push it aside. There were one or two frightening occasions when I heard it in broad daylight and found myself pressed against a wall, my hands covering my ears.

I always thought these kinds of psychiatric problems were suffered by other people, ordinary people, not by Navy SEALs. I now know the reality of them. I also doubt whether I will ever sleep through the night again.

Danny was dead. Mikey was now dead. And Axe was dying. Right now there were two of us, but only just. I resolved to walk down to where Axe was hiding and to die there with him. It was, I knew, unlikely there'd be a way out. There were still maybe fifty of the enemy, perhaps by now only hunting me.

It took me nearly ten minutes, firing back behind me sporadically to try to pin them down . . . just in case. I was firing on the wild chance there was a shot at survival—that somehow Mikey's phone call might yet have the guys up in here in time for a last-ditch rescue.

When I reached Axe, he was sitting in a hollow, and he'd fixed a temporary bandage on the side of his head. I stared at him, wondering where those cool blue eyes had gone. The eyes in which I could now see my own reflection were blood-black, the sockets filled from the terrible wound in his skull.

I smiled at him because I knew we would not walk this way again, at least not together, not on this Earth. Axe did not have long. If he'd been in the finest hospital in North America, Axe would still not have had long. The life was ebbing out of him, and I could see this powerful superathlete growing weaker by the second.

"Hey, man," I said, "you're all fucked up!" And I tried, pitifully, to fix the bandage.

"Marcus, they got us good, man." He spoke with difficulty, as if trying to concentrate. And then he said, "You stay alive, Marcus. And tell Cindy I love her."

Those were his last words. I just sat there, and that was where I planned to stay the night, right there with Axe so he wouldn't be alone when the end came. I didn't give a flying fuck what happened to me anymore. Quietly, I made peace with God, and thanked Him for protecting me and saving my rifle. Which, somehow, I still had. I never took my eyes off Axe, who was semiconscious but still breathing.

Along with the other two, Axe will always be a hero to me. Throughout this brief but brutal conflict, he'd fought like a wounded tiger. Like Audie Murphy, like Sergeant York. They shot away his body, crippled his brain, but not his spirit. They never got that.

Matthew Gene Axelson, husband of Cindy, fired at the enemy until he could no longer hold his rifle. He was just past his twenty-ninth birthday. And in his dying moments, I never took my eyes off him. I don't think he could hear me any longer. But his eyes were open, and we were still together, and I refused to allow him to die alone.

Right then, they must have seen us. Because one of those superpowerful Russian grenades came in, landed close, and blew me sideways, right out of the hollow and across the rough ground, and over the edge of the goddamned ravine. I lost consciousness before I hit the bottom, and when I came to, I was in a different hollow, and my first thought was, I'd been blinded by the explosion, because I couldn't see a thing.

However, after a few seconds, I gathered my wits and realized I was upside down in the freakin' hole. I still had my eyesight and a few other working parts, but my left leg seemed paralyzed and, to a lesser degree, so was my right. It took me God knows how long to wriggle out onto flat ground and claw my way into the cover of a rock.

My ears were zinging, I guess from the blast of the grenade. I looked up and saw I had fallen a pretty good way down, but I was too disoriented to put a number on it. The main difference between now and when I'd been sitting with Axe was that the gunfire had ceased.

If they'd reached Axe, who could not possibly have lived through the blast, they might not have bothered to go on shooting. They obviously had not found me, and I would have been real hard to locate, upside down in the hole. But, whatever, no one seemed to be looking. For the first time in maybe an hour and a half, I was apparently not being actively hunted.

Aside from being unable to stand, I had two other very serious problems. The first was the total loss of my pants; they'd been blown right off me. The second was the condition of my left leg, which I could scarcely feel but which was a horrific sight, bleeding profusely and full of shrapnel.

I had no bandages, nothing medical. I had been able to do nothing for my teammates, and I could do nothing for myself, except try to stay hidden. It was not a promising situation. I was damn sure I'd broken my back and probably my shoulder; I'd broken my nose, and my face was a total mess. I couldn't stand up, never mind walk. At least one leg was wrecked, and maybe the other. I was paralyzed in both thighs, and the only way I could move was to belly-crawl.

Unsurprisingly, I was dazed. And through this personal fog of war, there was yet one more miracle for me to recognize. Not two feet from me where I was lying, half hidden by dirt and shale, well out of sight of my enemy, was my Mark 12 rifle, and I still had one and a half magazines left. I prayed before I grabbed it, because I thought it might just be a mirage and that when I tried to hold it . . . well, it might just disappear.

But it did not. And I felt the cold steel in the hot air as my fingers clasped it. I listened again for His voice. I prayed again, imploring Him for guidance. But there was no sound, and all I knew was that somehow I had to make it out to the right, where I'd be safe, at least for a while.

My God had not spoken again. But neither had He forsaken me. I knew that. For damned sure, I knew that.

I knew one other thing as well. For the first time, I was entirely alone. Here in these Taliban-controlled hostile mountains, there was no earthly teammate for me, and my enemy was all around. Had they heeded the words of the goatherds? That there were four of us, and that right now they had only three bodies? Or did they assume I had been blown to pieces by the blast of the final Russian RPG?

I had no answer to these questions, only hope. With absolutely no one to turn to, no Mikey, no Axe, no Danny, I had to face the final battle by myself, maybe lonely, maybe desolate, maybe against formidable odds. But I was not giving up.

I had only one Teammate. And He moved, as ever, in mysterious ways. But I was a Christian, and He had somehow saved me from a thousand AK-47 bullets on this day. No one had shot me, which was well nigh beyond all comprehension.

And I still believed He did not wish me to die. And I would still try my best to uphold the honor of the United States Navy SEALs as I imagined they would have wished. No surrender. Fuck that.

When I judged I had fully gathered my senses and checked my watch, it was exactly 1342 local time. For a few minutes there was no gunfire, and I was beginning to assume they thought I was dead. Wrong, Marcus. The Taliban opened up again, and suddenly there were bullets flying everywhere, all around, just like before.

My enemy was coming up on me from the lower levels and from both sides, firing rapidly but inaccurately. Their bullets were ripping into the earth and shale across a wide range, most of them, thank Christ, well away from me.

It was clear they thought I might be still alive but equally clear they had not yet located me. They were conducting a kind of recon by fire, trying to flush me out, blazing away right across the spectrum, hoping someone would finally hit me and finish me. Or better yet, that I would come out with my hands high so the murdering little bastards could cut my head off or indulge in one of their other attractive little idiosyncrasies before telling that evil little television station Al Jazeera how they had conquered the infidels.

I think I've mentioned my view about surrender. I rammed another magazine into the breech of my miraculous rifle and somehow crawled over this little hill, through the hail of bullets, right into the side of the mountain. No one saw me. No one hit me. I wedged myself into a rocky crevasse with my legs sticking out into a clump of bushes.

There were huge rocks to both sides, protecting me. Overall I judged I was jammed into a fifteen-foot-wide ledge on the mountain. It was not a cave, not even a shallow cave, because it had a kind of open top way above me. Rocks and sand kept falling down on me as the Taliban warriors scrambled around above my position. But this crevasse provided sensational cover and camouflage. Even I realized I would be pretty hard to spot. They'd have to get real lucky, even with their latest policy of trying to flush me out with sheer volume of fire.

My line of vision was directly ahead. I realized I couldn't move or change position, at least in broad daylight I couldn't, and it was imperative I hide the blood which was leaking from my battered body. I took stock of my injuries. My left leg was still bleeding pretty bad, and I packed the wounds with mud. I had a bug cut on my forehead, which I also packed with mud. Both legs were numb. I was not going anywhere. At least for a while.

I had no medical kit, no maps, no compass. I had my bullets, and I had my gun, and I had a decent view off my mountain. I had no pants, no buddies, but no one could see me. I was wedged in tight, my back to the wall in every possible sense.

I eased myself into a relatively comfortable position, checked my rifle, and laid it down the length of my body, aiming outward. If enough of them discovered me, I guess I'd quickly be going to join Danny, Axe, and Mikey. But not before I'd killed a whole lot more of them. I was, I knew, in a perfect position for a stubborn, defensive military action, protected on all sides, vulnerable to a frontal assault only, and that would have to be by weight of numbers.

I could still hear gunfire, and it was growing closer. They were definitely coming this way. I just thought, Don't move, don't breathe, do not make a sound. I think it was about then I understood how utterly alone I was for the very first time. And the Taliban was hunting me. They were not hunting for a SEAL platoon. They were hunting for me alone. Despite my injuries, I knew I had to reach deep. I was starting to lose track of time. But I stayed still. I actually did not move an inch for eight hours.

As the time passed, I could see the Taliban guys right across the canyon, running up and down, seemed like hundreds of them, plainly searching, scouring the mountain they knew so well, looking for me. I had some feeling back in my legs, but I was bleeding real bad, and was in a lot of pain. I think the loss of blood may have started to make me feel light-headed.

Also I was scared to death. It was the first time in my entire six-year career as a Navy SEAL that I had been really scared. At one point, late in the afternoon, I thought they were all leaving. Across the canyon, the mountainside cleared, everyone running hard to the right, swarms of them, all headed for the same place. At least that's how it seemed to me across my narrow vision.

I now know where they were going. While I was lying in my crevasse, I had no idea what the hell was going on. But now I shall recount, to the best of my gathered knowledge, what happened elsewhere on that saddest of afternoons, that most shocking massacre high in the Hindu Kush, the worst disaster ever to befall the SEALs in any conflict in our more than forty-year history.

The first thing to remember is that Mikey had succeeded in getting through to the quick reaction force (QRF) in Asadabad, a couple of mountain ranges over from where I was still holding out. That last call, the one on his cell phone that essentially cost him his life, was successful. From all accounts, his haunting words—*My guys are dying out here . . . we need help*—ripped around our base like a flash fire. SEALs are dying! That's a five-alarm emergency that stops only just on the north side of frenzy.

Lieutenant Commander Kristensen, our acting CO, sounded the alarm. It's always a decision for the QRF, to launch or not to launch. Eric took a billionth of a second to make it. I know the vision of us four—his buddies, his friends and teammates, Mikey, Axe, Danny, and me, fighting for our lives, hurt, possibly dead, surrounded by a huge fighting force of bloodthirsty Afghan tribesmen—flashed through his mind as he summoned the boys to action stations.

And the vision of terrible loss stood stark before him as he roared down the phone, ordering the men of the 160th Special Operations Aviation Regiment (SOAR), the fabled Night Stalkers, to get the big army MH-47 helo ready, right there on the runway. It was the same one that had taken off just before us on the previous day, the one we tracked in our ops area.

Guys I've already introduced charged into position, desperate to help, cramming as much ammunition as they could into their pouches, grabbing rifles and running for the Chinook, its rotors already screaming. My SDV Team 1 guys were instantly there. Petty officers James Suh and Shane Patton reached the helo first. Then, scrambling aboard, came the massively built senior chief Dan Healy, the man who had masterminded Operation Redwing, who apparently looked as if he'd been shot as he left the barracks.

Then came the SEAL Team 10 guys, Lt. Mike McGreevy Jr. of New York, chief Jacques Fontan of New Orleans, petty officers first class Jeff Lucas from Oregon and Jeff Taylor from West Virginia. Finally, still shouting that his boys needed every gun they could get, came Lt. Cdr. Eric Kristensen, the man who knew perhaps better than anyone that the eight SEALs in that helo were about to risk a lethal daytime insertion in a high mountain pass, right into the jaws of an enemy that might outnumber them by dozens to one.

Kristensen knew he did not have to go. In fact, perhaps he should not have gone, stayed instead at his post, central to control and command. Right then, we had the skipper in the QRF, which was, at best, a bit unorthodox. But Kristensen was a SEAL to his fingertips. And what he knew above all else was that he had heard a desperate cry for help. From his brothers, from a man he knew well and trusted.

There was no way Eric was not going to answer that call. Nothing on God's Earth could have persuaded him not to go. He must have known we were barely holding on, praying for help to arrive. There were, after all, only four of us. And to everyone's certain knowledge, there were a minimum of a hundred Taliban.

Eric understood the stupendous nature of the risk, and he never blinked. Just grabbed his rifle and ammunition and raced aboard that aircraft, yelling at everyone else to hurry. . . . "Move it, guys! Let's really move it!" That's what he always said under pressure. Sure, he was a commanding officer, and a hell of a good one. But more than that, he was a SEAL, a part of that brotherhood forged in blood. Even more important, he was a man. And right now he was answering an urgent, despairing cry from the very heart of his own brotherhood. There was only one way Eric Kristensen was headed: straight up the mountain, guns blazing, command or no command.

Inside the MH-47, the men of the 160th SOAR waited quietly, as they had done so many times before on these hair-raising air-rescue ops, often at night. They were led by a terrific man, Maj. Steve Reich of Connecticut, with chief warrant officers Chris Scherkenbach of Jacksonville, Florida, and Corey J. Goodnature of Clarks Grove, Minnesota.

Master sergeant James W. Ponder was there, with sergeants first class Marcus Muralles of Shelbyville, Indiana, and Mike Russell of Stafford, Virginia. Their group was completed by staff sergeant Shamus Goare of Danville, Ohio, and sergeant Kip Jacoby of Pompano Beach, Florida. By any standards, it was a crack army fighting force.

The MH-47 took off and headed over the two mountain ranges. I guess it seemed to take forever. Those kinds of rescues always do. It came in to land at just about the same spot we had fast-roped in at the start of the mission, around five miles from where I was now positioned.

The plan was for the rescue team to rope it down just the same, and when the "Thirty seconds!" call came, I guess the lead guys edged toward the stern ramp. What no one knew was that the Taliban had some kind of bunker back there, and as the MH-47 tilted back for the insert and the ropes fell away for the climb down, the Taliban fired a rocket-propelled grenade straight through the open ramp.

It shot clean past the heads of the lead group and blew with a shattering blast against the fuel tanks, turning the helo into an inferno, stern and midships. Several of the guys were blown out and fell, some of them burning, to their deaths, from around thirty feet. They smashed into the mountainside and tumbled down. The impact was so violent, our search-and-rescue parties later found gun barrels snapped in half among the bodies.

The helicopter pilot fought for control, unaware of the carnage behind him, but certainly aware of the raging fire around and above him. Of course there was nothing he could do. The big MH-47 just fell out of the sky and crashed with thunderous impact onto the mountainside, swayed, and then rolled with brutal force over and over, smashing itself into pieces on a long two-hundred-yard downhill trail to extinction.

There was nothing left except scattered debris when our guys finally got up there to investigate. And, of course, no survivors. My close SDV Team 1 buddies James, chief Dan, and young Shane were all gone. It was just as well I did not know this as I lay there in my crevasse. I'm not sure I could have coped with it. It was nothing less than a massacre. Weeks later I broke down when I saw the photographs, mostly because it was me they were trying to rescue.

As I explained, at the time I knew nothing of this. I only knew something had happened that had caused a lot of Taliban to get very obviously excited. And soon I could see US aircraft flying right along the canyon in front of me, A-10s and AH-64 Apache helicopters. Some of them were so close I could see the pilots.

I pulled my PRC-148 radio out of my pouch and tried to make contact. But I could not speak. My throat was full of dirt, my tongue was sticking to the roof of my mouth, and I had no water. I was totally unable to transmit. But I knew I was in contact because I could hear the aircrew talking. So I fired up my emergency distress beacon on the radio and transmitted that.

They picked it up. I know they did because I could hear them plainly. "Hey, you getting that beacon?" "Yeah, we got it . . . but no further information." Then they just flew off, over to my right, where I now know the MH-47 had gone down.

The trouble was, the Taliban steal those radios if they can, and they often used them to lure the US helicopters down. I was unaware of this at the time, but now it's obvious to me: The American pilots were extremely jumpy about trying to put down a response to a US beacon because they did not know who the hell was aiming that beacon, and they might get shot down.

Which would have been, anyway, little comfort to me, lying there on the mountainside only half alive, bleeding to death and unable to walk. And now it was growing dark, and I was plainly running out of options. I guessed my only chance was to attract the attention of one of the pilots who were still flying down my canyon at pretty regular intervals.

My radio headset had been ripped away during my fall down the mountain, but I still had the wires. And I somehow rigged up two of my chem lights, which glow when you break them in half, and fixed them to the defunct radio wires. And then I whirled this homemade slingshot around my head in a kind of luminous buzz the first moment I saw a helicopter in the area.

I also had an infrared strobe light that I could fire up, and I had the laser from my rifle, which I took off and aimed at the regular US flyby. Jesus Christ! I was a living, breathing distress signal. *There's got to be someone watching these mountains. Someone's got to see me.* I was using this procedure only when I actually saw a helicopter. And soon my optimism turned to outright gloom. No one was paying attention. From where I was lying, it looked like I'd been abandoned for dead.

By now, with the sun declining behind the mountains, I had almost all of the feeling back in my legs. And this gave me hope that I might be able to walk, although I knew the pain might be a bit fierce. I was getting dangerously thirsty. I could not get the clogged dust and dirt out of my throat. It was all I could do to breathe, never mind speak. I had to find water, and I had to get the hell out of the death trap. But not until the veil of darkness fell over these mountains.

I knew I had to get myself out, first to water, and then to safety, because it sure as hell didn't look like anyone was going to find me. I remember Axe's final words. They still rang clearly in my mind: "You stay alive, Marcus. And tell Cindy I love her." For Axe, and for Danny, and above all, for Mikey, I knew I must stay alive.

I saw the last, long rays of the mountain sun cast their gigantic shadows through the canyon before me. And just as certainly, I saw the glint of the silver barrel of an AK-47 right across from me, dead ahead, on the far cliff face, maybe 150 yards. It caught the rays of the dying sun twice, which suggested the sonofabitch who was holding it was making a sweep across the wall of the mountain, right past the crevasse inside of which I was still lying motionless.

And now I could see the tribesman in question. He was just standing there, his shirtsleeves rolled up, wearing a blue-and-white-checked vest, holding his rifle in the familiar low-slung grip of the Afghans, a split second short of raising it to the firing position. The only conclusion was he was looking for me.

I did not know how many of his buddies were within shouting range. But I did know if he got a clear sight across that canyon and somehow spotted me, I was essentially history. He could hardly miss, and he kept staring across, but he did not raise his rifle. Yet.

I decided this was not a risk I was prepared to take. My own rifle was loaded and suppressed. There would be little noise to attract anyone else's attention. And very carefully, hardly daring to breathe, I raised the Mark 12 into the firing position and drew down on the little man on the far ridge. He was bang in the crosshairs of my telescopic sight.

I squeezed the trigger and hit him straight between the eyes. I just had time to see the blood bloom out into the center of his forehead, and then I watched him topple over the edge, down into the canyon. He must have fallen two hundred feet, screaming with his dying breath all the way. I was not in any way moved, except to thank God there was one less.

Almost immediately two of his colleagues ran into the precise spot where he had been standing, directly across from me. They were dressed more or less the same, except for the different colors of their vests. They stood there staring down into the canyon where the first man had fallen. They both carried AKs, held in the firing position, but not fully raised.

I thought they might just take off, but they stood there, now looking hard across the void which separated my mountain from theirs. From where I was, they seemed to be looking right at me, scanning the cliff face for any sign of movement. I knew they had no idea if their pal had been shot, simply fallen, or perhaps committed suicide.

However, I think option one was their instinct. And right now they were trying to find out precisely who had shot him. I remained motion-less, but those little black eyes were looking straight at me, and I realized if they both opened fire at once on my rocky redoubt, the chances of an

AK-47 bullet, or bullets, hitting me were good to excellent. They had to go. Both of them.

Once more, I slowly raised my rifle and drew a bead on an armed Taliban tribesman. My first shot killed the one on the right instantly, and I watched him tumble over the edge. The second one, understanding now there was an enemy at large, raised his gun and scanned the cliff face where I was still flat on my back.

I hit him straight in the chest, then I fired a second time in case he was still breathing and able to cry out. He fell forward without a sound and went to join his two buddies on the canyon floor. Which left me all alone and thus far undiscovered.

Just a few hours previously, Mike Murphy and I had made a military judgment which cost three lives, the lives of some of the best SEALs I had ever met. Lying here on my ledge, surrounded on all sides by hostile Taliban warriors, I could not afford another mistake. I'd somehow, by the grace of God, been spared from the consequences of the first one, made way up there on that granite outcrop which ought to be named for Mikey, our superb leader. The Battle of Murphy's Ridge.

Every decision I made from now on would involve my own life or death. I needed to fight my way out, and I did not give a damn how many of the Taliban enemy I had to kill in order to achieve that. The key point was, I could not make another mistake. I could take no chances.

The far side of the canyon remained silent as the sun disappeared behind the high western peaks of the Hindu Kush. I figured the Taliban had probably split their search party in this particular area and that I'd gotten rid of one half. Out there, somewhere, in the deathly silence of the twilight, there would almost certainly be three more, looking for the one surviving American from that original four-man platoon that had inflicted such damage on their troops.

The friendly clatter of the US Apaches had gone now. No one was looking for me. And by far my biggest problem was water. Aside from the fact that I was still bleeding and couldn't stand up, the thirst was becoming desperate. My tongue was still clogged with dust and dirt, and I still could not speak. I'd lost my water bottle on the mountain during the first crashing fall with Mikey, and it had now been nine hours since I'd had a drink.

Also, I was still soaking wet from when I'd fallen in the river. I understood I was very light-headed from loss of blood, but I still tried to concentrate. And the one conclusion I reached was that I had to stand up—even though I knew that if a couple of those Taliban came around that corner to my left, the only way to approach me, and they had any form of light, I'd be like a jackrabbit caught in someone's headlights.

My redoubt had served me well, but I had to get out of it right now. When the bodies of those three guys were found at first light, this mountain would be swarming with Taliban. I dragged myself to my feet and stood there in my boxers in the freezing cold mountain air. I tested my right leg. Not too bad. Then I tested my left, and that hurt like a devil. I tried to brush some of the shale and dirt away from where I'd packed the wound, but the shards of the shrapnel were jutting out of my thigh, and whenever I touched one, I nearly jumped through the ceiling. At least I would have, if there'd been one.

One of my main problems was that I had no handle on the terrain. Of course I knew that the mountain reared up behind me and that I was trapped on the cliff face with no way to go except up. Which from where I stood, almost unable to hobble, was a seriously daunting task. I tested my left leg again, and at least it wasn't worse.

But my back hurt like hell. I never realized how much pain three cracked vertebrae could inflict on a guy. Of course, I never realized I had three cracked vertebrae either. I could move my right shoulder despite a torn rotator cuff, which I also didn't realize I had. And my broken nose throbbed a bit, which was kid's stiff compared with the rest. I knew one side of my face was shredded by the fall down the mountain, and the big cut on my forehead was pretty sore.

But my overriding thought was my thirst. I was only slightly comforted by the closeness of several mountain streams up here. I had to find one, fast, both to clean my wounds and to drink. That way I had a shot at yelling through the radio and locating an American helicopter or fighter aircraft in the morning.

I gathered up my gear, radio, strobes, and laser and repacked them into my pouch. I checked my rifle, which had about twenty rounds left in the magazine, with a full magazine remaining in the harness I still wore across my chest.

Then I stepped out of my redoubt, into absolute pitch black and the deadly silence of the Hindu Kush. There was no moon, and it was just starting to rain, which meant there wasn't going to be a moon in the foreseeable future.

I tested the leg again. It held my weight without giving way. I felt my direction around the huge rock which had been guarding my left flank all day. And then, with the smallest, most timid strides I had ever taken, I stepped out onto the mountain.

In 2007, Murphy was posthumously awarded the Medal of Honor for his actions during the battle.

FROM THE CITATION

For conspicuous gallantry and intrepidity at the risk of his life above and beyond the call of duty as the leader of a special reconnaissance element with Naval Special Warfare Task Unit Afghanistan on 27 and 28 June 2005. While leading a mission to locate a high-level anti-coalition militia leader, Lieutenant Murphy demonstrated extraordinary heroism in the face of grave danger in the vicinity of Asadabad, Kunar Province, Afghanistan. On 28 June 2005, operating in an extremely rugged enemy-controlled area, Lieutenant Murphy's team was discovered by anti-coalition militia sympathizers, who revealed their position to Taliban fighters. As a result, between 30 and 40 enemy fighters besieged his four-member team. Demonstrating exceptional resolve, Lieutenant Murphy valiantly led his men in engaging the large enemy force. The ensuing fierce firefight resulted in numerous enemy casualties, as well as the wounding of all four members of the team. Ignoring his own wounds and demonstrating exceptional composure, Lieutenant Murphy continued to lead and encourage his men. When the primary communicator fell mortally wounded, Lieutenant Murphy repeatedly attempted to call for assistance for his beleaguered teammates. Realizing the impossibility of communicating in the extreme terrain, and in the face of almost certain death, he fought his way into open terrain to gain a better position to transmit a call. This deliberate, heroic act deprived him of cover, exposing him to direct enemy fire. Finally achieving contact with his headquarters, Lieutenant Murphy maintained his exposed position while he provided his location and requested immediate support for his team. In his final act of bravery, he continued to engage the enemy until he was mortally wounded, gallantly giving his life for his country and for the cause of freedom. By his selfless leadership, courageous actions, and extraordinary devotion to duty, Lieutenant Murphy reflected great credit upon himself and upheld the highest traditions of the United States Naval Service.

CHAPTER TWO

San Juan Hill: Teddy Roosevelt

Theodore Roosevelt

JUST BEFORE LEAVING TAMPA WE HAD BEEN BRIGADED WITH THE FIRST (white) and Tenth (colored) Regular Cavalry under Brigadier-General S. B. M. Young. We were the Second Brigade, the First Brigade consisting of the Third and Sixth (white), and the Ninth (colored) Regular Cavalry under Brigadier-General Sumner. The two brigades of the cavalry division were under Major-General Joseph Wheeler, the gallant old Confederate cavalry commander.

General Young was—and is—as fine a type of the American fighting soldier as a man can hope to see. He had been in command, as Colonel, of the Yellowstone National Park, and I had seen a good deal of him in connection therewith, as I was President of the Boone and Crockett Club, an organization devoted to hunting big game, to its preservation, and to forest preservation. During the preceding winter, while he was in Washington, he had lunched with me at the Metropolitan Club, Wood being one of the other guests. Of course, we talked of the war, which all of us present believed to be impending, and Wood and I told him we were going to make every effort to get in, somehow; and he answered that we must be sure to get into his brigade, if he had one, and he would guarantee to show us fighting. None of us forgot the conversation. As soon as our regiment was raised, General Young applied for it to be put in his brigade. We were put in; and he made his word good; for he fought and won the first fight on Cuban soil.

Yet, even though under him, we should not have been in this fight at all if we had not taken advantage of the chance to disembark among the first troops, and if it had not been for Wood's energy in pushing our regiment to the front.

On landing we spent some active hours in marching our men a quarter of a mile or so inland, as boat-load by boat-load they disembarked. Meanwhile one of the men, Knoblauch, a New Yorker, who was a great athlete and a champion swimmer, by diving in the surf off the dock, recovered most of the rifles which had been lost when the boat-load of colored cavalry capsized. The country would have offered very great difficulties to an attacking force had there been resistance. It was little but a mass of rugged and precipitous hills, covered for the most part by dense jungle. Five hundred resolute men could have prevented the disembarkation at very little cost to themselves. There had been about that number of Spaniards at Daiquiri that morning, but they had fled even before the ships began shelling. In their place we found hundreds of Cuban insurgents, a crew of as utter tatterdemalions as human eyes ever looked on, armed with every kind of rifle in all stages of dilapidation. It was evident, at a glance, that they would be no use in serious fighting, but it was hoped that they might be of service in scouting. From a variety of causes, however, they turned out to be nearly useless, even for this purpose, so far as the Santiago campaign was concerned.

We were camped on a dusty, brush-covered flat, with jungle on one side, and on the other a shallow, fetid pool fringed with palm-trees. Huge land-crabs scuttled noisily through the underbrush, exciting much interest among the men. Camping was a simple matter, as each man carried all he had, and the officers had nothing. I took a light mackintosh and a tooth-brush. Fortunately, that night it did not rain; and from the palm-leaves we built shelters from the sun.

General Lawton, a tall, fine-looking man, had taken the advance. A thorough soldier, he at once established outposts and pushed reconnoitering parties ahead on the trails. He had as little baggage as the rest of us. Our own Brigade-Commander, General Young, had exactly the same impedimenta that I had, namely, a mackintosh and a tooth-brush.

Next morning we were hard at work trying to get the stuff unloaded from the ship, and succeeded in getting most of it ashore, but were utterly unable to get transportation for anything but a very small quantity. The great shortcoming throughout the campaign was the utterly inadequate transportation. If we had been allowed to take our mule-train, we could have kept the whole cavalry division supplied.

In the afternoon word came to us to march. General Wheeler, a regular game-cock, was as anxious as Lawton to get first blood, and he was bent upon putting the cavalry division to the front as quickly as possible. Lawton's advance guard was in touch with the Spaniards, and there had been a skirmish between the latter and some Cubans, who were repulsed. General Wheeler made a reconnaissance in person, found out where the enemy was, and directed General Young to take our brigade and move forward so as to strike him next morning. He had the power to do this, as when General Shafter was afloat he had command ashore.

I had succeeded in finding Texas, my surviving horse, much the worse for his fortnight on the transport and his experience in getting off, but still able to carry me.

It was mid-afternoon and the tropic sun was beating fiercely down when Colonel Wood started our regiment—the First and Tenth Cavalry and some of the infantry regiments having already marched. Colonel Wood himself rode in advance, while I led my squadron, and Major Brodie followed with his. It was a hard march, the hilly jungle trail being so narrow that often we had to go in single file. We marched fast, for Wood was bound to get us ahead of the other regiments, so as to be sure of our place in the body that struck the enemy next morning. If it had not been for his energy in pushing forward, we should certainly have missed the fight. As it was, we did not halt until we were at the extreme front.

The men were not in very good shape for marching, and moreover they were really horsemen, the majority being cowboys who had never done much walking. The heat was intense and their burdens very heavy. Yet there was very little straggling. Whenever we halted they instantly took off their packs and threw themselves on their backs. Then at the word to start they would spring into place again. The captains and lieutenants tramped along, encouraging the men by example and word. A good part of the time I was by Captain Llewellen, and was greatly pleased to see the way in which he kept his men up to their work. He never pitied or coddled his troopers, but he always looked after them. He helped them whenever he could, and took rather more than his full share of hardship and danger, so that his men naturally followed him with entire devotion. Jack Greenway was under him as lieutenant, and to him the entire march was nothing but an enjoyable outing, the chance of fight on the morrow simply adding the needed spice of excitement.

It was long after nightfall when we tramped through the darkness into the squalid coast hamlet of Siboney. As usual when we made a night camp, we simply drew the men up in column of troops, and then let each man lie down where he was. Black thunder-clouds were gathering. Before they broke, the fires were made and the men cooked their coffee and pork, some frying the hardtack with the pork. The officers, of course, fared just as the men did. Hardly had we finished eating when the rain came, a regular tropic downpour. We sat about, sheltering ourselves as best we could, for the hour or two it lasted; then the fires were relighted and we closed around them, the men taking off their wet things to dry them, so far as possible, by the blaze.

Wood had gone off to see General Young, as General Wheeler had instructed General Young to hit the Spaniards, who were about four miles away, as soon after daybreak as possible. Meanwhile, I strolled over to Captain Capron's troop. He and I, with his two lieutenants, Day and Thomas, stood around the fire, together with two or three non-commissioned officers and privates; among the latter were Sergeant Hamilton Fish and Trooper Elliot Cowdin, both of New York. Cowdin, together with two other troopers, Harry Thorpe and Munro Ferguson, had been on my Oyster Bay Polo Team some years before. Hamilton Fish had already shown himself one of the best non-commissioned officers we had. A huge fellow, of enormous strength and endurance and dauntless courage, he took naturally to a soldier's life. He never complained and never shirked any duty of any kind, while his power over his men was great. So good a sergeant had he made that Captain Capron, keen to get the best men under him, took him when he left Tampa—for Fish's troop remained behind. As we stood around the flickering blaze that night I caught myself admiring the splendid bodily vigor of Capron and Fish—the captain and the sergeant. Their frames seemed of steel, to withstand all fatigue; they were flushed with health; in their eyes shone high resolve and fiery desire. Two finer types of the fighting man, two better representatives of the American soldier, there were not in the whole army. Capron was going over his plans for the fight when we should meet the Spaniards on the morrow, Fish occasionally asking a question. They were both filled with eager longing to show their mettle, and both were rightly confident that if they lived they would win honorable renown and would rise high in their chosen profession. Within twelve hours they both were dead.

I had lain down when toward midnight Wood returned. He had gone over the whole plan with General Young. We were to start by sunrise toward Santiago, General Young taking four troops of the Tenth and four troops of the First up the road which led through the valley; while Colonel Wood was to lead our eight troops along a hill-trail to the left, which joined the valley road about four miles on, at a point where the road went over a spur of the mountain chain and from thence went downhill toward Santiago. The Spaniards had their lines at the junction of the road and the trail.

Before describing our part in the fight, it is necessary to say a word about General Young's share, for, of course, the whole fight was under his direction, and the fight on the right wing under his immediate supervision. General Young had obtained from General Castillo, the commander of the Cuban forces, a full description of the country in front. General Castillo promised Young the aid of eight hundred Cubans, if he made a reconnaissance in force to find out exactly what the Spanish strength was. This promised Cuban aid did not, however, materialize, the Cubans, who had been beaten back by the Spaniards the day before, not appearing on the firing-line until the fight was over.

General Young had in his immediate command a squadron of the First Regular Cavalry, two hundred and forty-four strong, under the command of Major Bell, and a squadron of the Tenth Regular Cavalry, two hundred and twenty strong, under the command of Major Norvell. He also had two Hotchkiss mountain guns, under Captain Watson of the Tenth. He started at a quarter before six in the morning, accompanied by Captain A. L. Mills, as aide. It was at half-past seven that Captain Mills, with a patrol of two men in advance, discovered the Spaniards as they lay across where the two roads came together, some of them in pits, others simply lying in the heavy jungle, while on their extreme right they occupied a big ranch. Where General Young struck them they held a high ridge a little to the left of his front, this ridge being separated by a deep ravine from the hill-trail still farther to the left, down which the Rough Riders were advancing. That is, their forces occupied a range of high hills in the form of an obtuse angle, the salient being toward the space between the American forces, while there were advance parties along both roads. There were stone breastworks flanked by block-houses on that part of the ridge where the two trails came together. The place was called Las Guasimas, from trees of that name in the neighborhood.

General Young, who was riding a mule, carefully examined the Spanish position in person. He ordered the canteens of the troops to be filled, placed the Hotchkiss battery in concealment about nine hundred yards from the Spanish lines, and then deployed the white regulars, with the colored regulars in support, having sent a Cuban guide to try to find Colonel Wood and warn him. He did not attack immediately, because he knew that Colonel Wood, having a more difficult route, would require a longer time to reach the position. During the delay General Wheeler arrived; he had been up since long before dawn, to see that everything went well. Young informed him of the dispositions and plan of attack he made. General Wheeler approved of them, and with excellent judgment left General Young a free hand to fight his battle.

So, about eight o'clock Young began the fight with his Hotchkiss guns, he himself being up on the firing-line. No sooner had the Hotchkiss one-pounders opened than the Spaniards opened fire in return, most of the time firing by volleys executed in perfect time, almost as on parade. They had a couple of light guns, which our people thought were quick firers. The denseness of the jungle and the fact that they used absolutely smokeless powder, made it exceedingly difficult to place exactly where they were, and almost immediately Young, who always liked to get as close as possible to his enemy, began to push his troops forward. They were deployed on both sides of the road in such thick jungle that it was only here and there that they could possibly see ahead, and some confusion, of course, ensued, the support gradually getting mixed with the advance. Captain Beck took a troop of the Tenth in on the left, next Captain Galbraith's troop of the First; two other troops of the Tenth were on the extreme right. Through the jungle ran wire fences here and there, and as the troops got to the ridge they encountered precipitous heights. They were led most gallantly, as American regular officers always lead their men; and the men followed their leaders with the splendid courage always shown by the American regular soldier. There was not a single straggler among them, and in not one instance was an attempt made by any trooper to fall out in order to assist the wounded or carry back the dead, while so cool were they and so perfect their fire discipline, that in the entire engagement the expenditure of ammunition was not over ten rounds per man. Major Bell, who commanded the squadron, had his leg broken by a shot as he was leading his men. Captain Wainwright succeeded to the command of the squadron. Captain Knox was shot in the abdomen. He continued for some time giving orders to his troops, and refused to allow a man in the firing-line to assist him to the rear. His First Lieutenant, Byram, was himself shot, but continued to lead his men until the wound and the heat overcame him and he fell in a faint. The advance was pushed forward under General Young's eye with the utmost energy, until the enemy's voices could be heard in the entrenchments. The Spaniards kept up a very heavy firing, but the regulars would not be denied, and as they climbed the ridges the Spaniards broke and fled.

Meanwhile, at six o'clock, the Rough Riders began their advance. We first had to climb a very steep hill. Many of the men, foot-sore and weary from their march of the preceding day, found the pace up this hill too hard, and either dropped their bundles or fell out of line, with the result that we went into action with less than five hundred men—as, in addition to the stragglers, a detachment had been left to guard the baggage on shore. At the time I was rather inclined to grumble to myself about Wood setting so fast a pace, but when the fight began I realized that it had been absolutely necessary, as otherwise we should have arrived late and the regulars would have had very hard work indeed.

Tiffany, by great exertions, had corralled a couple of mules and was using them to transport the Colt automatic guns in the rear of the regiment. The dynamite gun was not with us, as mules for it could not be obtained in time.

Captain Capron's troop was in the lead, it being chosen for the most responsible and dangerous position because of Capron's capacity. Four men, headed by Sergeant Hamilton Fish, went first; a support of twenty men followed some distance behind; and then came Capron and the rest of his troop, followed by Wood, with whom General Young had sent Lieutenants Smedburg and Rivers as aides. I rode close behind, at the head of the other three troops of my squadron, and then came Brodie at the head of his squadron. The trail was so narrow that for the most part the men marched in single file, and it was bordered by dense, tangled jungle, through which a man could with difficulty force his way; so that to put out flankers was impossible, for they could not possibly have kept up with the march of the column. Every man had his canteen full. There was a Cuban guide at the head of the column, but he ran away as soon as the fighting began. There were also with us, at the head of the column, two men who did not run away, who, though non-combatants—newspaper correspondents—showed as much gallantry as any soldier in the field. They were Edward Marshall and Richard Harding Davis.

After reaching the top of the hill, the walk was very pleasant. Now and then we came to glades or rounded hill-shoulders, whence we could look off for some distance. The tropical forest was very beautiful, and it was a delight to see the strange trees, the splendid royal palms and a tree which looked like a flat-topped acacia, and which was covered with a mass of brilliant scarlet flowers. We heard many bird-notes, too, the cooing of doves and the call of a great brush cuckoo. Afterward we found that the Spanish guerrillas imitated these bird-calls, but the sounds we heard that morning, as we advanced through the tropic forest, were from birds, not guerrillas, until we came right up to the Spanish lines. It was very beautiful and very peaceful, and it seemed more as if we were off on some hunting excursion than as if we were about to go into a sharp and bloody little fight.

Of course, we accommodated our movements to those of the men in front. After marching for somewhat over an hour, we suddenly came to a halt, and immediately afterward Colonel Wood sent word down the line that the advance guard had come upon a Spanish outpost. Then the order was passed to fill the magazines, which was done.

The men were totally unconcerned, and I do not think they realized that any fighting was at hand; at any rate, I could hear the group nearest me discussing in low murmurs, not the Spaniards, but the conduct of a certain cow-puncher in quitting work on a ranch and starting a saloon in some New Mexican town. In another minute, however, Wood sent me orders to deploy three troops to the right of the trail, and to advance when we became engaged; while, at the same time, the other troops, under Major Brodie, were deployed to the left of the trail where the ground was more open than elsewhere—one troop being held in reserve in the centre, besides the reserves on each wing. Later all the reserves were put into the firing-line.

To the right the jungle was quite thick, and we had barely begun to deploy when a crash in front announced that the fight was on. It was evidently very hot, and L Troop had its hands full; so I hurried my men up abreast of them. So thick was the jungle that it was very difficult to keep together, especially when there was no time for delay, and while I got up Llewellen's troops and Kane's platoon of K Troop, the rest of K Troop under Captain Jenkins, which, with Bucky O'Neill's troop, made up the right wing, were behind, and it was some time before they got into the fight at all.

Meanwhile, I had gone forward with Llewellen, Greenway, Kane, and their troopers until we came out on a kind of shoulder, jutting over a ravine, which separated us from a great ridge on our right. It was on this ridge that the Spaniards had some of their entrenchments, and it was just beyond this ridge that the Valley Road led, up which the regulars were at that very time pushing their attack; but, of course, at the moment we knew nothing of this. The effect of the smokeless powder was remarkable. The air seemed full of the rustling sound of the Mauser bullets, for the Spaniards knew the trails by which we were advancing, and opened heavily on our position. Moreover, as we advanced we were, of course, exposed, and they could see us and fire. But they themselves were entirely invisible. The jungle covered everything, and not the faintest trace of smoke was to be seen in any direction to indicate from whence the bullets came. It was some time before the men fired; Llewellen, Kane, and I anxiously study-ing the ground to see where our opponents were, and utterly unable to find out.

We could hear the faint reports of the Hotchkiss guns and the reply of two Spanish guns, and the Mauser bullets were singing through the trees over our heads, making a noise like the humming of telephone wires; but exactly where they came from we could not tell. The Spaniards were firing high and for the most part by volleys, and their shooting was not very good, which perhaps was not to be wondered at, as they were a long way off. Gradually, however, they began to get the range and occasion-ally one of our men would crumple up. In no case did the men make any outcry when hit, seeming to take it as a matter of course; at the outside, making only such a remark as: "Well, I got it that time." With hardly an exception, there was no sign of flinching. I say with hardly an excep-tion, for though I personally did not see an instance, and though all the men at the front behaved excellently, yet there were a very few men who lagged behind and drifted back to the trail over which we had come. The character of the fight put a premium upon such conduct, and afforded a very severe test for raw troops; because the jungle was so dense that as we advanced in open order, every man was, from time to time, left almost alone and away from the eyes of his officers. There was unlimited oppor-tunity for dropping out without attracting notice, while it was peculiarly hard to be exposed to the fire of an unseen foe, and to see men dropping under it, and yet to be, for some time, unable to return it, and also to be entirely ignorant of what was going on in any other part of the field.

It was Richard Harding Davis who gave us our first opportunity to shoot back with effect. He was behaving precisely like my officers, being on the extreme front of the line, and taking every opportunity to study with his glasses the ground where we thought the Spaniards were. I had tried some volley firing at points where I rather doubtfully believed the Spaniards to be, but had stopped firing and was myself studying the jungle-covered mountain ahead with my glasses, when Davis suddenly said: "There they are, Colonel; look over there; I can see their hats near that glade," pointing across the valley to our right. In a minute I, too, made out the hats, and then pointed them out to three or four of our best shots, giving them my estimate of the range. For a minute or two no result followed, and I kept raising the range, at the same time getting more men on the firing-line. Then, evidently, the shots told, for the Spaniards suddenly sprang out of the cover through which we had seen their hats, and ran to another spot; and we could now make out a large number of them.

I accordingly got all of my men up in line and began quick firing. In a very few minutes our bullets began to do damage, for the Spaniards retreated to the left into the jungle, and we lost sight of them. At the same moment a big body of men who, it afterward turned out, were Spaniards, came in sight along the glade, following the retreat of those whom we had just driven from the trenches. We supposed that there was a large force of Cubans with General Young, not being aware that these Cubans had failed to make their appearance, and as it was impossible to tell the Cubans from the Spaniards, and as we could not decide whether these were Cubans following the Spaniards we had put to flight, or merely another troop of Spaniards retreating after the first (which was really the case), we dared not fire, and in a minute they had passed the glade and were out of sight.

At every halt we took advantage of the cover, sinking down behind any mound, bush, or tree trunk in the neighborhood. The trees, of course, furnished no protection from the Mauser bullets. Once I was standing behind a large palm with my head out to one side, very fortunately; for a bullet passed through the palm, filling my left eye and ear with the dust and splinters.

No man was allowed to drop out to help the wounded. It was hard to leave them there in the jungle, where they might not be found again until the vultures and the land-crabs came, but war is a grim game and there was no choice. One of the men shot was Harry Heffner of G Troop, who was mortally wounded through the hips. He fell without uttering a sound, and two of his companions dragged him behind a tree. Here he propped himself up and asked to be given his canteen and his rifle, which I handed to him. He then again began shooting, and continued loading and firing until the line moved forward and we left him alone, dying in the gloomy shade. When we found him again, after the fight, he was dead.

At one time, as I was out of touch with that part of my wing commanded by Jenkins and O'Neill, I sent Greenway, with Sergeant Russell, a New Yorker, and trooper Rowland, a New Mexican cow-puncher, down in the valley to find out where they were. To do this the three had to expose themselves to a very severe fire, but they were not men to whom this mattered. Russell was killed; the other two returned and reported to me the position of Jenkins and O'Neill. They then resumed their places on the firing-line. After a while I noticed blood coming out of Rowland's side and discovered that he had been shot, although he did not seem to be taking any notice of it. He said the wound was only slight, but as I saw he had broken a rib, I told him to go to the rear to the hospital. After some grumbling he went, but fifteen minutes later he was back on the firing-line again and said he could not find the hospital—which I doubted. However, I then let him stay until the end of the fight.

After we had driven the Spaniards off from their position to our right, the firing seemed to die away so far as we were concerned, for the bullets no longer struck around us in such a storm as before, though along the rest of the line the battle was as brisk as ever. Soon we saw troops appearing across the ravine, not very far from where we had seen the Spaniards whom we had thought might be Cubans. Again we dared not fire, and carefully studied the new-comers with our glasses; and this time we were right, for we recognized our own cavalry-men. We were by no means sure that they recognized us, however, and were anxious that they should, but it was very difficult to find a clear spot in the jungle from which to signal; so Sergeant Lee of Troop K climbed a tree and from its summit waved the troop guidon. They waved their guidon back, and as our right wing was now in touch with the regulars, I left Jenkins and O'Neill to keep the connection, and led Llewellen's troop back to the path to join the rest of the regiment, which was evidently still in the thick of the fight. I was still very much in the dark as to where the main body of the Spanish forces were, or exactly what lines the battle was following, and was very uncertain what I ought to do; but I knew it could not be wrong to go forward, and I thought I would find Wood and then see what he wished me to do. I was in a mood to cordially welcome guidance, for it was most bewildering to fight an enemy whom one so rarely saw.

I had not seen Wood since the beginning of the skirmish, when he hurried forward. When the firing opened some of the men began to curse. "Don't swear—shoot!" growled Wood, as he strode along the path leading his horse, and everyone laughed and became cool again. The Spanish outposts were very near our advance guard, and some minutes of the hottest kind of firing followed before they were driven back and slipped off through the jungle to their main lines in the rear.

Here, at the very outset of our active service, we suffered the loss of two as gallant men as ever wore uniform. Sergeant Hamilton Fish at the extreme front, while holding the point up to its work and firing back where the Spanish advance guards lay, was shot and instantly killed; three of the men with him were likewise hit. Captain Capron, leading the advance guard in person, and displaying equal courage and coolness in the way that he handled them, was also struck, and died a few minutes afterward. The command of the troop then devolved upon the First Lieutenant, young Thomas. Like Capron, Thomas was the fifth in line from father to son who had served in the American army, though in his case it was in the volunteer and not the regular service; the four preceding generations had furnished soldiers respectively to the Revolutionary War, the War of 1812, the Mexican War, and the Civil War. In a few minutes Thomas was shot through the leg, and the command devolved upon the Second Lieutenant, Day (a nephew of "Albemarle" Cushing, he who sunk the great Confederate ram). Day, who proved himself to be one of our most efficient officers, continued to handle the men to the best possible advantage, and brought them steadily forward. L Troop was from the Indian Territory. The whites, Indians, and half-breeds in it, all fought with equal courage. Captain McClintock was hurried forward to its relief with his Troop B of Arizona men. In a few minutes he was shot through the leg and his place was taken by his First Lieutenant, Wilcox, who handled his men in the same soldierly manner that Day did.

Among the men who showed marked courage and coolness was the tall color-sergeant, Wright; the colors were shot through three times.

When I had led G Troop back to the trail I ran ahead of them, passing the dead and wounded men of L Troop, passing young Fish as he lay with glazed eyes under the rank tropic growth to one side of the trail. When I came to the front I found the men spread out in a very thin skirmish line, advancing through comparatively open ground, each man taking advantage of what cover he could, while Wood strolled about leading his horse, Brodie being close at hand. How Wood escaped being hit, I do not see, and still less how his horse escaped. I had left mine at the beginning of the action, and was only regretting that I had not left my sword with it, as it kept getting between my legs when I was tearing my way through the jungle. I never wore it again in action. Lieutenant Rivers was with Wood, also leading his horse. Smedburg had been sent off on the by no means pleasant task of establishing communications with Young.

Very soon after I reached the front, Brodie was hit, the bullet shattering one arm and whirling him around as he stood. He had kept on the extreme front all through, his presence and example keeping his men entirely steady, and he at first refused to go to the rear; but the wound was very painful, and he became so faint that he had to be sent. Thereupon, Wood directed me to take charge of the left wing in Brodie's place, and to bring it forward; so over I went.

I now had under me Captains Luna, Muller, and Houston, and I began to take them forward, well spread out, through the high grass of a rather open forest. I noticed Goodrich, of Houston's troop, tramping along behind his men, absorbed in making them keep at good intervals from one another and fire slowly with careful aim. As I came close up to the edge of the troop, he caught a glimpse of me, mistook me for one of his own skirmishers who was crowding in too closely, and called out, "Keep your interval, sir; keep your interval, and go forward."

A perfect hail of bullets was sweeping over us as we advanced. Once I got a glimpse of some Spaniards, apparently retreating, far in the front, and to our right, and we fired a couple of rounds after them. Then I became convinced, after much anxious study, that we were being fired at from some large red-tiled buildings, part of a ranch on our front. Smokeless powder, and the thick cover in our front, continued to puzzle us, and I more than once consulted anxiously the officers as to the exact whereabouts of our opponents. I took a rifle from a wounded man and began to try shots with it myself. It was very hot and the men were getting exhausted, though at this particular time we were not suffering heavily from bullets, the

Spanish fire going high. As we advanced, the cover became a little thicker and I lost touch of the main body under Wood; so I halted and we fired industriously at the ranch buildings ahead of us, some five hundred yards off. Then we heard cheering on the right, and I supposed that this meant a charge on the part of Wood's men, so I sprang up and ordered the men to rush the buildings ahead of us. They came forward with a will. There was a moment's heavy firing from the Spaniards, which all went over our heads, and then it ceased entirely. When we arrived at the buildings, panting and out of breath, they contained nothing but heaps of empty cartridge-shells and two dead Spaniards, shot through the head.

The country all around us was thickly forested, so that it was very difficult to see any distance in any direction. The firing had now died out, but I was still entirely uncertain as to exactly what had happened. I did not know whether the enemy had been driven back or whether it was merely a lull in the fight, and we might be attacked again; nor did I know what had happened in any other part of the line, while as I occupied the extreme left, I was not sure whether or not my flank was in danger. At this moment one of our men who had dropped out arrived with the informa-tion (fortunately false) that Wood was dead. Of course, this meant that the command devolved upon me, and I hastily set about taking charge of the regiment. I had been particularly struck by the coolness and courage shown by Sergeants Dame and McIlhenny, and sent them out with small pickets to keep watch in front and to the left of the left wing. I sent other men to fill the canteens with water, and threw the rest out in a long line in a disused sunken road, which gave them cover, putting two or three wounded men, who had hitherto kept up with the fighting-line, and a dozen men who were suffering from heat exhaustion—for the fighting and running under that blazing sun through the thick dry jungle was heart-breaking—into the ranch buildings. Then I started over toward the main body, but to my delight encountered Wood himself, who told me the fight was over and the Spaniards had retreated. He also informed me that other troops were just coming up. The first to appear was a squadron of the Ninth Cavalry, under Major Dimick, which had hurried up to get into the fight, and was greatly disappointed to find it over. They took post in front of our lines, so that our tired men were able to get a rest, Captain

McBlain, of the Ninth, good-naturedly giving us some points as to the best way to station our outposts. Then General Chaffee, rather glum at not having been in the fight himself, rode up at the head of some of his infantry, and I marched my squadron back to where the rest of the regiment was going into camp, just where the two trails came together, and beyond—that is, on the Santiago side of—the original Spanish lines.

The Rough Riders had lost 8 men killed and 34 wounded, aside from two or three who were merely scratched and whose wounds were not reported. The First Cavalry, white, lost 7 men killed and 8 wounded; the Tenth Cavalry, colored, 1 man killed and 10 wounded; so, out of 964 men engaged on our side, 16 were killed and 52 wounded. The Spaniards were under General Rubin, with, as second in command, Colonel Alcarez. They had two guns, and eleven companies of about 100 men each: three belonging to the Porto Rico regiment, three to the San Fernandino, two to the Talavero, two being so-called mobilized companies from the mineral districts, and one a company of engineers; over 1,200 men in all, together with two guns.

General Rubin reported that he had repulsed the American attack, and Lieutenant Tejeiro states in his book that General Rubin forced the Americans to retreat, and enumerates the attacking force as consisting of three regular regiments of infantry, the Second Massachusetts and the Seventy-first New York (not one of which fired a gun or were anywhere near the battle), in addition to the sixteen dismounted troops of cavalry. In other words, as the five infantry regiments each included twelve companies, he makes the attacking force consist of just five times the actual amount. As for the "repulse," our line never went back ten yards in any place, and the advance was practically steady; while an hour and a half after the fight began we were in complete possession of the entire Spanish position, and their troops were fleeing in masses down the road, our men being too exhausted to follow them.

General Rubin also reports that he lost but seven men killed. This is certainly incorrect, for Captain O'Neill and I went over the ground very carefully and counted eleven dead Spaniards, all of whom were actually buried by our burying squads. There were probably two or three men whom we missed, but I think that our official reports are incorrect in stating that forty-two dead Spaniards were found; this being based upon reports in which I think some of the Spanish dead were counted two or three times. Indeed, I should doubt whether their loss was as heavy as ours, for they were under cover, while we advanced, often in the open, and their main lines fled long before we could get to close quarters. It was a very difficult country, and a force of good soldiers resolutely handled could have held the pass with ease against two or three times their number. As it was, with a force half of regulars and half of volunteers, we drove out a superior number of Spanish regular troops, strongly posted, without suffering a very heavy loss. Although the Spanish fire was very heavy, it does not seem to me it was very well directed; and though they fired with great spirit while we merely stood at a distance and fired at them, they did not show much resolution, and when we advanced, always went back long before there was any chance of our coming into contact with them. Our men behaved very well indeed—white regulars, colored regulars, and Rough Riders alike. The newspaper press failed to do full justice to the white regulars, in my opinion, from the simple reason that everybody knew that they would fight, whereas there had been a good deal of question as to how the Rough Riders, who were volunteer troops, and the Tenth Cavalry, who were colored, would behave; so there was a tendency to exalt our deeds at the expense of those of the First Regulars, whose courage and good conduct were taken for granted. It was a trying fight beyond what the losses show, for it is hard upon raw soldiers to be pitted against an unseen foe, and to advance steadily when their comrades are falling around them, and when they can only occasionally see a chance to retaliate. Wood's experience in fighting Apaches stood him in good stead. An entirely raw man at the head of the regiment, conducting, as Wood was, what was practically an independent fight, would have been in a very trying position. The fight cleared the way toward Santiago, and we experienced no further resistance.

That afternoon we made camp and dined, subsisting chiefly on a load of beans which we found on one of the Spanish mules which had been shot. We also looked after the wounded. Dr. Church had himself gone out to the firing-line during the fight, and carried to the rear some of the worst wounded on his back or in his arms. Those who could walk had walked in to where the little field-hospital of the regiment was established on the trail. We found all our dead and all the badly wounded. Around one of the latter the big, hideous land-crabs had gathered in a gruesome ring, waiting for life to be extinct. One of our own men and most of the Spanish dead had been found by the vultures before we got to them; and their bodies were mangled, the eyes and wounds being torn.

The Rough Rider who had been thus treated was in Bucky O'Neill's troop; and as we looked at the body, O'Neill turned to me and asked, "Colonel, isn't it Whitman who says of the vultures that 'they pluck the eyes of princes and tear the flesh of kings'?" I answered that I could not place the quotation. Just a week afterward we were shielding his own body from the birds of prey.

One of the men who fired first, and who displayed conspicuous gallantry, was a Cherokee half-breed, who was hit seven times, and of course had to go back to the States. Before he rejoined us at Montauk Point he had gone through a little private war of his own; for on his return he found that a cowboy had gone off with his sweetheart, and in the fight that ensued he shot his rival. Another man of L Troop who also showed marked gallantry was Elliot Cowdin. The men of the plains and mountains were trained by life-long habit to look on life and death with iron philosophy. As I passed by a couple of tall, lank, Oklahoma cow-punchers, I heard one say, "Well, some of the boys got it in the neck!" to which the other answered with the grim plains proverb of the South: "Many a good horse dies."

Thomas Isbell, a half-breed Cherokee in the squad under Hamilton Fish, was among the first to shoot and be shot at. He was wounded no less than seven times. The first wound was received by him two minutes after he had fired his first shot, the bullet going through his neck. The second hit him in the left thumb. The third struck near his right hip, passing entirely through the body. The fourth bullet (which was apparently from a Remington and not from a Mauser) went into his neck and lodged against the bone, being afterward cut out. The fifth bullet again hit his left hand. The sixth scraped his head and the seventh his neck. He did not receive all of the wounds at the same time, over half an hour elapsing between the first and the last. Up to receiving the last wound he had declined to leave the firing-line, but by that time he had lost so much blood that he had to be sent to the rear. The man's wiry toughness was as notable as his courage.

We improvised litters, and carried the more sorely wounded back to Siboney that afternoon and the next morning; the others walked. One of the men who had been most severely wounded was Edward Marshall, the correspondent, and he showed as much heroism as any soldier in the whole army. He was shot through the spine, a terrible and very painful wound, which we supposed meant that he would surely die; but he made no complaint of any kind, and while he retained consciousness persisted in dictating the story of the fight. A very touching incident happened in the improvised open-air hospital after the fight, where the wounded were lying. They did not groan, and made no complaint, trying to help one another. One of them suddenly began to hum, "My Country, 'Tis of Thee," and one by one the others joined in the chorus, which swelled out through the tropic woods, where the victors lay in camp beside their dead. I did not see any sign among the fighting men, whether wounded or unwounded, of the very complicated emotions assigned to their kind by some of the realistic modern novelists who have written about battles. At the front everyone behaved quite simply and took things as they came, in a matter-of-course way; but there was doubtless, as is always the case, a good deal of panic and confusion in the rear where the wounded, the stragglers, a few of the packers, and two or three newspaper correspondents were, and in consequence the first reports sent back to the coast were of a most alarming character, describing, with minute inaccuracy, how we had run into ambush, etc. The packers with the mules which carried the rapid-fire guns were among those who ran, and they let the mules go in the jungle; in consequence the guns were never even brought to the firing-line, and only Fred Herrig's skill as a trailer enabled us to recover them. By patient work he followed up the mules' tracks in the forest until he found the animals.

Among the wounded who walked to the temporary hospital at Siboney was the trooper, Rowland, of whom I spoke before. There the doctors examined him, and decreed that his wound was so serious that he must go back to the States. This was enough for Rowland, who waited until nightfall and then escaped, slipping out of the window and making his way back to camp with his rifle and pack, though his wound must have made all movement very painful to him. After this, we felt that he was entitled to stay, and he never left us for a day, distinguishing himself again in the fight at San Juan.

Next morning we buried seven dead Rough Riders in a grave on the summit of the trail, Chaplain Brown reading the solemn burial service of the Episcopalians, while the men stood around with bared heads and joined in singing, "Rock of Ages." Vast numbers of vultures were wheeling round and round in great circles through the blue sky overhead. There could be no more honorable burial than that of these men in a common grave—Indian and cowboy, miner, packer, and college athlete—the man of unknown ancestry from the lonely Western plains, and the man who carried on his watch the crests of the Stuyvesants and the Fishes, one in the way they had met death, just as during life they had been one in their daring and their loyalty.

On the afternoon of the 25th we moved on a couple of miles, and camped in a marshy open spot close to a beautiful stream. Here we lay for several days. Captain Lee, the British attaché, spent some time with us; we had begun to regard him as almost a member of the regiment. Count von Gotzen, the German attaché, another good fellow, also visited us. General Young was struck down with the fever, and Wood took charge of the brigade. This left me in command of the regiment, of which I was very glad, for such experience as we had had is a quick teacher. By this time the men and I knew one another, and I felt able to make them do themselves justice in march or battle. They understood that I paid no heed to where they came from; no heed to their creed, politics, or social standing; that I would care for them to the utmost of my power, but that I demanded the highest performance of duty; while in return I had seen them tested, and knew I could depend absolutely on their courage, hardihood, obedience, and individual initiative.

There was nothing like enough transportation with the army, whether in the way of wagons or mule-trains; exactly as there had been no sufficient number of landing-boats with the transports. The officers' baggage had come up, but none of us had much, and the shelter-tents proved only a partial protection against the terrific downpours of rain. These occurred almost every afternoon, and turned the camp into a tarn, and the trails into torrents and quagmires. We were not given quite the proper amount of food, and what we did get, like most of the clothing issued us, was fitter for the Klondyke than for Cuba. We got enough salt pork and hardtack for the men, but not the full ration of coffee and sugar, and nothing else. I organized a couple of expeditions back to the seacoast, taking the strongest and best walkers and also some of the officers' horses and a stray mule or two, and brought back beans and canned tomatoes. These I got partly by great exertions on my part, and partly by the aid of Colonel Weston of the Commissary Department, a particularly energetic man whose services were of great value. A silly regulation forbade my purchasing canned vegetables, etc., except for the officers; and I had no little difficulty in getting round this regulation, and purchasing (with my own money, of course) what I needed for the men.

One of the men I took with me on one of these trips was Sherman Bell, the former Deputy Marshal of Cripple Creek, and Wells-Fargo Express rider. In coming home with his load, through a blinding storm, he slipped and opened the old rupture. The agony was very great and one of his comrades took his load. He himself, sometimes walking, and sometimes crawling, got back to camp, where Dr. Church fixed him up with a spike bandage, but informed him that he would have to be sent back to the States when an ambulance came along. The ambulance did not come until the next day, which was the day before we marched to San Juan. It arrived after nightfall, and as soon as Bell heard it coming, he crawled out of the hospital tent into the jungle, where he lay all night; and the ambulance went off without him. The men shielded him just as schoolboys would shield a companion, carrying his gun, belt, and bedding; while Bell kept out of sight until the column started, and then staggered along behind it. I found him the morning of the San Juan fight. He told me that he wanted to die fighting, if die he must, and I hadn't the heart to send him back. He did splendid service that day, and afterward in the trenches, and though the rupture opened twice again, and on each occasion he was within a hair's breadth of death, he escaped, and came back with us to the United States.

The army was camped along the valley, ahead of and behind us, our outposts being established on either side. From the generals to the privates all were eager to march against Santiago. At daybreak, when the tall palms began to show dimly through the rising mist, the scream of the cavalry trumpets tore the tropic dawn; and in the evening, as the bands of regiment after regiment played "The Star-Spangled Banner," all, officers and men alike, stood with heads uncovered, wherever they were, until the last strains of the anthem died away in the hot sunset air.

The Cavalry at Santiago

On June 30th we received orders to hold ourselves in readiness to march against Santiago, and all the men were greatly overjoyed, for the inaction was trying. The one narrow road, a mere muddy track along which the army was encamped, was choked with the marching columns. As always happened when we had to change camp, everything that the men could not carry, including, of course, the officers' baggage, was left behind.

About noon the Rough Riders struck camp and drew up in column beside the road in the rear of the First Cavalry. Then we sat down and waited for hours before the order came to march, while regiment after regiment passed by, varied by bands of tatterdemalion Cuban insurgents, and by mule-trains with ammunition. Every man carried three days' provisions. We had succeeded in borrowing mules sufficient to carry along the dynamite gun and the automatic Colts.

At last, toward mid-afternoon, the First and Tenth Cavalry, ahead of us, marched, and we followed. The First was under the command of Lieutenant-Colonel Veile, the Tenth under Lieutenant-Colonel Baldwin. Every few minutes there would be a stoppage in front, and at the halt I would make the men sit or lie down beside the track, loosening their packs. The heat was intense as we passed through the still, close jungle, which formed a wall on either hand. Occasionally we came to gaps or open spaces, where some regiment was camped, and now and then one of these regiments, which apparently had been left out of its proper place, would file into the road, breaking up our line of march. As a result, we finally found ourselves following merely the tail of the regiment ahead of us, an infantry regiment being thrust into the interval. Once or twice we had to wade streams. Darkness came on, but we still continued to march. It was about eight o'clock when we turned to the left and climbed El Poso hill, on whose summit there was a ruined ranch and sugar factory, now, of course, deserted. Here I found General Wood, who was arranging for the camping of the brigade. Our own arrangements for the night were simple. I extended each troop across the road into the jungle, and then the men threw down their belongings where they stood and slept on their arms. Fortunately, there was no rain. Wood and I curled up under our rain-coats on the saddle-blankets, while his two aides, Captain A. L. Mills and Lieutenant W. N. Ship, slept near us. We were up before dawn and getting breakfast. Mills and Ship had nothing to eat, and they breakfasted with Wood and myself, as we had been able to get some handfuls of beans, and some coffee and sugar, as well as the ordinary bacon and hardtack.

We did not talk much, for though we were in ignorance as to precisely what the day would bring forth, we knew that we should see fighting. We had slept soundly enough, although, of course, both Wood and I during the night had made a round of the sentries, he of the brigade, and I of the regiment; and I suppose that, excepting among hardened veterans, there is always a certain feeling of uneasy excitement the night before the battle.

Mills and Ship were both tall, fine-looking men, of tried courage, and thoroughly trained in every detail of their profession; I remember being struck by the quiet, soldierly way they were going about their work early that morning. Before noon one was killed and the other dangerously wounded.

General Wheeler was sick, but with his usual indomitable pluck and entire indifference to his own personal comfort, he kept to the front. He was unable to retain command of the cavalry division, which accordingly devolved upon General Samuel Sumner, who commanded it until midafternoon, when the bulk of the fighting was over. General Sumner's own brigade fell to Colonel Henry Carroll. General Sumner led the advance with the cavalry, and the battle was fought by him and by General Kent, who commanded the infantry division, and whose foremost brigade was led by General Hawkins.

As the sun rose the men fell in, and at the same time a battery of field-guns was brought up on the hill-crest just beyond, between us and toward Santiago. It was a fine sight to see the great horses straining under the lash as they whirled the guns up the hill and into position.

Our brigade was drawn up on the hither side of a kind of half basin, a big band of Cubans being off to the left. As yet we had received no orders, except that we were told that the main fighting was to be done by Lawton's infantry division, which was to take El Caney, several miles to our right, while we were simply to make a diversion. This diversion was to be made mainly with the artillery, and the battery which had taken position immediately in front of us was to begin when Lawton began.

It was about six o'clock that the first report of the cannon from El Caney came booming to us across the miles of still jungle. It was a very lovely morning, the sky of cloudless blue, while the level, shimmering rays from the just-risen sun brought into fine relief the splendid palms which here and there towered above the lower growth. The lofty and beautiful mountains hemmed in the Santiago plain, making it an amphitheatre for the battle.

Immediately our guns opened, and at the report great clouds of white smoke hung on the ridge crest. For a minute or two there was no response. Wood and I were sitting together, and Wood remarked to me that he wished our brigade could be moved somewhere else, for we were directly in line of any return fire aimed by the Spaniards at the battery. Hardly had he spoken when there was a peculiar whistling, singing sound in the air, and immediately afterward the noise of something exploding over our heads. It was shrapnel from the Spanish batteries. We sprung to our feet and leaped on our horses. Immediately afterward a second shot came which burst directly above us; and then a third. From the second shell one of the shrapnel bullets dropped on my wrist, hardly breaking the skin, but raising a bump about as big as a hickory-nut. The same shell wounded four of my regiment, one of them being Mason Mitchell, and two or three of the regulars were also hit, one losing his leg by a great fragment of shell. Another shell exploded right in the middle of the Cubans, killing and wounding a good many, while the remainder scattered like guinea-hens. Wood's lead horse was also shot through the lungs. I at once hustled my regiment over the crest of the hill into the thick underbrush, where I had no little difficulty in getting them together again into column.

Meanwhile, the firing continued for fifteen or twenty minutes, until it gradually died away. As the Spaniards used smokeless powder, their artillery had an enormous advantage over ours, and, moreover, we did not have the best type of modern guns, our fire being slow.

As soon as the firing ceased, Wood formed his brigade, with my regiment in front, and gave me orders to follow behind the First Brigade, which was just moving off the ground. In column of fours we marched down the trail toward the ford of the San Juan River. We passed two or three regiments of infantry, and were several times halted before we came to the ford. The First Brigade, which was under Colonel Carroll—Lieutenant-Colonel Hamilton commanding the Ninth Regiment, Major Wessels the Third, and Captain Kerr the Sixth—had already crossed and was marching to the right, parallel to, but a little distance from, the river. The Spaniards in the trenches and block-houses on top of the hills in front were already firing at the brigade in desultory fashion. The extreme advance of the Ninth Cavalry was under Lieutenants McNamee and Hartwick. They were joined by General Hawkins, with his staff, who was looking over the ground and deciding on the route he should take his infantry brigade.

Our orders had been of the vaguest kind, being simply to march to the right and connect with Lawton—with whom, of course, there was no chance of our connecting. No reconnaissance had been made, and the exact position and strength of the Spaniards was not known. A captive balloon was up in the air at this moment, but it was worse than useless. A previous proper reconnaissance and proper look-out from the hills would have given us exact information. As it was, Generals Kent, Sumner, and Hawkins had to be their own reconnaissance, and they fought their troops so well that we won anyhow.

I was now ordered to cross the ford, march half a mile or so to the right, and then halt and await further orders; and I promptly hurried my men across, for the fire was getting hot, and the captive balloon, to the horror of everybody, was coming down to the ford. Of course, it was a special target for the enemy's fire. I got my men across before it reached the ford. There it partly collapsed and remained, causing severe loss of life, as it indicated the exact position where the Tenth and the First Cavalry, and the infantry, were crossing.

As I led my column slowly along, under the intense heat, through the high grass of the open jungle, the First Brigade was to our left, and the firing between it and the Spaniards on the hills grew steadily hotter and hotter. After a while I came to a sunken lane, and as by this time the First Brigade had stopped and was engaged in a stand-up fight, I halted my men and sent back word for orders. As we faced toward the Spanish hills my regiment was on the right with next to it and a little in advance the First Cavalry, and behind them the Tenth. In our front the Ninth held the right, the Sixth the centre, and the Third the left; but in the jungle the lines were already overlapping in places. Kent's infantry were coming up, farther to the left.

Captain Mills was with me. The sunken lane, which had a wire fence on either side, led straight up toward, and between, the two hills in our front, the hill on the left, which contained heavy block-houses, being farther away from us than the hill on our right, which we afterward grew to call Kettle Hill, and which was surmounted merely by some large ranch buildings or haciendas, with sunken brick-lined walls and cellars. I got the men as well-sheltered as I could. Many of them lay close under the bank of the lane; others slipped into the San Juan River and crouched under its hither bank, while the rest lay down behind the patches of bushy jungle in the tall grass. The heat was intense, and many of the men were already showing signs of exhaustion. The sides of the hills in front were bare; but the country up to them was, for the most part, covered with such dense jungle that in charging through it no accuracy of formation could possibly be preserved.

The fight was now on in good earnest, and the Spaniards on the hills were engaged in heavy volley firing. The Mauser bullets drove in sheets through the trees and the tall jungle grass, making a peculiar whirring or rustling sound; some of the bullets seemed to pop in the air, so that we thought they were explosive; and, indeed, many of those which were coated with brass did explode, in the sense that the brass coat was ripped off, making a thin plate of hard metal with a jagged edge, which inflicted a ghastly wound. These bullets were shot from a .45-calibre rifle carrying smokeless powder, which was much used by the guerrillas and irregular Spanish troops. The Mauser bullets themselves made a small clean hole, with the result that the wound healed in a most astonishing manner. One or two of our men who were shot in the head had the skull blown open, but elsewhere the wounds from the minute steel-coated bullet, with its very high velocity, were certainly nothing like as serious as those made by the old large-calibre, low-power rifle. If a man was shot through the heart, spine, or brain he was, of course, killed instantly; but very few of the wounded died—even under the appalling conditions which prevailed, owing to the lack of attendance and supplies in the field-hospitals with the army.

While we were lying in reserve we were suffering nearly as much as afterward when we charged. I think that the bulk of the Spanish fire was practically unaimed, or at least not aimed at any particular man, and only occasionally at a particular body of men; but they swept the whole field of battle up to the edge of the river, and man after man in our ranks fell dead or wounded, although I had the troopers scattered out far apart, taking advantage of every scrap of cover.

Devereux was dangerously shot while he lay with his men on the edge of the river. A young West Point cadet, Ernest Haskell, who had taken his holiday with us as an acting second lieutenant, was shot through the stomach. He had shown great coolness and gallantry, which he displayed to an even more marked degree after being wounded, shaking my hand and saying: "All right, Colonel, I'm going to get well. Don't bother about me, and don't let any man come away with me." When I shook hands with him, I thought he would surely die; yet he recovered.

The most serious loss that I and the regiment could have suffered befell just before we charged. Bucky O'Neill was strolling up and down in front of his men, smoking his cigarette, for he was inveterately addicted to the habit. He had a theory that an officer ought never to take cover—a theory which was, of course, wrong, though in a volunteer organization the officers should certainly expose themselves very fully, simply for the effect on the men; our regimental toast on the transport running, "The officers; may the war last until each is killed, wounded, or promoted." As O'Neill moved to and fro, his men begged him to lie down, and one of the sergeants said, "Captain, a bullet is sure to hit you." O'Neill took his cigarette out of his mouth, and blowing out a cloud of smoke, laughed and said, "Sergeant, the Spanish bullet isn't made that will kill me." A little later he discussed for a moment with one of the regular officers the direction from which the Spanish fire was coming. As he turned on his heel a bullet struck him in the mouth and came out at the back of his head, so that even before he fell his wild and gallant soul had gone out into the darkness.

My orderly was a brave young Harvard boy, Sanders, from the quaint old Massachusetts town of Salem. The work of an orderly on foot, under the blazing sun, through the hot and matted jungle, was very severe, and finally the heat overcame him. He dropped; nor did he ever recover fully, and later he died from fever. In his place I summoned a trooper whose name I did not know. Shortly afterward, while sitting beside the bank, I directed him to go back and ask whatever general he came across if I could not advance, as my men were being much cut up. He stood up to salute and then pitched forward across my knees, a bullet having gone through his throat, cutting the carotid.

When O'Neill was shot, his troops, who were devoted to him, were for the moment at a loss whom to follow. One of their number, Henry Bardshar, a huge Arizona miner, immediately attached himself to me as my orderly, and from that moment he was closer to me, not only in the fight, but throughout the rest of the campaign, than any other man, not even excepting the color-sergeant, Wright.

Captain Mills was with me; gallant Ship had already been killed. Mills was an invaluable aide, absolutely cool, absolutely unmoved or flurried in any way.

I sent messenger after messenger to try to find General Sumner or General Wood and get permission to advance, and was just about making up my mind that in the absence of orders I had better "march toward the guns," when Lieutenant-Colonel Dorst came riding up through the storm of bullets with the welcome command "to move forward and support the regulars in the assault on the hills in front." General Sumner had obtained authority to advance from Lieutenant Miley, who was representing General Shafter at the front, and was in the thick of the fire. The General at once ordered the first brigade to advance on the hills, and the second to support it. He himself was riding his horse along the lines, superintending the fight. Later I overheard a couple of my men talking together about him. What they said illustrates the value of a display of courage among the officers in hardening their soldiers; for their theme was how, as they were lying down under a fire which they could not return, and were in consequence feeling rather nervous, General Sumner suddenly appeared on horseback, sauntering by quite unmoved; and, said one of the men, "That made us feel all right. If the General could stand it, we could."

The instant I received the order I sprang on my horse and then my "crowded hour" began. The guerrillas had been shooting at us from the edges of the jungle and from their perches in the leafy trees, and as they used smokeless powder, it was almost impossible to see them, though a few of my men had from time to time responded. We had also suffered from the hill on our right front, which was held chiefly by guerrillas, although there were also some Spanish regulars with them, for we found their dead. I formed my men in columns of troops, each troop extended in open skirmishing order, the right resting on the wire fences which bordered the sunken lane. Captain Jenkins led the first squadron, his eyes literally dancing with joyous excitement.

I started in the rear of the regiment, the position in which the colonel should theoretically stay. Captain Mills and Captain McCormick were both with me as aides; but I speedily had to send them off on special duty in getting the different bodies of men forward. I had intended to go into action on foot as at Las Guasimas, but the heat was so oppressive that I found I should be quite unable to run up and down the line and superintend matters unless I was mounted; and, moreover, when on horseback, I could see the men better and they could see me better.

A curious incident happened as I was getting the men started forward. Always when men have been lying down under cover for some time, and are required to advance, there is a little hesitation, each looking to see whether the others are going forward. As I rode down the line, calling to the troopers to go forward, and rasping brief directions to the captains and lieutenants, I came upon a man lying behind a little bush, and I ordered him to jump up. I do not think he understood that we were making a forward move, and he looked up at me for a moment with hesitation, and I again bade him rise, jeering him and saying: "Are you afraid to stand up when I am on horseback?" As I spoke, he suddenly fell forward on his face, a bullet having struck him and gone through him lengthwise. I suppose the bullet had been aimed at me; at any rate, I, who was on horseback in the open, was unhurt, and the man lying flat on the ground in the cover beside me was killed. There were several pairs of brothers with us; of the two Nortons one was killed; of the two McCurdys one was wounded.

I soon found that I could get that line, behind which I personally was, faster forward than the one immediately in front of it, with the result that the two rearmost lines of the regiment began to crowd together; so I rode through them both, the better to move on the one in front. This happened with every line in succession, until I found myself at the head of the regiment.

Both lieutenants of B Troop from Arizona had been exerting themselves greatly, and both were overcome by the heat; but Sergeants Campbell and Davidson took it forward in splendid shape. Some of the men from this troop and from the other Arizona troop (Bucky O'Neill's) joined me as a kind of fighting tail.

The Ninth Regiment was immediately in front of me, and the First on my left, and these went up Kettle Hill with my regiment. The Third, Sixth, and Tenth went partly up Kettle Hill (following the Rough Riders and the Ninth and First), and partly between that and the block-house hill, which the infantry were assailing. General Sumner in person gave the Tenth the order to charge the hills; and it went forward at a rapid gait. The three regiments went forward more or less intermingled, advancing steadily and keeping up a heavy fire. Up Kettle Hill Sergeant George Berry, of the Tenth, bore not only his own regimental colors but those of the Third, the color-sergeant of the Third having been shot down; he kept shouting, "Dress on the colors, boys, dress on the colors!" as he followed Captain Ayres, who was running in advance of his men, shouting and waving his hat. The Tenth Cavalry lost a greater proportion of its officers than any other regiment in the battle—eleven out of twenty-two.

By the time I had come to the head of the regiment we ran into the left wing of the Ninth Regulars, and some of the First Regulars, who were lying down; that is, the troopers were lying down, while the officers were walking to and fro. The officers of the white and colored regiments alike took the greatest pride in seeing that the men more than did their duty; and the mortality among them was great.

I spoke to the captain in command of the rear platoons, saying that I had been ordered to support the regulars in the attack upon the hills, and that in my judgment we could not take these hills by firing at them, and that we must rush them. He answered that his orders were to keep his men lying where they were, and that he could not charge without orders. I asked where the Colonel was, and as he was not in sight, said, "Then I am the ranking officer here and I give the order to charge"—for I did not want to keep the men longer in the open suffering under a fire which they could not effectively return. Naturally the captain hesitated to obey this order when no word had been received from his own Colonel. So I said, "Then let my men through, sir," and rode on through the lines, followed by the grinning Rough Riders, whose attention had been completely taken off the Spanish bullets, partly by my dialogue with the regulars, and partly by the language I had been using to themselves as I got the lines forward, for I had been joking with some and swearing at others, as the exigencies of the case seemed to demand.

When we started to go through, however, it proved too much for the regulars, and they jumped up and came along, their officers and troops mingling with mine, all being delighted at the chance. When I got to where the head of the left wing of the Ninth was lying, through the courtesy of Lieutenant Hartwick, two of whose colored troopers threw down the fence, I was enabled to get back into the lane, at the same time waving my hat, and giving the order to charge the hill on our right front. Out of my sight, over on the right, Captains McBlain and Taylor, of the Ninth, made up their minds independently to charge at just about this time; and at almost the same moment Colonels Carroll and Hamilton, who were off, I believe, to my left, where we could see neither them nor their men, gave the order to advance. But of all this I knew nothing at the time. The whole line, tired of waiting, and eager to close with the enemy, was straining to go forward; and it seems that different parts slipped the leash at almost the same moment. The First Cavalry came up the hill just behind, and partly mixed with my regiment and the Ninth. As already said, portions of the Third, Sixth, and Tenth followed, while the rest of the members of these three regiments kept more in touch with the infantry on our left.

By this time we were all in the spirit of the thing and greatly excited by the charge, the men cheering and running forward between shots, while the delighted faces of the foremost officers, like Captain C. J. Stevens, of the Ninth, as they ran at the head of their troops, will always stay in my mind. As soon as I was in the line I galloped forward a few yards until I saw that the men were well started, and then galloped back to help Goodrich, who was in command of his troop, get his men across the road so as to attack the hill from that side. Captain Mills had already thrown three of the other troops of the regiment across this road for the same purpose. Wheeling around, I then again galloped toward the hill, passing the shouting, cheering, firing men, and went up the lane, splashing through a small stream; when I got abreast of the ranch buildings on the top of Kettle Hill, I turned and went up the slope. Being on horseback I was, of course, able to get ahead of the men on foot, excepting my orderly, Henry Bardshar, who had run ahead very fast in order to get better shots at the Spaniards, who were now running out of the ranch buildings. Sergeant Campbell and a number of the Arizona men, and Dudley Dean, among others, were very close behind. Stevens, with his platoon of the Ninth, was abreast of us; so were McNamee and Hartwick. Some forty yards from the top I ran into a wire fence and jumped off Little Texas, turning him loose. He had been scraped by a couple of bullets, one of which nicked my elbow, and I never expected to see him again. As I ran up to the hill, Bardshar stopped to shoot, and two Spaniards fell as he emptied his magazine. These were the only Spaniards I actually saw fall to aimed shots by any one of my men, with the exception of two guerrillas in trees.

Almost immediately afterward the hill was covered by the troops, both Rough Riders and the colored troopers of the Ninth, and some men of the First. There was the usual confusion, and afterward there was much discussion as to exactly who had been on the hill first. The first guidons planted there were those of the three New Mexican troops, G, E, and F, of my regiment, under their Captains, Llewellen, Luna, and Muller, but on the extreme right of the hill, at the opposite end from where we struck it, Captains Taylor and McBlain and their men of the Ninth were first up. Each of the five captains was firm in the belief that his troop was first up. As for the individual men, each of whom honestly thought he was first on the summit, their name was legion. One Spaniard was captured in the buildings, another was shot as he tried to hide himself, and a few others were killed as they ran.

Among the many deeds of conspicuous gallantry here performed, two, both to the credit of the First Cavalry, may be mentioned as examples of the others, not as exceptions. Sergeant Charles Karsten, while close beside Captain Tutherly, the squadron commander, was hit by a shrapnel bullet. He continued on the line, firing until his arm grew numb; and he then refused to go to the rear, and devoted himself to taking care of the wounded, utterly unmoved by the heavy fire. Trooper Hugo Brittain, when wounded, brought the regimental standard forward, waving it to and fro, to cheer the men.

No sooner were we on the crest than the Spaniards from the line of hills in our front, where they were strongly entrenched, opened a very heavy fire upon us with their rifles. They also opened upon us with one or two pieces of artillery, using time fuses which burned very accurately, the shells exploding right over our heads.

On the top of the hill was a huge iron kettle, or something of the kind, probably used for sugar refining. Several of our men took shelter behind this. We had a splendid view of the charge on the San Juan block-house to our left, where the infantry of Kent, led by Hawkins, were climbing the hill. Obviously the proper thing to do was to help them, and I got the men together and started them volley-firing against the Spaniards in the San Juan block-house and in the trenches around it. We could only see their heads; of course, this was all we ever could see when we were firing at them in their trenches. Stevens was directing not only his own colored troopers, but a number of Rough Riders; for in a melee good soldiers are always prompt to recognize a good officer, and are eager to follow him.

We kept up a brisk fire for some five or ten minutes; meanwhile, we were much cut up ourselves. Gallant Colonel Hamilton, than whom there was never a braver man, was killed, and equally gallant Colonel Carroll wounded. When near the summit Captain Mills had been shot through the head, the bullet destroying the sight of one eye permanently and of the other temporarily. He would not go back or let any man assist him, sitting down where he was and waiting until one of the men brought him word that the hill was stormed. Colonel Veile planted the standard of the First Cavalry on the hill, and General Sumner rode up. He was fighting his division in great form, and was always himself in the thick of the fire. As the men were much excited by the firing, they seemed to pay very little heed to their own losses.

Suddenly, above the cracking of the carbines, rose a peculiar drumming sound, and some of the men cried, "The Spanish machine-guns!" Listening, I made out that it came from the flat ground to the left, and jumped to my feet, smiting my hand on my thigh, and shouting aloud with exultation, "It's the Gatlings, men, our Gatlings!" Lieutenant Parker was bringing his four Gatlings into action, and shoving them nearer and nearer the front. Now and then the drumming ceased for a moment; then it would resound again, always closer to San Juan Hill, which Parker, like ourselves, was hammering to assist the infantry attack. Our men cheered lustily. We saw much of Parker after that, and there was never a more welcome sound than his Gatlings as they opened. It was the only sound which I ever heard my men cheer in battle.

The infantry got nearer and nearer the crest of the hill. At last we could see the Spaniards running from the rifle-pits as the Americans came on in their final rush. Then I stopped my men for fear they should injure their comrades, and called to them to charge the next line of trenches, on the hills in our front, from which we had been undergoing a good deal of punishment. Thinking that the men would all come, I jumped over the wire fence in front of us and started at the double; but, as a matter of fact, the troopers were so excited, what with shooting and being shot, and shouting and cheering, that they did not hear, or did not heed me; and after running about a hundred yards I found I had only five men along with me. Bullets were ripping the grass all around us, and one of the men, Clay Green, was mortally wounded; another, Winslow Clark, a Harvard man, was shot first in the leg and then through the body. He made not the slightest murmur, only asking me to put his water canteen where he could get at it, which I did; he ultimately recovered.

There was no use going on with the remaining three men, and I bade them stay where they were while I went back and brought up the rest of the brigade. This was a decidedly cool request, for there was really no possible point in letting them stay there while I went back; but at the moment it seemed perfectly natural to me, and apparently so to them, for they cheerfully nodded, and sat down in the grass, firing back at the line of trenches from which the Spaniards were shooting at them. Meanwhile, I ran back, jumped over the wire fence, and went over the crest of the hill, filled with anger against the troopers, and especially those of my own regiment, for not having accompanied me. They, of course, were quite innocent of wrong-doing; and even while I taunted them bitterly for not having followed me, it was all I could do not to smile at the look of injury and surprise that came over their faces, while they cried out, "We didn't hear you, we didn't see you go, Colonel; lead on now, we'll sure follow you."

I wanted the other regiments to come too, so I ran down to where General Sumner was and asked him if I might make the charge; and he told me to go and that he would see that the men followed. By this time everybody had his attention attracted, and when I leaped over the fence again, with Major Jenkins beside me, the men of the various regiments which were already on the hill came with a rush, and we started across the wide valley which lay between us and the Spanish entrenchments. Captain Dimmick, now in command of the Ninth, was bringing it forward; Captain McBlain had a number of Rough Riders mixed in with his troop, and led them all together; Captain Taylor had been severely wounded. The long-legged men like Greenway, Goodrich, sharp-shooter Proffit, and others, outstripped the rest of us, as we had a considerable distance to go. Long before we got near them the Spaniards ran, save a few here and there, who either surrendered or were shot down. When we reached the trenches we found them filled with dead bodies in the light blue and white uniform of the Spanish regular army. There were very few wounded. Most of the fallen had little holes in their heads from which their brains were oozing; for they were covered from the neck down by the trenches.

It was at this place that Major Wessels, of the Third Cavalry, was shot in the back of the head. It was a severe wound, but after having it bound up, he again came to the front in command of his regiment. Among the men who were foremost was Lieutenant Milton F. Davis, of the First Cavalry. He had been joined by three men of the Seventy-first New York, who ran up, and, saluting, said, "Lieutenant, we want to go with you; our officers won't lead us." One of the brave fellows was soon afterward shot in the face. Lieutenant Davis's first sergeant, Clarence Gould, killed a Spanish soldier with his revolver, just as the Spaniard was aiming at one of my Rough Riders. At about the same time I also shot one. I was with Henry Bardshar, running up at the double, and two Spaniards leaped from the trenches and fired at us, not ten yards away. As they turned to run I closed in and fired twice, missing the first and killing the second. My revolver was from the sunken battleship *Maine*, and had been given me by my brother-in-law, Captain W. S. Cowles, of the Navy. At the time I did not know of Gould's exploit, and supposed my feat to be unique; and although Gould had killed his Spaniard in the trenches, not very far from me, I never learned of it until weeks after. It is astonishing what a limited area of vision and experience one has in the hurly-burly of a battle.

There was very great confusion at this time, the different regiments being completely intermingled—white regulars, colored regulars, and Rough Riders. General Sumner had kept a considerable force in reserve on Kettle Hill, under Major Jackson, of the Third Cavalry. We were still under a heavy fire and I got together a mixed lot of men and pushed on from the trenches and ranch-houses which we had just taken, driving the Spaniards through a line of palm-trees, and over the crest of a chain of hills. When we reached these crests we found ourselves overlooking Santiago. Some of the men, including Jenkins, Greenway, and Goodrich, pushed on almost by themselves far ahead. Lieutenant Hugh Berkely, of the First, with a sergeant and two troopers, reached the extreme front. He was, at the time, ahead of everyone; the sergeant was killed and one trooper wounded; but the lieutenant and the remaining trooper stuck to their post for the rest of the afternoon until our line was gradually extended to include them.

While I was re-forming the troops on the chain of hills, one of General Sumner's aides, Captain Robert Howze—as dashing and gallant an officer as there was in the whole gallant cavalry division, by the way—came up with orders to me to halt where I was, not advancing farther, but to hold the hill at all hazards. Howze had his horse, and I had some difficulty in making him take proper shelter; he stayed with us for quite a time, unable to make up his mind to leave the extreme front, and meanwhile jumping at the chance to render any service, of risk or otherwise, which the moment developed.

I now had under me all the fragments of the six cavalry regiments which were at the extreme front, being the highest officer left there, and I was in immediate command of them for the remainder of the afternoon and that night. The Ninth was over to the right, and the Thirteenth Infantry afterward came up beside it. The rest of Kent's infantry was to our left. Of the Tenth, Lieutenants Anderson, Muller, and Fleming reported to me; Anderson was slightly wounded, but he paid no heed to this. All three, like every other officer, had troopers of various regiments under them; such mixing was inevitable in making repeated charges through thick jungle; it was essentially a troop commanders', indeed, almost a squad leaders', fight. The Spaniards who had been holding the trenches and the line of hills, had fallen back upon their supports, and we were under a very heavy fire both from rifles and great guns. At the point where we were, the grass-covered hill-crest was gently rounded, giving poor cover, and I made my men lie down on the hither slope.

On the extreme left Captain Beck, of the Tenth, with his own troop, and small bodies of the men of other regiments, was exercising a practically independent command, driving back the Spaniards whenever they showed any symptoms of advancing. He had received his orders to hold the line at all hazards from Lieutenant Andrews, one of General Sumner's aides, just as I had received mine from Captain Howze. Finally, he was relieved by some infantry, and then rejoined the rest of the Tenth, which was engaged heavily until dark, Major Wint being among the severely wounded. Lieutenant W. N. Smith was killed. Captain Bigelow had been wounded three times.

Our artillery made one or two efforts to come into action on the firing-line of the infantry, but the black powder rendered each attempt fruitless. The Spanish guns used smokeless powder, so that it was difficult to place them. In this respect they were on a par with their own infantry and with our regular infantry and dismounted cavalry; but our only two volunteer infantry regiments, the Second Massachusetts and the Seventy-first New York, and our artillery, all had black powder. This rendered the two volunteer regiments, which were armed with the antiquated Springfield, almost useless in the battle, and did practically the same thing for the artillery wherever it was formed within rifle range. When one of the guns was discharged a thick cloud of smoke shot out and hung over the place, making an ideal target, and in a half minute every Spanish gun and rifle within range was directed at the particular spot thus indicated; the consequence was that after a more or less lengthy stand the gun was silenced or driven off. We got no appreciable help from our guns on July 1st. Our men were quick to realize the defects of our artillery, but they were entirely philosophic about it, not showing the least concern at its failure. On the contrary, whenever they heard our artillery open they would grin as they looked at one another and remark, "There go the guns again; wonder how soon they'll be shut up," and shut up they were sure to be. The light battery of Hotchkiss one-pounders, under Lieutenant J. B. Hughes, of the Tenth Cavalry, was handled with conspicuous gallantry.

On the hill-slope immediately around me I had a mixed force composed of members of most of the cavalry regiments, and a few infantrymen. There were about fifty of my Rough Riders with Lieutenants Goodrich and Carr. Among the rest were perhaps a score of colored infantrymen, but, as it happened, at this particular point without any of their officers. No troops could have behaved better than the colored soldiers had behaved so far; but they are, of course, peculiarly dependent upon their white officers. Occasionally they produce non-commissioned officers who can take the initiative and accept responsibility precisely like the best class of whites; but this cannot be expected normally, nor is it fair to expect it. With the colored troops there should always be some of their own officers; whereas, with the white regulars, as with my own Rough Riders, experience showed that the non-commissioned officers could usually carry on the fight by themselves if they were once started, no matter whether their officers were killed or not.

At this particular time it was trying for the men, as they were lying flat on their faces, very rarely responding to the bullets, shells, and shrapnel which swept over the hill-top, and which occasionally killed or wounded one of their number. Major Albert G. Forse, of the First Cavalry, a noted Indian fighter, was killed about this time. One of my best men, Sergeant Greenly, of Arizona, who was lying beside me, suddenly said, "Beg pardon, Colonel, but I've been hit in the leg." I asked, "Badly?" He said, "Yes, Colonel; quite badly." After one of his comrades had helped him fix up his leg with a first-aid-to-the-injured bandage, he limped off to the rear.

None of the white regulars or Rough Riders showed the slightest sign of weakening; but under the strain some other infantrymen (who had none of their officers) began to get a little uneasy and to drift to the rear, either helping wounded men, or saying that they wished to find their own regiments. This I could not allow, as it was depleting my line, so I jumped up, and walking a few yards to the rear, drew my revolver, halted the retreating soldiers, and called out to them that I appreciated the gallantry with which they had fought and would be sorry to hurt them, but that I should shoot the first man who, on any pretence whatever, went to the rear. My own men had all sat up and were watching my movements with utmost interest; so was Captain Howze. I ended my statement to the colored soldiers by saying: "Now, I shall be very sorry to hurt you, and you don't know whether or not I will keep my word, but my men can tell you that I always do"; whereupon my cow-punchers, hunters, and miners solemnly nodded their heads and commented in chorus, exactly as if in a comic opera, "He always does; he always does!"

This was the end of the trouble, for the "smoked Yankees"—as the Spaniards called the colored soldiers—flashed their white teeth at one another, as they broke into broad grins, and I had no more trouble with them, they seeming to accept me as one of their own officers. The colored cavalry-men had already so accepted me; in return, the Rough Riders, although for the most part Southwesterners, who have a strong color prejudice, grew to accept them with hearty good-will as comrades, and were entirely willing, in their own phrase, "to drink out of the same canteen."

69

Where all the regular officers did so well, it is hard to draw any distinction; but in the cavalry division a peculiar need of praise should be given to the officers of the Ninth and Tenth for their work, and under their leadership the colored troops did as well as any soldiers could possibly do.

In the course of the afternoon the Spaniards in our front made the only offensive movement which I saw them make during the entire campaign; for what were ordinarily called "attacks" upon our lines consisted merely of heavy firing from their trenches and from their skirmishers. In this case they did actually begin to make a forward movement, their cavalry coming up as well as the marines and reserve infantry, while their skirmishers, who were always bold, redoubled their activity. It could not be called a charge, and not only was it not pushed home, but it was stopped almost as soon as it began, our men immediately running forward to the crest of the hill with shouts of delight at seeing their enemies at last come into the open. A few seconds' firing stopped their advance and drove them into the cover of the trenches.

They kept up a very heavy fire for some time longer, and our men again lay down, only replying occasionally. Suddenly we heard on our right the peculiar drumming sound which had been so welcome in the morning, when the infantry were assailing the San Juan block-house. The Gatlings were up again! I started over to inquire, and found that Lieutenant Parker, not content with using his guns in support of the attacking forces, had thrust them forward to the extreme front of the fighting-line, where he was handling them with great effect. From this time on, throughout the fighting, Parker's Gatlings were on the right of my regiment, and his men and mine fraternized in every way. He kept his pieces at the extreme front, using them on every occasion until the last Spanish shot was fired. Indeed, the dash and efficiency with which the Gatlings were handled by Parker was one of the most striking features of the campaign; he showed that a first-rate officer could use machine-guns, on wheels, in battle and skirmish, in attacking and defending trenches, alongside of the best troops, and to their great advantage.

As night came on, the firing gradually died away. Before this happened, however, Captains Morton and Boughton, of the Third Cavalry, came over to tell me that a rumor had reached them to the effect that there had been some talk of retiring and that they wished to protest in the strongest manner. I had been watching them both, as they handled their troops with the cool confidence of the veteran regular officer, and had been congratulating myself that they were off toward the right flank, for as long as they were there, I knew I was perfectly safe in that direction. I had heard no rumor about retiring, and I cordially agreed with them that it would be far worse than a blunder to abandon our position.

To attack the Spaniards by rushing across open ground, or through wire entanglements and low, almost impassable jungle, without the help of artillery, and to force unbroken infantry, fighting behind earthworks and armed with the best repeating weapons, supported by cannon, was one thing; to repel such an attack ourselves, or to fight our foes on anything like even terms in the open, was quite another thing. No possible number of Spaniards coming at us from in front could have driven us from our position, and there was not a man on the crest who did not eagerly and devoutly hope that our opponents would make the attempt, for it would surely have been followed, not merely by a repulse, but by our immediately taking the city. There was not an officer or a man on the firing-line, so far as I saw them, who did not feel this way.

As night fell, some of my men went back to the buildings in our rear and foraged through them, for we had now been fourteen hours charging and fighting without food. They came across what was evidently the Spanish officers' mess, where their dinner was still cooking, and they brought it to the front in high glee. It was evident that the Spanish officers were living well, however the Spanish rank and file were faring. There were three big iron pots, one filled with beef-stew, one with boiled rice, and one with boiled peas; there was a big demijohn of rum (all along the trenches which the Spaniards held were empty wine and liquor bottles); there were a number of loaves of rice-bread; and there were even some small cans of preserves and a few salt fish. Of course, among so many men, the food, which was equally divided, did not give very much to each, but it freshened us all.

Soon after dark, General Wheeler, who in the afternoon had resumed command of the cavalry division, came to the front. A very few words with General Wheeler reassured us about retiring. He had been through too much heavy fighting in the Civil War to regard the present fight as very serious, and he told us not to be under any apprehension, for he had sent word that there was no need whatever of retiring, and was sure we would stay where we were until the chance came to advance. He was second in command; and to him more than to any other one man was due the prompt abandonment of the proposal to fall back—a proposal which, if adopted, would have meant shame and disaster.

Shortly afterward General Wheeler sent us orders to entrench. The men of the different regiments were now getting in place again and sifting themselves out. All of our troops who had been kept at Kettle Hill came forward and rejoined us after nightfall. During the afternoon Greenway, apparently not having enough to do in the fighting, had taken advantage of a lull to explore the buildings himself, and had found a number of Spanish entrenching tools, picks, and shovels, and these we used in digging trenches along our line. The men were very tired indeed, but they went cheerfully to work, all the officers doing their part.

Crockett, the ex-Revenue officer from Georgia, was a slight man, not physically very strong. He came to me and told me he didn't think he would be much use in digging, but that he had found a lot of Spanish coffee and would spend his time making coffee for the men, if I approved. I did approve very heartily, and Crockett officiated as cook for the next three or four hours until the trench was dug, his coffee being much appreciated by all of us.

So many acts of gallantry were performed during the day that it is quite impossible to notice them all, and it seems unjust to single out any; yet I shall mention a few, which it must always be remembered are to stand, not as exceptions, but as instances of what very many men did. It happened that I saw these myself. There were innumerable others, which either were not seen at all, or were seen only by officers who happened not to mention them; and, of course, I know chiefly those that happened in my own regiment.

Captain Llewellen was a large, heavy man, who had a grown-up son in the ranks. On the march he had frequently carried the load of some man who weakened, and he was not feeling well on the morning of the fight. Nevertheless, he kept at the head of his troop all day. In the charging and rushing, he not only became very much exhausted, but finally fell, wrenching himself terribly, and though he remained with us all night, he was so sick by morning that we had to take him behind the hill into an improvised hospital. Lieutenant Day, after handling his troop with equal gallantry and efficiency, was shot, on the summit of Kettle Hill. He was hit in the arm and was forced to go to the rear, but he would not return to the States, and rejoined us at the front long before his wound was healed. Lieutenant Leahy was also wounded, not far from him. Thirteen of the men were wounded and yet kept on fighting until the end of the day, and in some cases never went to the rear at all, even to have their wounds dressed. They were Corporals Waller and Fortescue and Trooper McKinley of Troop E; Corporal Roades of Troop D; Troopers Albertson, Winter, McGregor, and Ray Clark of Troop F; Troopers Bugbee, Jackson, and Waller of Troop A; Trumpeter McDonald of Troop L; Sergeant Hughes of Troop B; and Trooper Gievers of Troop G.

One of the Wallers was a cow-puncher from New Mexico, the other, the champion Yale high-jumper. The first was shot through the left arm so as to paralyze the fingers, but he continued in battle, pointing his rifle over the wounded arm as though it had been a rest. The other Waller, and Bugbee, were hit in the head, the bullets merely inflicting scalp wounds. Neither of them paid any heed to the wounds except that after nightfall each had his head done up in a bandage. Fortescue I was at times using as an extra orderly. I noticed he limped, but supposed that his foot was skinned. It proved, however, that he had been struck in the foot, though not very seriously, by a bullet, and I never knew what was the matter until the next day I saw him making wry faces as he drew off his bloody boot, which was stuck fast to the foot. Trooper Rowland again distinguished himself by his fearlessness.

For gallantry on the field of action Sergeants Dame, Ferguson, Tiffany, Greenwald, and, later on, McIlhenny, were promoted to second lieutenancies, as Sergeant Hayes had already been. Lieutenant Carr, who commanded his troop, and behaved with great gallantry throughout the day, was shot and severely wounded at nightfall. He was the son of a Confederate officer; his was the fifth generation which, from father to son, had fought in every war of the United States. Among the men whom

I noticed as leading in the charges and always being nearest the enemy, were the Pawnee, Pollock; Simpson of Texas; and Dudley Dean. Jenkins was made major; Woodbury Kane, Day, and Frantz, captains; and Greenway and Goodrich, first lieutenants, for gallantry in action, and for the efficiency with which the first had handled his squadron, and the other five their troops—for each of them, owing to some accident to his superior, found himself in command of his troop.

Dr. Church had worked quite as hard as any man at the front in caring for the wounded; as had Chaplain Brown. Lieutenant Keyes, who acted as adjutant, did so well that he was given the position permanently. Lieutenant Coleman similarly won the position of quartermaster.

We finished digging the trench soon after midnight, and then the worn-out men laid down in rows on their rifles and dropped heavily to sleep. About one in ten of them had blankets taken from the Spaniards. Henry Bardshar, my orderly, had procured one for me. He, Goodrich, and I slept together. If the men without blankets had not been so tired that they fell asleep anyhow, they would have been very cold, for, of course, we were all drenched with sweat, and above the waist had on nothing but our flannel shirts, while the night was cool, with a heavy dew. Before anyone had time to wake from the cold, however, we were all awakened by the Spaniards, whose skirmishers suddenly opened fire on us. Of course, we could not tell whether or not this was the forerunner of a heavy attack, for our Cossack posts were responding briskly. It was about three o'clock in the morning, at which time men's courage is said to be at the lowest ebb; but the cavalry division was certainly free from any weakness in that direction. At the alarm everybody jumped to his feet and the stiff, shivering, haggard men, their eyes only half-opened, all clutched their rifles and ran forward to the trench on the crest of the hill.

The sputtering shots died away and we went to sleep again. But in another hour dawn broke and the Spaniards opened fire in good earnest. There was a little tree only a few feet away, under which I made my head-quarters, and while I was lying there, with Goodrich and Keyes, a shrapnel burst among us, not hurting us in the least, but with the sweep of its bullets killing or wounding five men in our rear, one of whom was a singularly gallant young Harvard fellow, Stanley Hollister. An equally gallant young fellow from Yale, Theodore Miller, had already been mortally wounded. Hollister also died.

The Second Brigade lost more heavily than the First; but neither its brigade commander nor any of its regimental commanders were touched, while the commander of the First Brigade and two of its three regimental commanders had been killed or wounded.

In this fight our regiment had numbered 490 men, as, in addition to the killed and wounded of the first fight, some had had to go to the hospital for sickness and some had been left behind with the baggage, or were detailed on other duty. Eighty-nine were killed and wounded: the heaviest loss suffered by any regiment in the cavalry division. The Spaniards made a stiff fight, standing firm until we charged home. They fought much more stubbornly than at Las Guasimas. We ought to have expected this, for they have always done well in holding entrenchments. On this day they showed themselves to be brave foes, worthy of honor for their gallantry.

In the attack on the San Juan hills our forces numbered about 6,600. There were about 4,500 Spaniards against us. Our total loss in killed and wounded was 1,071. Of the cavalry division there were, all told, some 2,300 officers and men, of whom 375 were killed and wounded. In the division over a fourth of the officers were killed or wounded, their loss being relatively half as great again as that of the enlisted men—which was as it should be.

I think we suffered more heavily than the Spaniards did in killed and wounded (though we also captured some scores of prisoners). It would have been very extraordinary if the reverse was the case, for we did the charging; and to carry earthworks on foot with dismounted cavalry, when these earthworks are held by unbroken infantry armed with the best modern rifles, is a serious task.

On January 16, 2001—four days before he would leave office—President Bill Clinton held a ceremony in the Roosevelt Room of the White House. Attended by many Roosevelt family members, the president presented the Medal of Honor to Tweed Roosevelt, Teddy's great-grandson.

FROM THE CITATION

Lieutenant Colonel Theodore Roosevelt distinguished himself by acts of bravery on 1 July 1898, near Santiago de Cuba, Republic of Cuba, while leading a daring charge up San Juan Hill. Lieutenant Colonel Roosevelt, in total disregard for his personal safety, and accompanied by only four or five men, led a desperate and gallant charge up San Juan Hill, encouraging his troops to continue the assault through withering enemy fire over open countryside. Facing the enemy's heavy fire, he displayed extraordinary bravery throughout the charge, and was the first to reach the enemy trenches, where he quickly killed one of the enemy with his pistol, allowing his men to continue the assault. His leadership and valor turned the tide in the Battle for San Juan Hill. Lieutenant Colonel Roosevelt's extraordinary heroism and devotion to duty are in keeping with the highest traditions of military service and reflect great credit upon himself, his unit, and the United States Army.

CHAPTER THREE

Single-Handed: Tibor "Teddy" Rubin

Daniel M. Cohen

In the first ten days of combat, the First Cav Division lost over five thousand men. North Korea lost five times that number, but continued to push the Americans farther south, testing their resolve to hold the Pusan perimeter. At the end of July, General Walton Walker issued a stand-or-die order, the tone and substance of which was unmistakable.

"There is no line behind which we can retreat . . . a retreat to Pusan would be one of the greatest butcheries in history. We must fight until the end . . . if some of us die, we will die fighting together."

By mid-August the loose talk of kicking Korean ass and pushing the "gooks" back to where they came from had ended. Staff Sergeant Randall Briere, who constantly reviewed the strengths and weaknesses of his men, described his company as "scattered, tired, and beaten . . . a bunch of animals, each trying to survive." He'd buried a dozen or more enlisted men, but the officers had taken even heavier losses. Since the day they landed, three company commanders had been killed in action, all three 1950 West Point graduates. The toll was simply overwhelming.

Unlike the vast majority of his company, Briere was a Massachusetts-born Yankee, although his parents had emigrated from Canada. When they fell on hard times, Randall and his sister, who grew up speaking French, were placed in a Catholic orphanage, where a strict code of conduct kept the two siblings apart. He joined the army in the late 1930s, underage by two years, but intent on escaping disagreeable foster parents and a troubled biological family.

Korea was not Randall's first encounter with war. He had been stationed at the barracks adjoining Wheeler Air Field when the Japanese bombed it on their way to Pearl Harbor, and fought in the Solomon Islands before being sent to Europe as part of the postwar occupation. He came back to the States with sergeant stripes and a tattoo of a naked girl in a champagne glass on his left forearm. In spite of lengthy combat and a yearlong bout with malaria, he planned a career in the army.

In 1946, Randall Briere met Esther Daldry, from Eustis, Florida, and married her six weeks later. It didn't matter to him that his tight-lipped, clannish, New England family disapproved of him marrying a small-town girl from the South. Randall rebuffed them and moved his new bride onto an army base. He figured with the war behind them that the country had entered a time of enduring peace and that he, his wife, and their new baby would be safe under the protective wing of the military. The army would take good care of them.

Then Korea exploded.

Back at Guadalcanal, Randall became accustomed to long stretches of grinding boredom punctuated by sudden bursts of lethal combat. He appreciated how hard it was for untested boys to remain on the alert when there was no sign of the enemy for days on end. In that regard the Korean War was similar to the Pacific Theater [of World War II]. But Korea's mountainous badlands and feverishly hot climate, along with its brutal civil war, struck him as more treacherous than the humid jungles of the Solomon Islands, where he'd fought the Japanese and contracted malaria.

Item Company was deployed around the town of Chirye, about thirty miles north of the provisional capital, Taegu. After hearing General Walker's statement, Briere realized that Item and several other undermanned companies were facing three crack North Korean divisions, and that they had no choice but to hold the route to the capital. To make matters worse, the shrewd and determined In Min Gun usually made their assaults at dawn—when there was enough light for troops to see, but not yet enough for the airplanes to detect and strike at them. Conflict veterans like Briere realized that if the In Min Gun took out their machine guns or if grenades failed to stop them, his men were seconds away from an onslaught of fearsome, screw-shaped bayonets. Briere hoped and prayed the still-tender recruits of Item Company never had to face that horror. He didn't think they could survive it. But he knew that there was no giving up the road or the rail line to Taegu, which was only a few miles behind them. Thinking about the dilemma kept him up at night. And while there was talk of reinforcements from Pusan, including the marines, Briere had yet to see any sign of them.

Item Company spent several stifling and airless days on a nameless hill, waiting for an attack that never came. Then the order came to pull back. North Korean patrols had been spotted on the move, to the north, east, and west of them. There was also talk of an enemy assault from the valley below.

The rest of the battalion had already been relocated several miles south, into a tighter formation. The big guns had been moved to better defend Taegu. Now Item Company was hanging out in the open, on this thumb-like ridge. If the In Min Gun decided to take it, there was nothing to stop them. The order to pull back came not a minute too soon.

Item had come to the hill with a large stockpile of ammunition and equipment. The initial plan was for them to hold this and several other ridges that made up a more or less straight line facing the north. But now the plan had changed. Other companies, to their right and left, had already pulled back, leaving Item holding more ammo than they could transport on their own. Before Briere had a chance to talk to anybody about the issue, master sergeant Arthur Peyton called his sergeants and a few corporals to gather at the problematic munitions dump.

"Battalion wants us out by night," Peyton said matter-of-factly. "They can't spare the vehicles right now, so somebody's got to stay and look after all this stuff. I need a few volunteers."

The others shrugged and looked away; nobody wanted to sit in a foxhole while the rest of the company moved to a safer position. Peyton then looked to Briere.

"Find me the Hungarian," he barked.

The last thing Briere wanted to do was assign this job to Private Rubin; he'd already been "volunteered" for more than his fair share of hazardous duty. But Peyton's fixation on Private Rubin was beyond Briere's control. Peyton outranked Briere, and his word was law.

Tibor Rubin's platoon was positioned in a series of foxholes that ran the entire length of the crest. Peyton cracked that the Jew was probably burrowed as far to the rear as possible, hiding his ass. But Briere found Rubin on the front line. In spite of his misgivings, Briere delivered Rubin to the mean-spirited, anti-Semitic master sergeant.

Peyton walked Rubin back to the rear of the crest and pointed to the hip-high cache of grenades, machine-gun ammo, carbine clips, and mortar shells.

"You're gonna stay here and watch this stuff while we get to our next position," Peyton said, gesturing toward Taegu.

Tibor was puzzled. "How far over there?"

"Command hasn't said yet. A few miles, I guess. I'll let you know when I get the heads-up."

It sounded to Tibor like the whole company was leaving the hill, while he alone was ordered to stay behind. Peyton continued: "Battalion's gonna come back and get all this stuff as soon as they can free up a few trucks. Probably between fourteen and sixteen hours. Before dark, anyway. If not, I'll send a jeep to get you."

Peyton talked too fast for Tibor to fully understand. Was his master sergeant really saying he was leaving Tibor all alone on the hill? Before Tibor could formulate the right words, Peyton clarified.

"I'll leave a couple gooks to keep you company, if you want," he said, almost like an afterthought.

Tibor shook his head no. Keeping watch over the ammunition was enough; he didn't want the extra burden of Koreans who regarded GIs with cold stares and didn't speak a word of English.

"Your decision," Peyton stated. "You understand?"

Tibor nodded yes.

Randall Briere complained when he heard that Peyton intended to leave Rubin completely alone. Worse than unfair, it struck him as unprofessional. Peyton informed Briere that he had offered Rubin help, but he'd turned it down. He ordered Briere to prepare the men to move out.

The company left the hill by midafternoon. As the last platoon skittered down the rear face of the incline, Peyton visited Tibor's foxhole and patted him on the shoulder.

"We'll be back for you before dark," he said. "Before you know it."

Then he was gone.

As the sun dropped closer to the horizon, Tibor grew tense. Nights on the hilltops were haunting, even with an entire company around you. The quiet of the craggy hills was distressing; they couldn't be read like the forests, where the telling sounds of nature could tell you who was out there or how close they were. Korea's rocky foothills were naked and dead still—virtual obstacle courses—unyielding heaps of stone with no place to hide. Worse yet, the terrain itself posed a hazard. No matter how careful you were, you could trip on a rock and stumble into a crevasse, making just enough noise to reveal your position to a waiting sniper.

When there was no moon, it was impossible to see ten feet in front of you; when the moon was bright your own shadow could give you away. Your only defense was to lie perfectly still in your foxhole and pray the enemy didn't see you.

Every time Tibor glanced at his watch, another hour had slipped away; another hour when the company failed to retrieve him. He quietly recited the Hebrew prayer that began every service: "Blessed are You, Lord our God, sovereign of the universe ..." Then he made a personal plea for God to protect him. After that he cursed Him for leaving one of his "chosen people" alone on the damn hill.

Two a.m. came and went. It remained hot, dark, and quiet. Too quiet.

Fear invaded Tibor's gut and sent a bitter taste from his gullet to his mouth. In a heartbeat it would be dawn, and if he was unlucky, the In Min Gun would be somewhere nearby, preparing to capture one more plot of useless real estate. One guy could not protect the hill—not even one guy with an arsenal.

The In Min Gun had been trained to keep coming at a target until their bodies gave out or artillery turned them to hamburger meat. And now that Item had retreated, Tibor was certain that there was no artillery behind him.

Tibor's situation was crazy; straight out of a Looney Tunes or a Merrie Melodies cartoon. Like Daffy Duck or Bugs Bunny or Popeye going single-handed against Hitler or the entire Japanese Army. Except that when a bomb went off, all it did was singe Daffy's face and feathers, turning him cross-eyed for a few seconds. It wasn't going to work that way when bullets and bombs started flying at Tibor. And yet it was just as absurd.

Because it remained so still, and because he didn't know what else to do, Tibor popped out of his foxhole and loped back to the weapons dump. Acknowledging the hopelessness of the situation, he felt free to deal with it accordingly. He dragged two boxes of grenades into the middle of a cluster of empty foxholes and plunked a half-dozen of them into each one. With the naive hope that he had somehow improved his chances of survival, Tibor also grabbed as many 250-round belts of machine-gun ammo as he could, then placed them next to the two guns with the best vantage point looking down the hill. After that, he grabbed as many mortar shells as he could, staggering back to the launcher. Next, he collected thirty clips for his carbine, then another thirty for good measure. After he had adequately stocked a half-dozen of the most forward foxholes, he still had time on his hands, so he doubled up on the previous supply. Then, just by accident, he found a cache of C rations that included a stash of his favorite candy, Butterfingers. He filled his pockets with enough for a week.

Tiber tried to calculate the time it would take for the enemy to arrive within striking distance of his position. That would probably be the next ridge over, which was currently blanketed in velvety black. The enemy would have to send flares up just to make out the contours of Tibor's hill.

He reasoned he could probably hold off a platoon or two, provided that a bullet or shell didn't find him first. Once he dropped enough attackers to slow the rest behind them, he might be able to fall back toward Item's new line—on the odd chance that he could locate it. But as he played out several possible scenarios, a troubling thought occurred to him. He had been in numerous firefights, but he had never been close enough to a living, enemy soldier to see his face. Had he ever hit a man? Probably, but there was no way to be sure of it. Whenever Tibor had spotted the In Min Gun, they were off in the distance. The jumble of variables confused him. He tried to put it out of his mind by stuffing an entire Butterfinger in his mouth.

It was the kind of night that he hated most. The moon was parked behind a heavy cloud bank, handing the enemy a decided advantage. An entire company could crawl up the hill or creep through the valley unnoticed. As long as the men were on foot and quiet, the deep darkness was their friend.

As the hours between one and four a.m. shriveled to nothing, Tibor gave up on the slim chance that anyone was coming for him. The time was fast approaching when the enemy generally made his move. Tibor figured he might be as many as five miles in front of his lines, and that nobody in his right mind was crazy enough to travel that far at night to retrieve one little Jew. He said another prayer and ate two more Butterfingers.

Desperate for any hint of movement, Tibor wriggled to the outlying ledge and trained his eyes where the valley floor might be. He squinted and strained, but it was futile. Beyond the precipice it was all darkness. He turned to study the sky. Any moment it would soften and turn gray.

Then the moon briefly wrested itself from the clouds. Its pale yellow face seemed to wink at Tibor, abruptly offering a merciless glimpse into his future: a hundred or more uniformed soldiers slinking across the valley floor. As the light played on them, they seemed to pause, as one. Then, like a nest of cockroaches suddenly lit up by a flashlight, they scattered over the uneven ground and began to scale the hill.

Whistles shrieked. A bugle called out. A ragged chorus of human voices, crying out like coyotes, came in response.

Yeye Yeye Yeye Yeye Yeye Yeye Yeye! they shouted like ravenous animals.

The rational part of Tibor Rubin's brain shut down. His body began to act on its own orders, with no regard to will or reason. He began to hurl grenades, one after another, fast as he could pull the pins. The screaming from below grew louder. In the endless second before the report from the first grenade, one fleeting thought ran across his mind: that North Koreans rarely fired their weapons until they had a man in the crosshairs. For one moment he was comforted by the notion that North Korean officers would sacrifice entire companies before they'd waste ammunition. Was it possible if they couldn't see him, they wouldn't shoot at him?

Tibor continued to pitch grenades into the dark. After the first thunderous volley, he couldn't tell if the North Koreans were shooting at him or not. If so, he couldn't hear their fire; the chorus of so many explosions was like a solid wall. In his mind, the ruckus had created a buffer between him and the attackers. As it blotted out their battle cries, he took a fleeting moment to reflect. Even if his grenades did block the first wave of attackers, the soldiers to follow would be mad as hell, but he could use this chaotic moment to move to a different position. Tibor slid into another foxhole; arms trembling, he started on another pile of grenades.

The Koreans were either holding their fire or Tibor was deaf to it, he wasn't sure which. But he could still hear them yelling as he crawled behind a machine gun. His hands mounted the stock and fidgeted onto the trigger, but when he tried to aim it, there was nothing to see. Fighting the screaming fear in his head, he took a shallow breath and absently pointed the barrel into a haze of sand and smoke. As the gun went off, he glanced right and left, hoping to detect enemy movement before it was too late. But even in the gray dawn, he could only see flashes of the jagged rocks to either side of him.

His hands held fast to his weapon until the heat from the chamber flowed back and seared them. He let the trigger go, but the racket mysteriously continued. Was the gun firing on its own? Were his hands still working? He couldn't tell.

The moment Tibor abandoned the machine gun, the enemy's war whoops seemed to rise up again, louder and fiercer than before. It might have only been in his head, he wasn't sure, and he wasn't about to get closer to the ledge to find out. Overhead, the air was singing with small-weapons fire that seemed to call his name. Tibor ignored it and shimmied to yet another foxhole, where he greedily cuddled another pile of grenades. Sweat-drenched, his skin burning beneath his fatigues, he madly palmed the little bombs, yanked pin after pin, and flung them like baseballs, up and out, in every direction. One after another, a string of concussions jackhammered his helmet, forced his head down, and compressed his spine.

Tibor still couldn't see the attackers. Only in the very briefest gaps between blasts did he hear their cries, which barely broke through the ruckus. But now they were different. Something in their tone had changed. It had become more like a collective howl than a rallying call.

A new threat, the dull thud of mortar shells, echoed from below. The hill trembled. Wavelets of sand and gravel crashed on Tibor's back. Panic seized his chest. He forced his gaze downward, but he couldn't see the strike points; they were lost in a wall of smog. Tibor squirmed to the second machine gun and let loose; one, then two, then three bands of .30 caliber shells. As the gun's vibration punished his hands, another bugle call rose up, turned faint, and then fell silent. What stopped it, or why, he couldn't tell. And it didn't make any difference. He just kept at it.

When daylight fully bloomed, Tibor was still launching grenades as fast as his rubbery arms allowed. He wasn't thinking, but moving to a rush that coursed through like a continuous electric shock. He couldn't feel anything, his cheeks swollen, like he'd just endured a prize fight, mouth caked with dust, but still he kept up the barrage.

A rolling peal of thunder rose up so quickly that it was in front of him before he realized that it was actually coming from overhead, and that it was the roar of God's appointed servants, come to deliver him from his attackers. They had come in the form of US Air Force Corsairs.

Suddenly chills of elation and relief shook him from head to toe. He felt free to attend to the awful burning in his mouth and throat. He grabbed his canteen and uncapped it. He pitched his head back and inhaled. He then doused his face with what was left in the canteen and gazed at the sky. He saw the white trails of screaming planes.

Almost unconsciously Tibor began to pray again, his lips trembling with garbled Hebrew. When he was through giving thanks, he numbly took hold of a carbine and a last few clips. His hands swelled and clumsily attached eight grenades to his neck and belt. He grabbed a canteen and took another great swig, turning his back to the ongoing carnage in the valley. He was done with this god-awful hill, forever.

His feet felt like deadweights. He couldn't lift his boots high enough to keep from stumbling over every rock and small gully in his path. He rode his heels halfway down the hill, almost like they were skis.

Once planted on level ground, Tibor was at a loss for direction. The road appeared familiar; it was most likely the one Item Company had taken when it first arrived at the hill. But he wasn't sure. He checked his compass and trudged south.

Trucks zoomed by Tibor; a driver called out to him, but his words were drowned by the sound of the engine. Tibor absently shook his head and the truck went on. He might have missed the opportunity for a ride, but it was no longer an effort to walk. His body felt like it was floating.

When Sergeant Briere first saw a figure in the distance, he had no idea who it was. Then he looked through his binoculars and realized that it was Rubin, shuffling like a sleepwalker.

Before Briere could say a word, Rubin came to a sharp halt in front of him, sweat-drenched, grimy, and slit-eyed. The sergeant asked Tibor what happened.

"I was stopping these gook bastards, sir," he stammered. He sat down, put his head in his hands, and buttoned his lips.

Briere took Rubin by the arm and took him to company headquarters, where Peyton glanced at him and said, "Looks like he just got out of a Turkish steam bath."

"I just killed thousands of gooks, maybe more," Rubin muttered blankly.

Peyton chuckled and turned to his clerks. "Rubin had a Hungarian nightmare."

Tibor's lips curled into a tired grin. "I want to see the company commander."

"Well, he doesn't want to see you."

"I want to see the CO," Tibor repeated solemnly.

Peyton glanced at Briere and the other half-dozen enlisted men within earshot.

Before Rubin could utter a single word, Peyton apologized to the CO for pestering him.

"It's probably a case of shell shock," he said.

But as Tibor rambled on, about how he had filled the foxholes full of grenades, and how the enemy had attacked the hill, and how he had somehow, inexplicably, held them at bay, the officer became interested. He turned to Peyton.

"Since we have to go back to the hill for the weapons and ammo, we might as well check it out."

The CO, Peyton, and several other men made curious by Rubin's rambling piled into three jeeps. After parking the vehicles, they dug their boots into the gravel and bent their knees into the incline. Briere stayed close to Rubin, who continued to move like a sleepwalker, like he didn't know where he was.

There was no mistaking what had happened. The far side of the hill was carpeted with dead and dying North Koreans. Many were sprawled among the shredded remains of others, as if they had tripped and become stuck in their own ravaged flesh. Hands and feet lay scattered about like empty weapons that had been absently dropped.

Tibor began to cry. He hadn't pictured what the battlefield would look like—that death could appear in so many horrid forms. Up to that second, the entire experience had seemed fuzzy and distant, but now there were scores of bodies in front of him, some positioned like question marks, their dead asking him why he had killed them. Tortured voices of the wounded called for water or their mothers, just like so many American GIs after they had been hit.

Tibor's thoughts went to one of the central values of his faith. Long ago he had been taught that the worst shame came from vile deeds forced upon you by your enemies. You had reached the lowest point of existence when you struck back at those who had struck at you. As Tibor faced the destruction that he had single-handedly visited on so many young people, young people not so different from him, he felt the deep hurt of failure that went beyond the personal, and that violated the most sacred laws of God. Then he began to sob, in a way that he had never done before, not even when he'd heard the sad news of his parents being left in Europe.

The CO put his arm around Tibor's shoulder.

"You didn't have any choice, Rubin. If you hadn't killed them, they would have killed you." He said that Tibor would receive a medal for his bravery, and that he would have leave time away from the battlefield to rest and recuperate.

Then he told Peyton to take down his instructions:

"Tibor Rubin is recommended for the Medal of Honor for distinguishing himself conspicuously by gallantry, at the risk of his life, above and beyond the call of duty, to kill hundreds of enemy soldiers, stopping their advance," and "securing the only road from Taegu to Pusan, saving the lives of countless soldiers of ours and our allies, so that our only main road will be open at least for the next twenty-four hours."

The CO instructed the staff sergeant to draw up the papers for a Medal of Honor and to deliver them for his signature. After a review, the commander would send the documents through the proper channels.

Tibor could not grasp that he had been nominated for his adopted country's highest military honor. He had no context within which to understand it, not to mention that he was too disoriented and upset to even consider its meaning. A medal, the way Tibor conceived it, would only make it easier for snipers to get him.

Briere kept a close watch on Private Rubin over the next few days. The sergeant took it as a bad sign that Rubin had turned so glum. It was unlike him. His typically animated, open features had turned slack and dark, and he had stopped talking. In Briere's opinion, the events on the hill had left the private distant and self-absorbed, a danger to himself and others around him.

Finally, Tibor confessed to Briere that he was ashamed of what had happened on the hill. He explained that his family and his religion found such killing sorrowful and repugnant, and that his actions had changed him forever. Briere, who had seen this before, advised Rubin to take the CO's offer to spend a week in the city of Pusan, to rest and recuperate. Tibor said he could not do that; it was his duty to stay with the company until the war was over. He refused to even consider leaving.

There was no more mention of the medal. Peyton never finished the paperwork, and carried on as if Rubin's bravery on the hill had never happened. Then the company's CO was killed in action a few days later. If there had been a chance of official recognition for Rubin's act of valor, it died with that officer.

Harold Speakman, a friend to both Rubin and Briere, found out what Peyton had done. Speakman saw this as an injustice—not only to Tibor, but to the whole company. Speakman knew that Peyton had done this solely because Rubin was a Jew. There would be no medal in Rubin's immediate future, but this injustice would be rectified later on.

The feeling around the company spread, that Peyton had had no business leaving Rubin on that hill alone, especially after frequently assigning Rubin to a number of other life-threatening details in the past. In Speakman's opinion, the fact that Rubin had taken them on with so few complaints had actually incensed the sergeant. Peyton seemed to take Rubin's goodwill as an invitation to amplify the abuse.

Harold Speakman was wounded on the Pusan perimeter, badly enough to be sent back to the United States. He would later say that it was his honor to have served alongside a soldier whom he called "the Jewish gentleman." But after he was wounded, Speakman lost touch with Rubin for thirty years. In that way he was like a lot of the guys in Item Company: Each man had his own special injuries and losses, and the corporal was no exception. Survival meant leaving the past behind, and Tibor Rubin soon receded into Speakman's past.

FROM THE CITATION

For conspicuous gallantry and intrepidity at the risk of his life, above and beyond the call of duty:

On 30 October 1950, Chinese forces attacked his unit at Unsan, North Korea, during a massive nighttime assault. That night and throughout the next day, he manned a .30 caliber machine gun at the south end of the unit's line after three previous gunners became casualties. He continued to man his machine gun until his ammunition was exhausted. His determined stand slowed the pace of the enemy advance in his sector, permitting the remnants of his unit to retreat southward. As the battle raged, Corporal Rubin was severely wounded and captured by the Chinese. Choosing to remain in the prison camp despite offers from the Chinese to return him to his native Hungary, Corporal Rubin disregarded his own personal safety and immediately began sneaking out of the camp at night in search of food for his comrades. Breaking into enemy food storehouses and gardens, he risked certain torture or death if caught. Corporal

Rubin provided not only food to the starving soldiers, but also desperately needed medical care and moral support for the sick and wounded of the POW camp. His brave, selfless efforts were directly attributed to saving the lives of as many as forty of his fellow prisoners. Corporal Rubin's gallant actions in close contact with the enemy and unyielding courage and bravery while a prisoner of war are in the highest traditions of military service, and reflect great credit upon himself and the United States Army.

CHAPTER FOUR

The Siege of Fort Wagner: William Harvey Carney

Luis F. Emilio

EDITOR'S NOTE: THE STORY OF THE 54TH MASSACHUSETTS IS ONE OF courage and the visceral struggle of death and survival that accompanies any battle. This account of one of the 54th's first tastes of action is filled with almost cinematic heroism, a fact not lost on the producers of the 1989 film, *Glory,* which told the story of the African-American regiment and its and bravery in the face of unrelenting Confederate opposition. Understated in this account, but astounding in any regard, are the actions of Sgt. William Harvey Carney, who won a Congressional Medal of Honor for saving the American flag under fire. With his commander and the flag bearer both mortally wounded and pinned down, Sergeant Carney seized the flag and prevented it from touching the ground. Seriously wounded himself, he kept the flag aloft. When he made it back to the protection of his lines, he said, "Boys, I only did my duty; the old flag never touched the ground."

This is a story of bravery beyond the comprehension of anyone who has not been in battle and felt its savage effects.

On the *General Hunter,* the officers procured breakfast; but the men were still without rations. Refreshed, the officers were all together for the last time socially; before another day three were dead, and three wounded who never returned.

Captain Simpkins, whose manly appearance and clear-cut features were so pleasing to look upon, was, as always, quiet and dignified; Captain Russel was voluble and active as ever, despite all fatigue. Neither appeared to have any premonition of their fate. It was different with Colonel Shaw, who again expressed to Lieutenant-Colonel Hallowell his apprehension of speedy death.

Running up Folly River, the steamer arrived at Pawnee Landing, where, at 9 a.m., the Fifty-fourth disembarked. Crossing the island through woods, the camps of several regiments were passed, from which soldiers ran out, shouting, "Well done! We heard your guns!" Others cried, "Hurrah, boys! You saved the Tenth Connecticut!"

Leaving the timber, the Fifty-fourth came to the sea beach, where marching was easier. Stretching away to the horizon, on the right, was the Atlantic; to the left, sand hillocks, with pine woods farther inland. Occasional squalls of rain came, bringing rubber blankets and coats into use. At one point on the beach, a box of water-soaked hard bread was discovered, and the contents speedily divided among the hungry men. Firing at the front had been heard from early morning, which toward noon was observed to have risen into a heavy cannonade.

After a march of some six miles, we arrived at Lighthouse Inlet and rested, awaiting transportation. Tuneful voices about the colors started the song, "When this Cruel War Is Over," and the pathetic words of the chorus were taken up by others. It was the last song of many, but few then thought it a requiem. By ascending the sandhills, we could see the distant vessels engaging Wagner. When all was prepared, the Fifty-fourth boarded a small steamer, landed on Morris Island, about 5 p.m., and remained near the shore for further orders.

General Gillmore, on the 13th, began constructing four batteries, mounting forty-two guns and mortars, to damage the slopes and guns of Wagner, which were completed under the enemy's fire, and in spite of a sortie at night, on the 14th. He expected to open with them on the 16th; but heavy rains so delayed progress that all was not prepared until the 18th. Beyond this siege line, which was 1,350 yards south of Wagner, stretched a narrow strip of land between the sea and Vincent's Creek, with its marshes. At low tide, the beach sand afforded a good pathway to the enemy's position; but at high tide, it was through deep, loose sand, and over low sand hillocks. This stretch of sand was unobstructed, until at a point two hundred yards in front of Wagner, the enemy had made a line of rifle tranches. Some fifty yards nearer Wagner, an easterly bend of the marsh extended to within twenty-five yards of the sea at high tide, forming a defile, through which an assaulting column must pass.

Nearly covered by this sweep of the marsh, and commanding it as well as the stretch of sand beyond to the Federal line, was "Battery Wagner," so named by the Confederates, in memory of Lt. Col. Thomas M. Wagner, First South Carolina Artillery, killed at Fort Sumter. This field work was constructed of quartz sand, with turf and palmetto log revetment, and occupied the whole width of the island there—some six hundred and thirty feet. Its southern and principal front was double-bastioned. Next [to] the sea was a heavy traverse and curtain covering a sally-port. Then came the southeast bastion, prolonged westerly by a curtain connected with the southwest bastion. At the western end was another sally-port. An infantry parapet closed the rear or north face. It had large bomb-proofs, magazines, and heavy traverses.

Wagner's armament was reported to its commander, on July 15, as follows: on sea face, one ten-inch Columbiad, and two smooth-bore thirty-two-pounders; on southeast bastion, operating on land and sea, one rifled thirty-two-pounder; on south point of bastion operating on land, one forty-two-pounder carronade; in the curtain, with direct fire on land approach to embrasure, two eight-inch naval shell-guns, one eight-inch sea-coast howitzer, and one thirty-two-pounder smooth-bore; on the flank defences of the curtain, two thirty-two-pounder carronades in embrasures; on the southerly face, one thirty-two-pounder carronade in embrasure; in southwest angle, one ten-inch sea-coast mortar; on bastion gorge, one thirty-two-pounder carronade. There were also four twelve-pounder howitzers. All the northerly portion of Morris Island was in range of Fort Sumter, the eastern James Island and the Sullivan's Island batteries, besides Fort Gregg, on the northerly extremity of Morris Island, which mounted three guns.

Brig. Gen. William B. Taliaferro, an able officer, who had served with distinction under "Stonewall" Jackson, was in command of Morris Island, for the Confederates. Wagner's garrison, on the 18th, consisted of the Thirty-first and Fifty-first North Carolina, the Charleston Battalion, two companies Sixty-third Georgia Heavy Artillery, and two companies First South Carolina Infantry, acting as artillery, and two guns each of the Palmetto and Blake's Artillery—a total force of seventeen hundred men.

Such was the position, armament, and garrison of the strongest single earthwork known in the history of warfare.

About 10 a.m., on the 18th, five wooden gunboats joined the land batteries in shelling Wagner, lying out of the enemy's range. At about 12:30 p.m., five monitors and the "New *Ironsides*" opened, and the land batteries increased their fire. A deluge of shot was now poured into the work, driving the main portion of its garrison into the bombproofs, and throwing showers of sand from the slopes of Wagner into the air but to fall back in place again. The enemy's flag was twice shot away, and, until replaced, a battle-flag was planted with great gallantry by daring men. From Gregg, Sumter, and the James Island and Sullivan's Island batteries, the enemy returned the iron compliments; while for a time Wagner's cannoneers ran out at intervals, and served a part of the guns, at great risk.

A fresh breeze blew that day; at times the sky was clear; the atmosphere, lightened by recent rains, resounded with the thunders of an almost incessant cannonade. Smoke clouds hung over the naval vessels, our batteries, and those of the enemy. During this terrible bombardment, the two infantry regiments and the artillery companies, except gun detachments, kept in the bombproofs. But the Charleston Battalion lay all day under the parapets of Wagner—a terrible ordeal, which was borne without demoralization. In spite of the tremendous fire, the enemy's loss was only eight men killed and twenty wounded, before the assault.

General Taliaferro foresaw that this bombardment was preliminary to an assault, and had instructed his force to take certain assigned positions when the proper time came. To three companies of the Charleston Battalion was given the Confederate right along the parapet; the Fifty-first North Carolina, along the curtain; and the Thirty-first North Carolina, the left, including the south-east bastion. Two companies of the Charleston Battalion were placed outside the work, covering the gorge. A small reserve was assigned to the body of the fort. Two field-pieces were to fire from the traverse flanking the beach face and approach. For the protection of the eight-inch shell-guns in the curtain and the field-pieces, they were covered with sand-bags, until desired for service. Thoroughly conversant with the ground, the Confederate commander rightly calculated that the defile would break up the formation of his assailants at a critical moment, when at close range.

General Gillmore, at noon, ascended the lookout on a hill within his lines, and examined the ground in front. Throughout the day this high point was the gathering-place of observers. The tide turned to flow at 4 p.m., and about the same time firing from Wagner ceased, and not a man was to be seen there. During the afternoon the troops were moving from their camps toward the front. Late in the day the belief was general that the enemy had been driven from his shelter, and the armament of Wagner rendered harmless. General Gillmore, after calling his chief officers together for conference, decided to attack that evening, and the admiral was so notified. Firing from land and sea was still kept up with decreased rapidity, while the troops were preparing.

Upon arriving at Morris Island, Colonel Shaw and Adjutant James walked toward the front to report to General Strong, whom they at last found, and who announced that Fort Wagner was to be stormed that evening.

Knowing Colonel Shaw's desire to place his men beside white troops, he said, "You may lead the column, if you say 'yes.' Your men, I know, are worn out, but do as you choose." Shaw's face brightened, and before replying, he requested Adjutant James to return and have Lieutenant-Colonel Hallowell bring up the Fifty-fourth. Adjutant James, who relates this interview, then departed on his mission. Receiving this order, the regiment marched on to General Strong's headquarters, where a halt of five minutes was made about 6 p.m. Noticing the worn look of the men, who had passed two days without an issue of rations, and no food since morning, when the weary march began, the general expressed his sympathy and his great desire that they might have food and stimulant. It could not be, however, for it was necessary that the regiment should move on to the position assigned.

General Strong sent the Fifty-fourth forward under the lieutenant-colonel toward the front, moving by the middle road west of the sand-hills. Gaining a point where these elevations gave place to low ground, the long blue line of the regiment advancing by the flank attracted the attention of the enemy's gunners on James Island. Several solid shots were fired at the column, without doing any damage, but they rico-cheted ahead or over the line in dangerous proximity. Realizing that the national colors and the white flag of the State especially attracted the enemy's fire, the bearers began to roll them up on the staves. At the same moment, Captain Simpkins, commanding the color company (K), turned to observe his men. His quick eye noted the half-furled flags, and his gallant spirit took fire in a moment at the sight. Pointing to the flags with uplifted sword, he commanded in imperative tones, "Unfurl those colors!" It was done, and the fluttering silks again waved, untrammeled, in the air.

Colonel Shaw, at about 6:30 p.m., mounted and accompanied General Strong toward the front. After proceeding a short distance, he turned back, and gave to Mr. Edward L. Pierce, a personal friend, who had been General Strong's guest for several days, his letters and some papers, with a request to forward them to his family if anything occurred to him requir-ing such service. That sudden purpose accomplished, he galloped away, overtook the regiment, and informed Lieutenant-Colonel Hallowell of what the Fifty-fourth was expected to do. The direction was changed to the right, advancing east toward the sea. By orders, Lieutenant-Colonel Hallowell broke the column at the sixth company, and led the companies of the left wing to the rear of those of the right wing. When the sea beach was reached, the regiment halted and came to rest, awaiting the coming up of the supporting regiments.

General Gillmore had assigned to General Seymour the command of the assaulting column, charging him with its organization, forma-tion, and all the details of the attack. His force was formed into three brigades of infantry: the first under General Strong, composed of the Fifty-fourth Massachusetts, Sixth Connecticut, Forty-eighth New York, Third New Hampshire, Ninth Maine, and Seventy-sixth Pennsylvania; the second, under Col. Haldimand S. Putnam, of his own regiment—the

Seventh New Hampshire—One Hundredth New York, Sixty-Second and Sixty-seventh Ohio; the third, or reserve brigade, under Brig.-Gen. Thomas G. Stevenson, of the Twenty-fourth Massachusetts, Tenth Connecticut, Ninety-seventh Pennsylvania, and Second South Carolina. Four companies of the Seventh Connecticut, and some regular and volunteer artillery-men, manned and served the guns of the siege line.

Formed in column of wings, with the right resting near the sea, at a short distance in advance of the works, the men of the Fifty-fourth were ordered to lie down, their muskets loaded but not capped, and bayonets fixed. There the regiment remained for half an hour, while the formation of the storming column and reserve was perfected. To the Fifty-fourth had been given the post of honor, not by chance, but by deliberate selection. General Seymour has stated the reasons why this honorable but dangerous duty was assigned the regiment in the following words:

> *It was believed that the Fifty-fourth was in every respect as efficient as any other body of men; and as it was one of the strongest and best officered, there seemed to be no good reason why it should not be selected for the advance. This point was decided by General Strong and myself.*

In numbers the Fifty-fourth had present but six hundred men, for besides the large camp guard and the sick left at St. Helena Island, and the losses sustained on James Island, on the 16th, a fatigue detail of eighty men under Lt. Francis L. Higginson, did not participate in the attack.

The formation of the regiment for the assault was with Companies B and E on the right of the respective wings. Surgeon Stone and Quartermaster Ritchie were present on the field. Both field officers were dismounted; the band and musicians acted as stretcher-bearers. To many a gallant man these scenes upon the sands were the last of earth; to the survivors they will be ever present. Away over the sea to the eastward the heavy sea-fog was gathering, the western sky bright with the reflected light, for the sun had set. Faraway thunder mingled with the occasional boom of cannon. The gathering host all about, the silent lines stretching away to the rear, the passing of a horseman now and then carrying orders—all was ominous of the impending onslaught.

Far and indistinct in front was the now silent earthwork, seamed, scarred, and ploughed with shot, its flag still waving in defiance. Among the dark soldiers who were to lead veteran regiments which were equal in drill and discipline to any in the country, there was a lack of their usual light-heartedness, for they realized, partially at least, the dangers they were to encounter. But there was little nervousness and no depression observable. It took but a touch to bring out their irrepressible spirit and humor in the old way. When a cannon-shot from the enemy came toward the line and passed over, a man or two moved nervously, calling out a sharp reproof from Lieutenant-Colonel Hallowell, whom the men still spoke of as "the major." Thereupon one soldier quietly remarked to his comrades, "I guess the major forgets what kind of balls them is!" Another added, thinking of the foe, "I guess they kind of 'spec's we're coming!"

Naturally the officers' thoughts were largely regarding their men. Soon they would know whether the lessons they had taught of soldierly duty would bear good fruit. Would they have cause for exultation or be compelled to sheathe their swords, rather than lead cowards? Unknown to them, the whole question of employing three hundred thousand colored soldiers hung in the balance. But few, however, doubted the result. Wherever a white officer led that night, even to the gun-muzzles and bayonet-points, there, by his side, were black men as brave and steadfast as himself.

At last the formation of the column was nearly perfected. The Sixth Connecticut had taken position in column of companies just in rear of the Fifty-fourth. About this time, Colonel Shaw walked back to Lieutenant-Colonel Hallowell, and said, "I shall go in advance with the National flag. You will keep the State flag with you; it will give the men something to rally round. We shall take the fort or die there! Good-bye!"

Presently, General Strong, mounted upon a spirited gray horse, in full uniform, with a yellow handkerchief bound around his neck, rode in front of the Fifty-fourth, accompanied by two aides and two orderlies. He addressed the men, and his words, as given by an officer of the regiment, were: "Boys, I am a Massachusetts man, and I know you will fight for the honor of the State. I am sorry you must go into the fight tired and hungry, but the men in the fort are tired too. There are but three hundred behind those walls, and they have been fighting all day. Don't fire a musket on the way up, but go in and bayonet them at their guns."

Calling out the color-bearer, he said, "If this man should fall, who will lift the flag and carry it on?" Colonel Shaw, standing near, took a cigar from between his lips, and said quietly, "I will." The men loudly responded to Colonel Shaw's pledge, while General Strong rode away to give the signal for advancing.

Colonel Shaw calmly walked up and down the line of his regiment. He was clad in a close-fitting staff-officer's jacket, with a silver eagle denoting his rank on each shoulder. His trousers were light blue; a fine narrow silk sash was wound round his waist beneath the jacket. Upon his head was a high felt army hat with cord. Depending from his sword-belt was a field-officer's sword of English manufacture, with the initials of his name worked into the ornamentation of the guard. On his hand was an antique gem set in a ring. In his pocket was a gold watch, marked with his name, attached to a gold chain.

Although he had given certain papers and letters to his friend, Mr. Pierce, he retained his pocket-book, which doubtless contained papers which would establish his identity. His manner, generally reserved before his men, seemed to unbend to them, for he spoke as he had never done before. He said, "Now I want you to prove yourselves, men," and reminded them that the eyes of thousands would look upon the night's work. His bearing was composed and graceful; his cheek had somewhat paled; and the slight twitching of the corners of his mouth plainly showed that the whole cost was counted, and his expressed determination to take the fort or die was to be carried out.

Meanwhile, the twilight deepened, as the minutes, drawn out by waiting, passed, before the signal was given. Officers had silently grasped one another's hands, brought their revolvers round to the front, and tightened their sword-belts. The men whispered last injunctions to comrades, and listened for the word of command. The preparations usual in an assault were not made. There was no provision for cutting away obstructions, filling the ditch, or spiking the guns. No special instructions were given the stormers; no line of skirmishers or covering party was thrown out; no engineers or guides accompanied the column; no artillery-men to serve captured guns; no plan of the work was shown company officers. It was understood that the fort would be assaulted with the bayonet, and that the Fifty-fourth would be closely supported.

While on the sands a few cannon-shots had reached the regiment, one passing between the wings, another over to the right. When the inaction had become almost unendurable, the signal to advance came. Colonel Shaw walked along the front to the centre, and giving the command, "Attention!" the men sprang to their feet. Then came the admonition, "Move in quick time until within a hundred yards of the fort; then double quick, and charge!" A slight pause, followed by the sharp command, "Forward!" and the Fifty-fourth advanced to the storming.

There had been a partial resumption of the bombardment during the formation, but now only an occasional shot was heard. The enemy in Wagner had seen the preparations, knew what was coming, and were awaiting the blow. With Colonel Shaw leading, sword in hand, the long advance over three-quarters of a mile of sand had begun, with wings closed up and company officers admonishing their men to preserve the alignment. Guns from Sumter, Sullivan's Island, and James Island, began to play upon the regiment. It was about 7:45 p.m., with darkness coming on rapidly, when the Fifty-fourth moved.

With barely room for the formation from the first, the narrowing way between the sand hillocks and the sea soon caused a strong pressure to the right, so that Captains Willard and Emilio on the right of the right companies of their wings were with some of their men forced to march in water up to their knees, at each incoming of the sea.

Moving at quick time, and preserving its formation as well as the difficult ground and narrowing way permitted, the Fifty-fourth was approaching the defile made by the easterly sweep of the marsh. Darkness was rapidly coming on, and each moment became deeper. Soon men on the flanks were compelled to fall behind, for want of room to continue in line. The centre only had a free path, and with eyes strained upon the colonel and the flag, they pressed on toward the work, now only two hundred yards away.

At that moment Wagner became a mound of fire, from which poured a stream of shot and shell. Just a brief lull, and the deafening explosions of cannon were renewed, mingled with the crash and rattle of musketry. A sheet of flame, followed by a running fire, like electric sparks, swept along the parapet, as the Fifty-first North Carolina gave a direct, and the Charleston Battalion a left-oblique, fire on the Fifty-fourth. Their Thirty-first North Carolina had lost heart, and failed to take position in the southeast bastion—fortunately, too, for had its musketry fire been added to that delivered, it is doubtful whether any Federal troops could have passed the defile.

When this tempest of war came, before which men fell in numbers on every side, the only response the Fifty-fourth made to the deadly challenge was to change step to the double-quick, that it might the sooner close with the foe. There had been no stop, pause, or check at any period of the advance, nor was there now. As the swifter pace was taken, and officers sprang to the fore with waving swords barely seen in the darkness, the men closed the gaps, and with set jaws, panting breath, and bowed heads, charged on.

Wagner's wall, momentarily lit up by cannon-flashes, was still the goal toward which the survivors rushed in sadly diminished numbers. It was now dark, the gloom made more intense by the blinding explosions in the front. This terrible fire which the regiment had just faced, probably caused the greatest number of casualties sustained by the Fifty-fourth in the assault; for nearer the work the men were somewhat sheltered by the high parapet. Every flash showed the ground dotted with men of the regiment, killed or wounded. Great holes, made by the huge shells of the navy or the land batteries, were pitfalls into which the men stumbled or fell.

Colonel Shaw led the regiment to the left toward the curtain of the work, thus passing the southeast bastion, and leaving it to the right hand. From that salient no musketry fire came; and some Fifty-fourth men first entered it, not following the main body by reason of the darkness. As the survivors drew near the work, they encountered the flanking fire delivered from guns in the southwest salient, and the howitzers outside the fort, which swept the trench, where further severe losses were sustained. Nothing but the ditch now separated the stormers and the foe. Down into this they went, through the two or three feet of water therein, and mounted the slope beyond in the teeth of the enemy, some of whom, standing on the crest, fired down on them with depressed pieces.

Both flags were planted on the parapet, the national flag carried there and gallantly maintained by the brave Sgt. William H. Carney of Company C.

In the pathway from the defile to the fort many brave men had fallen. Lieutenant-Colonel Hallowell was severely wounded in the groin, Captain Willard in the leg, Adjutant James in the ankle and side, Lieutenant Homans in the shoulder. Lieutenants Smith and Pratt were also wounded. Colonel Shaw had led his regiment from first to last. Gaining the rampart, he stood there for a moment with uplifted sword, shouting, "Forward, Fifty-fourth!" and then fell dead, shot through the heart, besides other wounds.

Not a shot had been fired by the regiment up to this time. As the crest was gained, the crack of revolver-shots was heard, for the officers fired into the surging mass of upturned faces confronting them, lit up redly but a moment by the powder-flashes. Musket-butts and bayonets were freely used on the parapet, where the stormers were gallantly met. The garrison fought with muskets, handspikes, and gun-rammers, the officers striking with their swords, so close were the combatants. Numbers, however, soon told against the Fifty-fourth, for it was tens against hundreds. Outlined against the sky, they were a fair mark for the foe. Men fell every moment during the brief struggle.

Some of the wounded crawled down the slope to shelter; others fell headlong into the ditch below. It was seen from the volume of musketry fire, even before the walls were gained, that the garrison was stronger than had been supposed, and brave in defending the work. The first rush had failed, for those of the Fifty-fourth who reached the parapet were too few in numbers to overcome the garrison, and the supports were not at hand to take full advantage of their first fierce attack.

Repulsed from the crest after the short hand-to-hand struggle, the assailants fell back upon the exterior slope of the rampart. There the men were encouraged to remain by their officers, for by sweeping the top of the parapet with musketry, and firing at those trying to serve the guns, they would greatly aid an advancing force. For a time this was done, but at the cost of more lives. The enemy's fire became more effective as the numbers of the Fifty-fourth diminished. Hand grenades or lighted shells were rolled down the slope, or thrown over into the ditch.

All this time the remaining officers and men of the Fifty-fourth were firing at the hostile figures about the guns, or that they saw spring upon the parapet, fire, and jump away. One brave fellow, with his broken arm lying across his breast, was piling cartridges upon it for Lieutenant Emerson, who, like other officers, was using a musket he had picked up. Another soldier, tired of the enforced combat, climbed the slope to his fate; for in a moment his dead body rolled down again. A particularly severe fire came from the southwest bastion. There a Confederate was observed, who, stripped to the waist, with daring exposure for some time dealt out fatal shots; but at last three eager marksmen fired together, and he fell back into the fort, to appear no more. Capt. J. W-M. Appleton distinguished himself before the curtain. He crawled into an embrasure, and with his pistol prevented the artillery-men from serving the gun. Private George Wilson of Company A had been shot through both shoulders, but refused to go back until he had his captain's permission. While occupied with this faithful soldier, who came to him as he lay in the embrasure, Captain Appleton's attention was distracted, and the gun was fired.

In the fighting upon the slopes of Wagner, Captains Russel and Simpkins were killed or mortally wounded. Captain Pope there received a severe wound in the shoulder.

All these events had taken place in a short period of time. The charge of the Fifty-fourth had been made and repulsed before the arrival of any other troops. Those who had clung to the bloody slopes or were lying in the ditch, hearing fighting going on at their right, realized at last that the expected succor would not reach them where they were. To retire through the enveloping fire was as dangerous and deadly as to advance. Some that night preferred capture to the attempt at escaping; but the larger portion managed to fall back, singly or in squads, beyond the musketry fire of the garrison.

Captain Emilio, the junior of that rank, succeeded to the command of the Fifty-fourth on the field by casualties. After retiring from Wagner to a point where men were encountered singly or in small squads, he determined to rally as many as possible. With the assistance of Lieutenants Grace and Dexter, a large portion of the Fifty-fourth survivors were collected and formed in line, together with a considerable number of white soldiers of various regiments. While thus engaged, the national flag of the Fifty-fourth was brought to Captain Emilio; but as it was useless as a rallying point in the darkness, it was sent to the rear for safety. Sergeant Carney had bravely brought this flag from Wagner's parapet, at the cost of two grievous wounds. The State color was torn from the staff, the silk was found by the enemy in the moat, while the staff remained with us.

Finding a line of rifle trench unoccupied and no indication that dispositions were being made for holding it, believing that the enemy would attempt a sortie, which was indeed contemplated but not attempted, Captain Emilio there stationed his men, disposed to defend the line. Other men were collected as they appeared. Lieutenant Tucker, slightly wounded, who was among the last to leave the sandhills near the fort, joined this force. Desultory firing was still going on, and after a time, being informed that some troops were in the open ground, the force, numbering some two hundred, was formed by its commander, and advanced from the rifle trench. It is believed this was the only organized body of rallied men ready and able to support Stevenson's brigade, which alone was prepared after the repulse of the others to resist attack.

Presently the Twenty-fourth Massachusetts was encountered; but upon reporting, it was found that support was not required. Marching back to the still deserted trench, that line was again occupied.

By midnight firing entirely ceased. About 1 a.m., on the 19th, a mounted officer rode up, inquired what force held the trench, and asked for the commanding officer. Captain Emilio responded, and recognized General Stevenson, who thanked him for the support given the reserve brigade, and his dispositions for holding the line. He was also informed that a regiment would be sent to relieve his men, and shortly after, the Tenth Connecticut arrived for that purpose. When this was done, the white soldiers were formed into detachments by regiments, and sent to find their colors.

The Fifty-fourth men were then marched to the rear, and after proceeding a short distance down the beach, encountered Lieutenants Jewett,

Emerson, and Appleton, with some of the men. There the Fifty-fourth bivouacked for the night, under the shelter of the sand-bluffs. Although the storming column and supports did not move forward with a close formation and promptness in support of the Fifty-fourth, which might have won Wagner that night, their attacks when made were delivered with a gallantry and persistence that made their severe losses the more deplorable and fruitless, by reason of such faulty generalship.

When Strong's brigade advanced, it met the same devastating fire at the defile; but a considerable number of the survivors, mainly of the Sixth Connecticut and Forty-eighth New York, pushed on to the southeast bastion, feebly defended by the Thirty-first North Carolina, and entered, securing a portion of the salient. Farther they could not penetrate against superior numbers. General Strong accompanied his column, and, as always, exhibited the utmost bravery.

General Seymour, learning the failure of Strong's brigade to carry the work, ordered Colonel Putnam to advance his regiments. That officer gallantly led forward his brigade, meeting the same severe fire as he neared the fort. With survivors of the Seventh New Hampshire, he entered the disputed salient, followed by portions of the Sixty-second and Sixty-seventh Ohio. His One Hundredth New York advanced to a point near the work, in the confusion and darkness poured a volley into our own men in the salient, and then retired. It must be understood, however, that all these regiments suffered severe losses; but losses that night do not necessarily indicate effective regimental action. The greatest number of men in the salient at any time hardly equaled a regiment, and were of different organizations. They were fighting in a place unknown to them, holding their ground and repelling attacks, but were incapable of aggressive action. Fighting over traverses and sand-bags, hemmed in by a fire poured across their rear, as well as from the front and flanks, the struggle went on pitilessly for nearly two hours. Vainly were precious lives freely offered up, in heroic attempts to encourage a charge on the flanking guns. The enveloping darkness covered all; and the valiant, seeing how impotent were their efforts, felt like crying with Ajax, "Give us but light, Jove! and in the light, if thou seest fit, destroy us!"

Every field-officer in the bastion was at last struck down except Maj. Lewis Butler, Sixty-seventh Ohio. Colonel Putnam had been shot through the head. When all hope of expected support was gone, Major Butler sent out the regimental colors, and gave orders to leave the bastion. There were, according to his account, about one hundred men each of the Sixty-second and Sixty-seventh Ohio, about fifty of the Forty-eighth New York, and some small detachments of other regiments, some with and some without officers. When this force had departed, and the enemy had been re-enforced by the arrival of the Thirty-second Georgia, the wounded, those who feared to encounter the enclosing fire, and those who failed to hear or obey the order for abandonment, were soon surrounded and captured. General Stevenson's brigade had advanced toward the fort, but it was too late, and the men were withdrawn.

Upon the beach in front of the siege line, drunken soldiers of the regular artillery, with swords and pistol-shots, barred the passage of all to the rear. They would listen to no protestations that the regiments were driven back or broken up, and even brutally ordered wounded men to the front. After a time, their muddled senses came to them on seeing the host of arrivals, while the vigorous actions of a few determined officers who were prepared to enforce a free passage, made further opposition perilous.

Thus ended the great assault on Fort Wagner. It was the second and last attempted. The Confederate loss was 181 killed and wounded, including Lieut.-Col. J. C. Simkins, captains W. H. Eyan, W. T. Tatom, and P. II. Waring, and Lieut. G. W. Thompson, killed. Our loss was 1,515, including 111 officers, and embracing General Seymour wounded, General Strong mortally wounded, and Colonel Putnam (acting brigadier) killed. Of the ten regimental commanders, Colonel Shaw was killed, Col. J. L. Chatfield, Sixth Connecticut, mortally wounded, and five others wounded. Such severe casualties stamp the sanguinary character of the fighting, and mark the assault as one of the fiercest struggles of the war, considering the numbers engaged.

This is further evidenced by the fact that the losses exceeded those sustained by our forces in many much better-known actions during the Rebellion—notably Wilson's Creek, Pea Ridge, Cedar Mountain, Chantilly, Prairie Grove, Pleasant Hills, Sailor's Creek, Jonesborough,

Bentonville, and High Bridge, in most of which a much larger Federal force was engaged.

FROM THE CITATION

The President of the United States of America, in the name of Congress, takes pleasure in presenting the Medal of Honor to Sergeant William Harvey Carney, United States Army, for extraordinary heroism on 18 July 1863, while serving with Company C, 54th Massachusetts Colored Infantry, in action at Fort Wagner, South Carolina. When the color sergeant was shot down, Sergeant Carney grasped the flag, led the way to the parapet, and planted the colors thereon. When the troops fell back he brought off the flag, under a fierce fire in which he was twice severely wounded.

CHAPTER FIVE

Above and Beyond: Frank Luke Jr.

Keith Warren Lloyd

THE LATTER HALF OF AUGUST 1918 WAS A BUSY TIME FOR THE EAGLE Squadron. The United States First Army began plans for the first major offensive by American troops in the Great War. The objective was to reduce a salient in the front lines near the town of Saint-Mihiel.

A salient, or forward bulge in the battle line, is usually seen as a tactical liability, since the forces that occupy it are constantly under the threat of being attacked on their flanks. The Germans, however, had worked hard to maintain and fortify the order to interrupt the east–west lines of the French railway system and thus make it difficult for the Allies to keep their forces resupplied along the entire front.

The Allied attack was set for 12 September and would involve some 300,000 American soldiers and Marines, along with 110,000 French troops. The objective would be to roll back the salient and hopefully cut off and destroy the wary German army that was occupying it.

The Saint-Mihiel offensive would also be one of the earliest examples of infantry advancing with support from tanks, and of American combat aircraft providing close air support for ground forces in the attack. Over a thousand Allied aircraft were put to the task, under the command of Col. William Mitchell, the air commander for Gen. John Pershing's First Army.

In preparation for the offensive, Mitchell ordered the First Pursuit Group to relocate to new airfields closer to the front line. The 27th Aero

Squadron would move to the village of Rembercourt. The airfield there was meticulously camouflaged, and movements of the aircraft and equipment were carefully planned to avoid demolition or detection by the enemy.

By the time the move was complete, the 27th would have a new commanding officer. Colonel Mitchell selected Harold Hartney to command the First Pursuit Group and coordinate the efforts of its four squadrons during the offensive. Replacing Hartney at the head of Eagle Squadron would be Capt. Alfred A. Grant. On August 21, 1918, Grant assumed command of the unit.

Grant had a very different style of leadership than that of Hal Hartney. A member of the cadet corps in college, he insisted on military correctness, discipline, and strict adherence to regulations. If Hartney was the popular coach in the school of aerial combat, Grant was the stern headmaster.

An original member of the 27th Squadron, Grant was present during Frank Luke Jr.'s earliest days in the unit. For Luke, that meant Grant had shared the opinion of the Arizonan, also held by the rest of the squadron. Luke was commonly referred to among the men as the "Arizona Boaster." It would only be a matter of time before Grant and Luke butted heads.

On September 1, 1918, the squadron finished its move to the new aerodrome at Rembercourt and began receiving a new crop of replacement pilots to bring the roster up to full strength. On the evening of September 11, the officers met in the mess to discuss their part in the upcoming offensive.

"The Air Service will take the offensive at all points with the objective of destroying the enemy's air service, attacking his troops on the ground, and protecting our own air and ground troops," the operations order stated. The First Pursuit Group was to provide direct support to the First Army in Saint-Mihiel, and "attack hostile balloon positions, at the same time protecting Allied reconnaissance operating in the sector."

Observation balloons—called *drachens* (dragons) by the Germans, and nicknamed "sausages" by the Allies—became the focus of conversation. Used extensively by both sides during the war, balloons were set up just behind the front lines to gather reconnaissance information, and were highly effective in their task. When an enemy balloon floated nearby, you could expect a barrage of artillery and mortar fire. Needless to say, everyone from field marshals down to infantry privates hated the things. A First World War expression still used today in America's military is "The balloon's gone up," which means something bad is about to happen.

The great oblong canvas bags were filled with highly volatile hydrogen to make them lighter than air. A gondola was slung beneath the balloon with enough space for two trained observers and their communications equipment. The balloons were tethered by two-thousand-foot steel cables attached to flatbed trucks.

Observation balloons were not easy targets. Both sides placed high value on them, both militarily and financially. Great measures were taken to protect the balloons.

The balloons were surrounded by machine guns and mortar stations. In most cases, the observers had a machine gun swivel-mounted on the edge of the gondola. The balloons were also protected by air support circling high overhead, ready to pounce on any would-be attacker.

Firing at the balloon from a safe distance was not an option. The range and firepower of World War I–era weapons, particularly light machine guns used on aircraft, required the attacking pilot to get quite close to the "sausage" in order to hit it with enough incendiary ammunition to set it on fire. Then, if the balloon exploded, the pilot had to work fast in order to not be consumed by the flames. An attack on an observation balloon was, therefore, often considered to be a suicide mission.

The twelfth day of September was an important one for the soldiers of the American Expeditionary Force. Preparations for the Saint-Mihiel offensive had been made in painstaking detail. Pershing had promised the French that the German salient would be rolled back in less than a week. While the Americans had performed well in previous defensive actions, the credibility of the United States as a military power rested on this one attack. Everyone from Pershing down to the doughboys felt pressure to perform.

Before dawn, the First Pursuit pilots at Rembercourt heard the Allied artillery begin a massive preparatory barrage. Dark clouds hung low in the morning sky, and soon a heavy downpour added to the misery. The first patrol was grounded due to the lousy weather. To the east the sounds of artillery rumbled on, rolling with the thunder. Just after seven a.m. the rain began to slacken.

Eight Spads were rolled onto the muddy field, and a force of grimy mechanical riggers and armorers poured over the ships.

Joe Wehner was standing by his plane when Frank Luke sidled up alongside him.

"Remember what Vasconcelles said last night about attacking balloons?" he asked.

"Yeah," Wehner replied. "Why?"

"I'm going to get a balloon today," Luke said confidently.

So the cowboy is at it again, the pilots said to one another. More power to you, they said sarcastically, invoking the squadron motto. If he had the guts to try, which was doubtful, they had surely seen the last of the Arizona Boaster.

The inclement weather had made a shambles of the morning flight schedule. Anxious to get off the ground and start the show, the young lieutenants piloting the Spads of the Eagle Squadron scattered to the four winds.

Luke left Rembercourt and headed almost due east, toward the village of Lavignéville. As he neared the battle line, he spotted three enemy aircraft in the sky ahead and gave chase. Near the town of Pont-à-Mousson and the southernmost shoulder of the salient, the fleeing Germans turned north toward the larger city of Metz, entered a bank of clouds, and gave him the slip.

Undaunted, Luke flew over the battle and continued north, crossing into German territory. As he neared the smashed, rubble-strewn village of Marieulles, Luke spotted what he was looking for, bobbing on its tether beneath the rain clouds.

It was a *drachen*.

Luke put the Spad into a steady climb and scanned the sky for enemy aircraft before swooping in for the kill. Luke nosed the Spad into a steep dive, his Vickers gun chattering.

Immediately the sky around him began filling with black bursts of exploding antiaircraft shells, large incendiary rounds that looked like flaming tennis balls. They zipped past with streams of machine-gun tracer bullets. The German ground crew scrambled for the winch controls and started reeling the balloon earthward.

Luke kept firing, holding the screaming Spad in a dive for as long as he dared. Finally he eased back on the stick, cranked into a fast turn, and made another pass. The balloon jerked awkwardly at the end of its tether. Luke's gun stuttered and went silent. A feed jam.

Luke zoomed away, reaching forward to try and free the action of the two Vickers guns. The right gun remained jammed, but he got the left one functioning again. Luke started another run. The *drachen* was nearly at the ground and the enemy gunners were blazing away with everything they had. Luke pressed the trigger and fired a final burst. The observer, a young officer named Willi Klemm, slumped in the gondola. One of Frank's bullets had lanced through his chest, killing him instantly.

Suddenly, there was a terrific explosion as the balloon burst into flames and dropped into a burning mass on top of the winch. The Spad turned away from the withering antiaircraft fire and zoomed for the American lines.

Lt. Joseph M. Fox watched as a lean, blond youth emerged from the cockpit. Fox remarked that the flaming mass was hard to miss, and that there were probably a good number of Huns killed when the balloon exploded so close to the ground.

Fox watched as Frank Luke Jr. produced a pen and scratched out the details of the event on a blank affidavit for the purpose of confirming an aerial victory. Luke asked Fox and another witness to sign the document, thanked the balloon observers, and headed for his Spad. The airplane staggered and sputtered across the field. Luke saw how much damage was actually taken from enemy fire. The ship would go no further.

Frank spent the night with the balloon company, and in the morning hitched a ride back to Rembercourt in the sidecar of a motorcycle. Frank Luke, his face unshaven and smoke-stained, and his flying suit spattered with mud, reported to Grant's office and handed over the signed statement that confirmed his first kill.

When they were finally able to get Luke's plane back to Rembercourt, the maintenance chief shook his head. The Spad was full of shot holes. It was a wonder that Luke wasn't full of holes himself.

Frank just laughed. "They can't get me," he said.

By the third day it was evident that Pershing's attack was going to be a rout. Intelligence estimates claimed that German forces in the Saint-Mihiel region were strained to the breaking point. This proved to be correct. Within hours, the Germans were forced to withdraw from the territory that had cost them many days of hard fighting and many thousands of lives.

By September 14, 1918, although they had also suffered heavy casualties, the Americans were rounding up scores of German prisoners. That morning, a formation of twelve Spads of the Eagle Squadron departed the designation "shooters" to drop out of formation and attack observation balloons, while the remaining Spads kept watch for prowling enemy airplanes. The left guns of the shooters were loaded entirely with phosphorous tracer ammunition for igniting balloons. Frank Luke was one of the shooters.

Luke's victory two days earlier, and the manner in which he had confirmed it, did little to enhance his reputation. While it did raise some eyebrows, most felt that a Frank Luke without any kills to his credit was bad enough. A Frank Luke with a confirmed victory would be insufferable.

Still, the members of the squad had to have been questioning their initial impressions of Frank Luke. When they had first arrived in France, Luke was pegged as a coward; he had dropped out of previous flights due to engine trouble, and had seen little combat. But the attack on the balloon over Marieulles was anything but cowardly.

Unfortunately, Luke's relationship with his squad mates would worsen before it would improve.

The patrol crossed battle sites just west of Verdun and continued east. While flying over the hamlet of Abaucort, Luke spotted an enemy balloon and zoomed in for the attack.

Luke made his first pass with a steady stream of incendiary bullets pouring out of the Vickers gun. As he wheeled around for another run, he saw the observer drop his machine gun and jump from the gondola under the balloon. Luke kept firing until his gun got jammed.

Luke would attack the balloon four more times until the balloon started to rapidly deflate. The balloon sank to the ground, but somehow did not catch fire.

While Luke continued to strike at the antiaircraft gunfire, Lt. Leo Dawson dove into the fray. Lt. Thomas Lennon came in after him, firing a 100-round burst. Miraculously, the balloon still did not explode.

All twelve Spads returned safely to Rembercourt. The pilots inspected the damage done to their planes, and once again, Luke's Spad was liberally pockmarked with bullet holes.

Any good-natured, post-battle conversation came to an end when Luke, Dawson, and Lennon all claimed credit for destroying the balloon. The three filed separate reports detailing their attack, and stated that they saw the balloon on the ground in "very flabby condition."

The argument was ultimately settled by Captain Grant, who awarded all three men the victory. At the time there was no army policy to award partial credit for air-to-air victories.

The same day, reports began to arrive of another German observation balloon aloft near the village of Buzy. The enemy was attempting to take a stand against the headquarters of I Corps' right flank.

The report went down the chain of command to Harold Hartney's First Pursuit Group. The directive was clear: The balloon over Buzy had to go. After Hartney issued a warning to Grant, a delegation of officers from the 27th Squadron crossed the field to the Group operations shack.

There were four of them: Grant himself, 1st Lt. Kenneth Clapp (Luke's first flight leader and immediate superior), along with the disgruntled Dawson and Lennon.

They wanted Luke out of the Eagle Squadron.

Luke was a "menace to morale," Clapp told Hartney. Then, in less than delicate terms, he put forth a proposal. "Let Luke be the shooter on the next mission," said Clapp. "If he fails and survives, you can transfer him to another unit, but if he can do it, let him stay."

Hartney could scarcely believe what he was hearing, but instead of reprimanding the insubordinate Clapp and Grant, he went along with it. If the cowboy scored, they would have to learn to live with Luke. If he failed, a transfer would be easy enough.

At 2:30 in the afternoon the flight departed Rembercourt, crossed high over the Meuse and the carnage of the trenches near Verdun, then headed northeast for Buzy. Their target hung lazily in the air above the shell-shattered village. Luke signaled to Wehner and went off. Other members of the patrol watched while it looked as if Luke intended to ram his plane headfirst into the balloon. At the last possible moment Luke sent a stream of flaming .303 rounds, stitching the fabric of the balloon. Almost immediately it caught fire and begun fluttering earthward, its steel tether limp with slack.

Suddenly the wood and taut fabric of Luke's Spad was ripped with several crackling blows. From out of the sun came eight German Fokker D.VIIs. Two of them were right on his trail, the muzzles of their machine guns flickering. A hail of fire smashed through the wings and fuselage of the Spad, but the rugged aircraft continued to fly.

Luke looked out to see a stubby American pursuit plane plunge straight through the gang of Fokker D.VIIs, guns ablaze. While Luke raced for safety in his damaged aircraft, he was soon joined by the pilot that had saved him.

It was Joe Wehner.

Back at headquarters, the same officers who wanted Luke kicked off the squad were now offering emotional tributes to his bravery. In the confusion that often accompanies aerial combat, no one had actually seen Luke crash. The torching of the balloon was so extreme, and then being jumped by eight German planes made it seem obvious that Luke was dead.

"He's gone, poor kid, but he went down in a blaze of glory," said Clapp, choked with emotion.

The telephone rang. Luke wasn't just alive, he also wanted to trade in his Spad for a new one to go after another balloon. The mechanics were all shaking their heads. Luke's Spad had once again been shot to ribbons, and it was a wonder he had returned at all. Captain Grant and Major Hartney went out to the hangar to meet Luke. Luke was not going to get another plane, and he was crestfallen. Joe Wehner went after the next balloon without Luke, but arrived. The *drachen* was destroyed by the French ace-of-aces, René Fonck.

Luke seemed to be in a fine mood when he and his pal borrowed a squadron car and went souvenir hunting. Frank wanted to find a German machine gun, and they managed to locate two of them in a shell-damaged house near the front. After that they spent the rest of their day off happily shooting the breeze in one of the hangars at Rembercourt.

They took the scavenged machine guns and began taking them apart and cleaning them.

"You can't tell," Luke said jokingly. "Maybe there'll be another revolution in Mexico and we'll need them in Arizona. Maybe I'll start one when I get back!"

Captain Grant spent much of the day wondering what to do about Frank Luke. While Luke was a worthy combat pilot, he remained a commander's nightmare on the ground. The events of the last few days emboldened Luke to the point of showing a distinct lack of regard for authority, especially Grant's. Then there was the matter of Luke going around Grant and directly to Hartney to seek authorization for his twilight balloon-busting show.

Grant seemed to arrive at a solution. In a memo dated September 18, 1918, Grant recommended that Luke be advanced to first lieutenant, stating that "a vacancy exists in the new squadrons now being organized." While September 17 gave Luke and Wehner a chance to rest, it allowed the Germans to develop a deadly trap for the American balloon-busting team.

A 4:00 p.m. on September 18, Frank Luke and Joe Wehner took off from Rembercourt and headed east toward Saint-Mihiel in search of enemy balloons. Luke spotted a pair just over the new battle line near Three-Fingered Lake, a familiar pilot's landmark on the eastern edge of the former salient.

As usual, Frank was the shooter. He threaded the Spad through some high clouds. Wehner climbed to a height where he could keep watch for enemy patrols. Luke tipped the plane into a dive and dropped out of the clouds, firing steady bursts into the *drachen* below.

Tracers ripped across the balloon's fabric, spouting red flames. Luke pulled out of the dive, skimming the treetops as the enemy gunners blazed away with all they had.

Off to the west, Luke could see a flight of German Fokker D.VIIs angling downward to intercept him. He would have just enough time to make a single attack run on the second balloon before making his escape.

The target grew larger and larger before the Spad's whirling propeller. A burst of Luke's tracer slashed through it, and then it too erupted and wallowed to earth.

Luke put the Spad into a climb, searching for Joe.

Joe was still high above and some distance away. He had spotted the Fokkers going after Luke and had fired two red flares, but it is doubtful that Luke even saw the warning signs. Joe was rushing downward to help, as he had many times.

As Luke climbed to join his pal, the Fokkers caught up with him. Frank continued to climb higher, only to find Joe in trouble as well. Three German planes had pounced on Joe, meaning they were facing *two* groups of enemy planes. Luke was still too far away to help Joe, and the D.VIIs were closing in.

Joe's Spad burst into flames and began plummeting earthward.

Luke banked his plane in a tight climb and turned, roaring head-on at the Germans chasing him. Both Vickers guns hammered into the lead D.VII. The Fokker fell into a nosedive and smashed into the ground below. Frank took another sharp turn to repeat this on the second plane, and succeeded.

Luke determined how far east the fight had taken him, and he turned back to the American lines. Maybe Joe was nursing his wounded Spad home; maybe the burning Spad wasn't Joe at all.

As Luke neared Verdun, he saw white puffs of antiaircraft fire. It had to be an enemy plane on the Allied side of the lines. German *archie* was black; Allied antiaircraft fire tended to be white. It was an enemy plane, to be sure, a two-seater observation plane known as a Halberstadt. A short distance away Luke could see that a flight of Spads were stalking the enemy plane. They had stork emblems painted on their sides. It was a group of his French pals, the Cigognes.

The Storks seemed to be herding the enemy snooper into Allied territory, and its observer-gunner was probably busy watching them. Luke rapidly closed the gap, fired a burst of .303 slugs into the Halberstadt, and watched it fall from the sky.

A short while later, the telephone rang in the First Pursuit Group headquarters at the Rembercourt aerodrome. Frank Luke was safe, the caller said. He had landed after dark near the gun battery. They could put him up for the night, but someone from Rembercourt would have to come get him in the morning.

A witness reported seeing one of the Spads go down in flames near Saint Hilaire. Since Wehner had not returned and Frank was known to be safe, Hartney knew that Wehner had been killed.

Hartney decided that he better be the one to break the news to Frank.

Early the next morning, he asked the Group's YMCA representative, a Mrs. Welton, to accompany him while he performed the unpleasant duty.

They found the stone-faced Frank Luke sitting beside his shot-up Spad. When Luke saw who was coming out to collect him, it confirmed what he already knew.

"Wehner isn't back yet, is he, Major?" Luke said quietly.

Any attempt to console Frank Luke over the death of Joe Wehner was met with a stony silence. Any attempt to congratulate Luke on his recent success was met with the same. Even before their friendship had been tempered by the fires of combat, Frank had brushed aside the unfounded suspicion about Joe, and became his trusted pal when no one else would. In return he had received a type of loyalty that would cause Joe to deliberately sacrifice himself.

Among Joe's personal effects they found a brass pocket compass. The lid was engraved with the inscription: *For Frank Luke, "Balloon Buster," From J. W. Sept. 1919. 27th/1.* A gift intended for a buddy who had become the ace-of-aces.

There was a night of food, wine, and entertainment for the squadron, having as much as they could have despite being far from home in the middle of a war. Some of the men cheered Luke on to give a speech.

"Fellas," Frank began, "I haven't done anything except what all of us came here to do. We are all trying to get as many Huns as we can before they get us. I've been lucky. That's all there is to it."

Even more somberly, Frank added: "They got Joe. I'll make them pay for that. There's just one thing I want you to know: *They'll never take me alive.*"

The next day Hartney approved a week's leave in Paris for 2nd Lt. Frank Luke Jr. When Luke protested, Hartney made it an order. Still sullen, Luke left for Orly on his way to Paris.

On September 21, 1918, the *New York Times* printed the following headline:

11 GERMAN BALLOONS
HIS BAG IN 4 DAYS
Lieut. Luke Also Destroyed Three Airplanes in Same Period
USED INCENDIARY BULLETS
On One of His Flights the American Downed Two Foes on a Few
Gallons of Gasoline

Luke was soon back at headquarters.

"Aren't you back early?" Hartney asked him.

"Yes, sir."

Why?"

"There wasn't anything to do," Luke replied.

The exotic and enchanting City of Lights, the vibrant rush of revelers along gaslit cobblestone streets, kiosks and cafes, the music, the wine, the beautiful women . . . none of it had appealed to Frank Luke.

Luke remained grim and silent, his eyes containing that vacant look that a future generation of warriors would term "the thousand-yard stare." Joe Wehner's death changed Frank for the short time that he himself had left on earth. A twenty-one-year-old had been trained and commissioned and given a speedy pursuit plane to fly, and his resulting sense of invincibility seemed to have dissipated when Joe Wehner was killed.

Shortly after returning to the 27th Squadron, Frank received a telegram.

WE ARE PROUD. GOD BLESS YOU—MAMA

The cat was out of the bag, so to speak. Luke mentioned to a friend that he told his mother that aviation was the safest branch of the service.

On the night of Joe Wehner's death, he had said to Hartney, "My mother doesn't know I'm on the front yet."

On September 25, 1918, Frank penned a short explanation to Tillie Luke in Phoenix.

Dear Mother,

I have not written for some days now on account of being so busy, as no doubt you have already heard. This is only a line to let you know that I am O.K. Now, Mother, remember that I have passed the dangerous stages of being a new hand at the game, so don't worry, for I now know how to take care of myself.

Love to all,

Frank

While Luke was in Paris, the First Pursuit Group had established an advanced aerodrome near the front lines at Verdun. The air service would share the field with the naval gun batteries. The navy had been using the placement of a twelve-inch naval gun, the same type used in battleship turrets. Mounted to a flatbed railroad car, the weapon moved on a special spur line. It was capable of hurtling huge shells more than fifty miles and playing havoc with the enemy's rear echelon.

In the late afternoon of September 26, 1918, Luke departed Rembercourt to attack enemy balloons north of Verdun. With him was 2nd Lt. Ivan A. Roberts, who, like Wehner, hailed from Massachusetts. On their way they spotted a patrol of five Fokker D.VIIs and decided to attack.

Like most dogfights, the engagement forced the dueling planes closer and closer to the earth, and Luke found himself at only 100 meters by the time it was over. His fuel tank low and the Vickers guns plagued by stoppages, Luke turned for the Allied lines. No sign of Ivan Roberts. Roberts did not return that night, and was eventually listed as missing in action. The German ace Lt. Franz Büchner, of the Fokker D.VII pilots involved, was credited with shooting Roberts down, but neither the aircraft nor Roberts's body have ever been found.

When Ivan Roberts failed to return, Luke was once again stunned by the loss of a flying partner. The remainder of Luke's combat patrols would be flown alone.

Word would reach Captain Grant that Luke had requested a transfer out of the squadron to conduct lone-wolf missions. After confronting Luke himself, Grant informed him that he would be grounded until further notice. A few minutes later, a Spad bearing the number 26 on its fuselage taxied away from the hangar and lifted off.

Some brave soul informed Captain Grant that the departing Spad was being piloted by Frank Luke.

"Get Vasconcelles on the phone. Tell him that Luke is on the way. On his arrival he is to be placed under arrest."

"Then what?" the adjutant asked.

"First, I'm going to recommend him for the Distinguished Service Cross," Grant replied. "Then, by God, I'm going to court-martial him!"

Despite this, Hartney once again backed Luke up, making it look to Grant that Hartney allowed Luke to backchannel and circumvent Grant's orders.

Hartney found Luke at the forward aerodrome at Verdun on the evening of September 29.

"Major," Luke began, "there are three balloons north of here along the Meuse. I can get all three if you let me go now."

"Okay, Frank," Hartney answered, "but not until sundown, at 5:56."

Hartney and Luke repaired to the dugout command post. The field was very close to the front and had been shelled several times. Personnel assigned there kept their steel helmets and gas masks at arm's length. Luke paced nervously, and Hartney kept telling him to be patient.

When dusk finally settled, Luke took off from the Verdun field, but instead of flying up the Meuse he made a sudden detour toward the village of Souilly. Flying low over the headquarters of the American observation balloon unit there, he dropped a message:

WATCH THE THREE HUN BALLOONS ON THE MEUSE.
LT. LUKE

As instructed, the Yank observers did watch the three enemy balloons, and within minutes they saw the first one erupt into a bright orange glow. It was the balloon they noted on their map near Dun-sur-Meuse. It was very late into twilight and the Spad was barely visible. Within minutes a second *drachen* exploded over a farm, showering scraps of burning canvas.

At twelve minutes after the hour, a third rush of flame appeared just above the horizon and slowly sank out of sight. The First Pursuit Group received a call from the observers at Souilly. Confirmed: Luke had destroyed all three German balloons on the Meuse above Verdun.

The Rembercourt aerodrome was alerted to Luke's impending return. But as the night wore on, there was no sign of him. Most assumed he would arrive the following morning, after hitching a ride back to the airfield.

Correspondent Frederick Smith of the *Arizona Republican* was present at Rembercourt that night. Later he wrote in a dispatch: "There was still the forlorn hope that he would come roaring out of the northern sky with some new record of hairbreadth escape."

But Frank Luke did not.

Frank Luke Jr. was officially listed as missing in action on September 30, 1918. His name did not appear on any prisoner rolls provided to neutral authorities by the Germans. No Allied observers had seen him crash. Twelve days later, the Armistice officially ending the First World War went into effect. After four long years, the German people deposed their monarch and sued for peace. The "War to End All Wars" had been won, and the world was "safe for democracy." Or so it was thought.

FROM THE CITATION

After having previously destroyed a number of enemy aircraft within 17 days he voluntarily started on a patrol after German observation balloons. Though pursued by 8 German planes which were protecting the enemy balloon line, he unhesitatingly attacked and shot down in flames 3 German balloons, being himself under heavy fire from ground batteries and the hostile planes. Severely wounded, he descended to within 50 meters of the ground, and flying at this low altitude near the town of Murvaux, opened fire upon enemy troops, killing 6 and wounding as many more. Forced to make a landing and surrounded on all sides by the enemy, who called upon him to surrender, he drew his automatic pistol and defended himself gallantly until he fell dead from a wound in the chest.

CHAPTER SIX

Lasting Valor: Vernon J. Baker

Vernon J. Baker, Ken Olsen

I WAS FIERCELY PROUD OF THE FACT THAT MY PLATOON ALWAYS SHOWED up for the fight. We didn't have that much incentive. A great job hadn't earned black soldiers any special notice. Running away, however, earned infamy. And I made sure everyone knew it.

Runyon paced about the company while I agitated over the sparseness of our ranks. Not only was my platoon undermanned, Company C was at least seventy men short of the more than two hundred that should have been on hand. Again, casualties and the lack of replacement soldiers worked against us.

Once Runyon was satisfied the company was accounted for, he gave the order to move out. We walked a short distance up the road and then cut through several dew-heavy farm fields. We split into our separate platoons near the junction of two dirt tracks and made for our individual jumping-off spots.

Our starting point was another 250 yards from the junction, in a bombed-out grove of trees at the edge of a huge overgrown field. Even the most intrepid Italian wasn't going to cultivate this close to the German lines.

I motioned for my men to stop.

"No talking when we're going up that hill," I warned. "Hand signals only."

Inexplicably, I felt a rush of hope. "Today, we're going to do it," I added. My men nodded.

Doing nothing noisier than breathing, we squatted in the darkness and waited. The spring air was crisp and jaunty, welcome after several sultry days. It was a perfect day for a walk anywhere but into battle.

Italy's northwestern coast was mindful of Wyoming, the coastal plain meeting the Apennines much like the sagebrush prairie that embraces the Rocky Mountains. Italy was altogether different, with oceans, ancient ruins, and fast-talking, impatient natives. Still, spring between the Mediterranean and the mountains carried a sense of life and renewal. As long as you didn't contemplate the rest of the brutal picture.

Time ticked all too rapidly toward 4:45 a.m. My eyes were glued to my watch face. When the hands locked on the appointed time, the Allied artillery began its morning concert. This ritual had begun at exactly the same time, every day for a week, so the Germans would think that this was just another morning of gunnery practice.

Tanks, long-range guns from British battleships, howitzers, and mortars all played parts of the score, rhythmically rolling volleys up the steep Strettoia Hills. Eight months earlier, this kind of barrage would have had us cringing, no matter which side was launching it. Now we were numb to it. And on this morning, we focused on the hills ahead of us instead of the cataclysmic thundering. I kept my eyes on my watch. The rescue was far more important. A twenty-minute shelling intermission began at 5:00 a.m. This also was part of the weeklong performance, part of making the Germans believe this day was part of the same old routine.

I waited for the echo of the last explosion to ring back through the hills and gave my squad leader the high sign. We stood and rushed for the bottom of Hill X, a half-mile away over the most exposed countryside between ourselves and the Germans. Thank God for darkness.

We crossed the railroad tracks, Highway One, and one last small field smelling of alfalfa. The long slope of Hill X pitched 450 feet upward, one terrace at a time, although in this light we could see only a giant black knob. I spotted Captain Runyon as we closed the trail switchbacking to the top.

It was a good, solid dirt path, the outer edge delineated with rocks. And the captain, I'll bless him for this, was stepping rock to rock up the outside edge, probing the way with a stick. I admired Runyon's effort. He seemed coolheaded and a quick thinker. This showed he had spent a little bit of time studying the area and was aware of the Germans' reputation for paving it with mines.

I turned and whispered to the man behind me, "Walk only on the rocks. Pass it on back."

Single file, rock to rock, my men followed with .30 caliber light machine guns, 60mm mortars, and ammunition. I carried nine pounds of M1 rifle, stretched hand to hand in front of my waist. None of this using a sling to carry my weapon. Never. A sling meant I had to pull my rifle off my back when the bullets started flying—a shortcut to death.

A lighter-weight .30 caliber carbine was standard issue for officers. Experience cured my desire for this convenience. I once watched an American soldier, sitting on one of our tanks, unload five bullets from such a carbine into a German soldier who was charging him with a bazooka. The German never slowed. I immediately traded my carbine.

My next acquisition, a .45 caliber Thompson submachine gun, was great for throwing a lead shower if you didn't care about accuracy. I traded it away with the same speed it consumed ammunition. I preferred a solid weapon, one I could snap up and fire, like the rifle I had used when hunting deer and elk with my grandfather back in Wyoming. The M1 rifle, with a custom recoil pad, fulfilled my need.

With a methodical rhythm of stop, balance, step, stop, balance, step, we moved rapidly, rock to rock, one man after another, up the trail. Sweat, dust, and gun oil blended with the odor of well-worn army cloth and filled my nostrils.

Once we reached the top, I signaled for a quick break, so we could catch our breaths. But barely. Our artillery was scheduled to start lobbing shells again after giving us just enough time to cross the fields and get started climbing the advancing line of shells, to cover our push forward.

Suddenly the plan went awry. Explosions had already erupted on the slopes we had just climbed.

"Damn," I muttered, breaking my rule of silence, "we've outrun our own artillery."

We had to keep running or be smashed by friendly fire. With desperate energy, I stood, cranked by my arm windmill fashion, silently exclaiming, "Let's get the hell out of here."

My men pulled away and we spread out in a line along the olive trees and the stone pines at the crest of Hill X and moved west to the skirt of Hills Y and Z. Alpha Company was supposed to be on our left flank, Bravo Company on our right. We busted ahead to set up mortars and machine guns to cover their advance.

After I was temporarily satisfied we were safe from our own artillery, we paused again and I counted men. Our machine-gun crews were intact, but our mortar squads were nowhere to be seen. Running back into the murderous shellfire would be suicide. We had to push on without them.

During this respite a handful of men from the third platoon—my old rifle outfit—wandered into our flank. They had somehow gotten separated from the rest of their group. I ordered them to join us, and now we were a group of twenty-six, equivalent to the platoon I would have had if my mortar squads were there. We hiked.

The higher we moved, the less cover the trees provided. Leaves were almost nonexistent, and the light was just right for an attack. It wasn't total darkness, or the committed gray of dawn.

Sunup later showed this as one of the prettiest places in the world, a macabre contrast to the harsh ugliness of men killing other men for control of old castles, hillsides, and shell-shocked olive groves. At this hour, none of this showed. It was a shadowy maze.

My men placed their steps carefully, yet moved quickly over the level ground of the summit. We soon were stopped by yellow plastic lines snaking through the olive groves at about three inches off the ground. Without seeing their faces, I knew their body language. "What is this?" they silently asked.

Problem was, I had never seen this new invention called plastic either. But night patrols taught me to always carry a pair of wire cutters in my pocket to deal with barbed wire. I eased down and pulled them from my pocket. I took a bit off the line and exercised the cutter's jaws until it parted with a soft twang.

I pocketed the pliers, grabbed the plastic line, and scraped one end of the freshly cut yellow worm with my thumbnail. A solid copper core: German communications wire of some sort. We would foul this yellow spiderweb.

At my lead, we moved forward again, weaving in and out of the trees. We stayed close enough to each other, but far enough apart so a single 88mm cannon shell couldn't take out half the platoon. This distance from our fellow soldiers went against every desire. We wanted to be close to someone when we sensed death. The blessing of surviving a couple of battles is that we learned to operate on instinct and reflex while ignoring fear.

The taut yellow lines ran everywhere. I stopped to cut every wire we found. It felt good to inflict any sort of damage on the enemy.

I silently sidestepped away from my men, raised my rifle, and nestled the recoil pad into the natural slot between my arm and my clavicle. Two quick cracks and the helmets dropped like deer. I crept away from them for forty or fifty yards, and then made a half-circle back, trying to give myself shots. Instead I found two dead German machine gunners. We ditched their gun and replaced it with one of ours—one we had fired thousands of times, one we could resupply with ammunition, one we knew how to tear down, unjam, and reassemble even in the eye of a tornado.

A few hundred yards farther two more German helmets caught my eye. My M1 came up automatically. Muzzle flashes recorded two more shots. Another pair of Nazi machine gunners crumpled. Fortunately, the American artillery working the slopes muffled my fire. Not that there was a choice. It was better to risk a few rifle shots than to risk leaving live Germans.

I moved to the left of my remaining men. If I could reach the edge of the ridge, I could both keep a better view of the coming terrain and also keep better track of my troops. Perhaps I could spot our companies and figure out where the lagging mortar squads were.

I worked toward a buckle on the outer rim of the hill. Streaks of daylight started to creep up the horizon to my right, lifting our shield. It also lifted a portion of the German camouflage. I could see what appeared to be flared metal tubes poking from a horizontal hillside slit that was approximately two feet long and six inches wide. Flash suppressors for machine guns, I reasoned.

Reflexively, I melted into a crouch, then a crawl, and onto my belly. I inched toward the slit, propelled by my elbows. Once near enough, I came on my knees, raised my rifle above me, and as I stood up, I put the barrel in the opening and started working the trigger furiously.

The bolt whipsawed, taking cartridge after cartridge from the clip on the top of my gun. The bunker shouted back the muted echoes of each shot. The empty clip kicked off, telling me my last round was gone. I dropped back, tried to blend into the hillside, fingered a fresh clip from my pocket of the canvas bandoliers, and locked it in place. The solid click of a new clip nestling into the gun always gave me pleasure.

I counted off a minute, maybe less, then I moved back into the slit, stuck my rifle back through the opening, and peered inside. One German soldier slumped in a chair. Another was crawling toward a stash of grenades in the corner.

Spinning around the corner of the bunker, I grabbed a grenade from my chest with my left hand. I momentarily let my rifle rest on the ground as I pulled the pin with my right hand, and tossed the grenade through the opening serving as a door. The advantages of being ambidextrous. I could throw a grenade with either hand.

I caught my rifle on the fly, feeling as much as seeing the flash and the muffled thump-thump, tasting the bitter smoke and debris roiling out of the bunker as I ran. Fairly confident the wounded man hadn't survived, I returned almost immediately and ducked into the bunker, rifle at the ready.

The air had barely cleared, but it was enough. A cubbyhole built of rocks, dirt, and logs extended back about six feet. What I had taken for machine-gun flash suppressors were the twin barrels of a periscope-style binocular observation scope. I moved the eyepieces and dared to take the time for a hunter's appreciative glance through the powerful optics. Several American soldiers were clearly visible on the plains below, snuffling around with an artillery round. This observation scope was as lethal as machine guns or mortar rounds.

I glanced around the dugout and spotted two field telephones. Each sprouted a ribbon of the same yellow communications wire I had been cutting. This was a part of the yellow web. My wire cutters rendered both telephones useless.

Tearing loose another grenade, I went back to the observation scope. I balanced the grenade in the cradle where the eyepieces attached to the scope. After a quick, last look toward the dead man stitched into the observation chair with lead, I jerked the pin.

One thousand one . . . one thousand two . . . one thousand three . . . involuntarily trumpeted through my brain. I sprinted for the door, skidded down the face of the gentle slope and through the olive trees. There was no wasting time checking to see if the second grenade did the necessary work. I took it on faith and sound effects.

I reached my men and automatically scanned their surroundings. My eyes and ears searched for whatever hostilities my grenades might elicit. This couldn't go unchallenged all day.

There was no response. Our luck was holding.

I resumed walking through the trees, this time away from the ridge and back toward the castle. In a few hundred yards I had made my next jolt.

No more than fifty feet in front of me a ring of logs and rocks gave away a .50 caliber machine gun, ready to spit. The nest was so well disguised that the only way I could have found it was stumbling upon it.

Oh shit, I thought. *Prepare for heavy fire.*

But the gun was unmanned. Its attendants, two men in Nazi gray uniforms, sat at the back of the nest eating breakfast. I swung my rifle barrel forward and started shooting. The Germans staggered, one at a time and yet together, and pitched into their breakfast. Once convinced they were dead, I went back for one of our machine-gun squads and ordered it to take their place.

I was high on adrenaline. In a few hours, my platoon had stolen nearly three miles behind enemy lines. Three machine-gun nests and an observation post had been eliminated. German communication lines were reduced to a lifeless tangle. We hadn't suffered any casualties.

This might turn out to be easy stuff, I thought, reviewing the aerial photos in my mind. There was a deep draw between us and the castle. It was time to find Captain Runyon and the other platoons.

April 5, 1945, 6:30 a.m.

Three hundred yards across a deep V-shaped ravine, a steep knob rose. It contained the German stronghold: Castle Aghinolfi.

The morning sun gathered force over the Apennines and played on the ancient, crumbling fortress, giving it a mystical white luminescence. Towers staggered along the summit. Time, war, and neglect had eroded the tower-top parapets to the point where the castle looked more like a flat-topped monastery than a onetime medieval home to sword-and-shield-wielding warriors.

The remaining trees on the adjacent slopes had few branches and disfigured tops, casualties of the same artillery shells that had also scoured a jarring white scar in a rock outcropping fifty feet below the castle. All of this sat wrapped in morning quiet, eerie and beautiful—a peacefulness we didn't enjoy long.

It was not even 7:00 a.m. when Runyon and I perched at the edge of the draw to figure out how to traverse its steep slopes, scale the knob, and storm the castle. It was as formidable as its reputation. Brush covered all but the last seventy-five yards of ground between us and the castle. That critical space was rocky barren ground, but it was ringed with the ancient stone walls that had rigidly defended the castle for 1,500 years. A blind nitwit with any functioning rifle could wipe out half of any invading force brazen enough to try to scale the slope and the walls.

But orders were orders. And this was the only route to taking the castle and punching north.

Runyon and I agreed to move our machine guns to the lip of the draw to provide covering fire for the castle assault. We agonized over the absence of our mortar squads, still somewhere behind us. Our lack of mortars added great disadvantages to our daylight assault. The other ramification went unspoken between us. Holding our ground would be difficult in the face of the inevitable German counterattack. We banked on our mortar squads catching up soon. They wouldn't. They had been pinned down by German machine gunners or killed by mines on Hill X—but that realization was hours away.

As we contemplated, a German soldier emerged from the brush about twenty-five yards to our left and slightly below us. This was his backyard; it shouldn't have been anything startling. But it was. In surreal slow motion, the German started to heave one of the trademark Nazi potato-masher grenades. I started to bring my M1 around, instinctively trying to kill him before the grenade was airborne.

Runyon simultaneously yelped and scrambled to his feet, not noticing that my rifle was swinging across his midsection. In his haste to escape, Runyon knocked the barrel wide and nearly knocked the rifle into the ravine. I lunged.

The German soldier's arm reached the end of its windup. He leaned forward and launched the grenade, one foot coming off the ground in the fashion of an Olympic discus thrower. The moment the grenade cleared his fingertips he pivoted and started to run away.

I clawed the air to recover my rifle, not wanting to shoot him in the back, for some reason, but still very much wanting to kill him. The grenade tumbled toward me.

Three things happened—I cannot say in which order, or if they were simultaneous. The grenade landed five feet from me, bounced . . . but did not explode. I squeezed off two shots, slamming the German in the back. And Runyon disappeared.

I was livid. First this damn German, then Runyon goes hysterical, as if he'd seen an enemy soldier with a grenade, and as a result of those hysterics I had to adopt enough cowardice to shoot another soldier in the back. My honor was reparable. A battlefield commander so prone to panic was more unnerving.

Staff sergeant Willie Dickens, looking much more serious and disturbed than his normal, comical self, came running at the commotion.

"I think I nailed him," I told Dickens as I struggled to my feet, too full of adrenaline to fully realize how close I'd come to becoming a corpse. "But there's liable to be a few more where he came from."

"You want a patrol?" Dickens volunteered.

"No. Keep the guys up top," I said. "Pretty soon the Germans are going to figure out we're stirring around here. I want you guys here to cover each other when the shit gets thick. Trade me guns and I'll go see if this Kraut's got any cousins down in the draw."

I tossed my rifle to Dickens and he tossed me his Thompson machine gun.

"Wait," he said as I started off, and tossed me an extra thirty-round clip.

"Thanks—good idea," I said, glad that he was thinking when I was being hasty.

Despite my strong preference for the M1, this submachine gun was perfect for close-quarters fighting, especially when I expected to be outnumbered. I dropped into the ravine and scrambled after the grenade thrower. We needed to know where he came from and how many enemy soldiers might be with him. I found him facedown, and dead, almost at the entrance of a dugout. I stuck the submachine gun into the entrance and let loose with a dozen rounds and darted to the side. Nothing happened. I moved inside. The cavern was empty except for a few hand grenades strewn about the floor.

I stepped into the daylight and crouched next to the dead soldier, and studied the area. The dugout was on a path that continued around the hill. The path led away from the castle, as if going to overlook the coastal plain of the Cinquale Canal. I moved forward, where about a quarter-mile away, the narrow, chalky trail veered toward the face of the ravine—and found a partially concealed Volkswagen door, strangely hanging on the side of the draw. Another dugout, I reasoned.

I heaved on the door, ready to unleash the tommy gun the moment I cracked it open. It did not budge.

Not knowing what exactly I was up against, or when I could resupply, I retraced my steps back to the first dugout, dashed inside, and grabbed two of the German grenades. I returned to the Volkswagen door, nudged one of the grenades under it, pulled the pin, and dropped into cover. The grenade ripped the door off the hillside with the shriek of tormented metal. My gun came up in anticipation. Moments later, a dazed, half-dressed German soldier poked his head out of the entrance. I split his skull with a single burst and charged toward the entrance, pulled the pin from the second grenade, and tossed it in. A roar of dirt and rocks kicked out of the opening as I dove to the side. Without waiting for the entrance to clear completely, I rolled back to my feet. I went back to the doorway and emptied the submachine gun's magazine into the darkness.

Nothing.

Jamming a new magazine on the gun, I stepped over the dead soldier, through the entrance, and moved to one side, out of the light.

Nothing.

No Germans came bursting from whatever catacomb lay at the back of the dugout; none appeared from the outside to investigate. Other than the clack and clatter of rocks settling inside the dugout, all was quiet.

I inched ahead to see the rest of the cool, dark room. Three dead German soldiers had been heaped into opposite corners by the grenade blast. Breakfast was plastered against the walls and spewed all over the soldiers' faces. My second breakfast kill of the day, I noted, forcing myself to think mechanically, not emotionally. This luck wouldn't last. I bolted.

I retraced my path again, moving past the first dugout, and kept going until the trail led me to the top of the draw, almost right where Runyon and I had studied the castle. Had we seen the path, hidden by the thick brush, we might have anticipated company.

As I emerged at the top, rifle fire signaled that the Germans had discovered us. Then came mortar barrages. Then came chaos.

Our forward artillery observer, Second Lieutenant Walker, grabbed the handset from the radioman and barked coordinates. He repeated the instructions over and over. Shaking his head, he pulled the telephone-style handset away from his ear and looked at me.

"Goddamn, they ... goddamn, they don't believe we're here. They don't believe we're this far behind enemy lines. Goddammit!"

Walker looked as if he wanted to break the handset on the nearest rock. We desperately needed artillery fire on the German mortar positions. Our medics couldn't get our wounded because the air was saturated with shrapnel.

A moment of uneasy quiet punctuated the melee. I scanned the edge of the ridge, expecting attacking Germans.

"What's that?" one of my riflemen yelled. "Look at that flock of birds." He pointed to a cloud of black specks flying toward us.

"Cover!" I yelled, and dived for the dirt. Those weren't birds, they were mortar rounds. Explosions rumbled in rapid succession around us. Men screamed. This round of shells carved life out of three of my soldiers and left three others bleeding. I swore at the Germans and swore at the American intelligence officers who doubted our location.

The Germans continued warming up. The castle-side machine guns opened at full throttle. I crawled back toward Walker and grabbed the handset, this time screaming with all possible intensity, "Get me some goddamned artillery up here, *now!*"

Intense haggling followed. Walker took back the handset and shouted the same coordinates. It finally worked. Low-trajectory 90mm antiaircraft shells screeched from the far side of Hill X, skimmed in low over our heads, and smashed into the castle. We ducked with every round. The antiaircraft shells temporarily quieted the German mortars.

In the next moment of calm, my men started going for cover in the trees. Mortar rounds started winging in again; whish, whish, whish, KABOOM; whish, whish, whish, KABOOM. I woke to our folly and started into the trees, shouting and grabbing people. Trees were bursting. Those that weren't a hurricane of giant, jagged slivers toppled over to crush men.

"Move. Move. *Move!*" I yelled. "*Keep moving!*"

Men scattered. I grabbed, snagged, yelled, and prodded, trying to get control of them. In the distance I heard the bark of a German accent.

"*Feuer!*"

Fire! It was the German mortar battery commander giving the order to fire. I pulled at the man nearest to me and shouted, "*Move or die!*"

For the next several rounds we played this game of chicken. When I heard the German command to fire, we jumped and ran to a different place. For a time, it worked. The mortar rounds landed where we'd just left. The Germans stepped up their effort by adding artillery. The howls of shells, mortars, and wounded men intensified. The air was more burned explosives and bitter cordite than oxygen. A foggy kaleidoscope of dust, debris, and blood boiled around us.

Men dropped. A few pitched forward; others went bulleting backward, as if struck by a freight train. When I got to each man, I saw an arm or a leg or half of their face blown off. An hour before, charged with adrenaline, I'd felt born to fight, to do combat. I'd known I was an invincible giant. This slaughter jarred my immortality.

The mortars paused again. I checked for wounded and living. It was gruesome. Walker's radioman was dead, and the shell that killed him had demolished the artillery radio. Walker was at the moment alive and moving, though blood oozed from dozens of gashes.

I pointed to the radio questioningly.

"They promised reinforcements," he told me, of his final conversation with headquarters.

"When?" I asked.

"They said right away."

"Uh-huh," I replied. "Well, we gotta have them today." I yelled for Danny Belk.

"Where the hell's Runyon?" I asked.

Belk shook his head. He had no reason to know the name of a white officer who had only been around a week or two.

"Your captain, company commander," I said.

Belk pointed behind me.

"Over there, in the little stone house, the shed," he said. "He headed there the minute Jerry pitched a masher at you two."

I found Runyon sitting on the dirt floor, knees pulled up to his chest, his arms wrapped around his legs. His face was translucent, the color of bleached parchment.

"Baker," he said, with a note of disgust, "can't you get these men together?"

"I'm doing the best goddamned job I can, Captain," I snapped, boiling that he had the audacity to cower in here and still criticize us in the fray.

"*Feuer!*" echoed in the distance. Seconds later, the whish, whish of mortar rounds returned. I followed Runyon's gaze out the door. Lieutenant Botwinik was crouched behind a stone wall. A mortar cascaded into the top of the wall, right above Botwinik's head. Bricks spewed from a cloud of disintegrating wall.

Runyon gasped. I muttered a kind word for Botwinik's soul. And Botwinik stood up.

He staggered toward the shed. Runyon and I grabbed Botwinik, sat him inside the door, and checked for physical damage. The flash of the explosion had blinded him, and he was a bit dumb from shock.

Runyon cleared his throat. "Are we going to stay here?" he asked.

I couldn't believe the question. We had accomplished something four other assaults hadn't matched, and we were within conquering distance of the castle.

"We're staying," I replied. "We can do this."

Runyon blinked rapidly and looked at me as if I was crazy.

"Look, Baker, I'm going for reinforcements," he said, fighting to make his shaking voice sound flat and controlled.

A captain going for reinforcements? Wasn't this a task for a sergeant and a couple of privates? I kept my thoughts to myself. His face said it all. He hadn't stopped running since that grenade had come flying toward us.

"All right, Captain. We'll be here when you get back," I said, hoping my stare told him what my mouth had not.

Runyon waved his hand in front of Botwinik's face. Botwinik grabbed Runyon's arm and looked at him.

"My eyes are coming back, Captain."

Runyon helped Botwinik to his feet and signaled his personal radioman to take Botwinik's other arm.

"We're going for reinforcements and taking what wounded we can," Runyon announced.

A murmur rose from the remainder of the enlisted men.

"*Motherfucker!*" a disheartened voice called.

"I'll be back," he declared.

I waved for silence.

"Right, Captain," I repeated. "We'll be here when you get back."

I watched as Runyon, Botwinik, and the radioman—the only remaining radioman—trudged off into the late-morning haze. This stirred my outrage. The bastard had simply walked away. Here was a commander whose only thought was for himself, not for his men.

The moment of battle, however, did not allow time for such thoughts. Danny Belk needed me.

"Lieutenant, do you want a perimeter?" he asked.

"Right. Yes. Up here," I said.

We turned and I pointed out what seemed the most protected spot—a depression shielded by a slight rise on the outer edge of the ridge. Belk gave orders. The men gathered rifles and spare ammunition from the mortally wounded and dead. I followed them. When I reached a dead man, I pulled his helmet off, lifted his head with one hand, and gingerly slipped his dog tags off with the other. I tried not to look into the faces, their eyes not quite vacant, still holding a small hint of life. Some faces shouted terror, others shouted pain, but these men had fought to their last pulse anyway.

Gathering the dog tags maybe required fifteen minutes, but took the energy of fifteen hours. Dirty, smudged with the blood of others, but imbued with anger and determination, I rejoined my men, and we built our perimeter using whatever logs and rocks we could scrounge. I sent a man back for our machine gunners and their weapons. They were out of ammunition, so they each drew an M1 pulled from a casualty.

The last spare rifle was barely checked when the Germans renewed our acquaintance with their mortars. And so began the pattern.

Mortar rounds came first, followed by heavy machine-gun crossfire. The German soldiers attacked us from out of nowhere. Dirt, exploding trees, and dust roiled so thickly that the first thing we saw were shapes, not men. We distinguished between friend and foe based upon motion. We lay still. The Germans moved. When we saw movement, we shot, albeit methodically, so as not to waste precious ammunition. The M1 saved our butts.

A third wave of mortars cascaded in. By now, fine dust of exploding everything made a boiling cloud six or seven feet tall. We stayed burrowed in our little depression and strained to see what was next. An uncomfortably long silence.

My soldiers reached into their pockets or a dead man's bandoliers, pulled out an extra clip, and stacked them by their sides. It made for faster reloading. It made their ammunition more accessible to a fellow soldier if they were killed. We gripped our rifles more tightly and scrutinized the smoke.

A flag with a red cross came trotting out of the haze and slowly connected itself to a flag bearer. He was followed by a platoon of Germans, most carrying stretchers. All of the men had red crosses on their helmets.

"We've got to fire ... we've *got* to fire." The panicked whispers ran down our ranks toward me. My men's eyes pleaded. I held my hand up, signaling for calm, and kept my eyes on the advancing stretcher bearers.

"You don't want them shooting your medics," I replied sharply. "We're not going to shoot theirs."

The gray shapes grew closer, a hundred yards, seventy-five yards, seventy, then fifty. The German entourage stopped.

The stretchers dropped to the ground and the blankets were stripped off—revealing machine guns. One stretcher bearer reached for the gun while the second reached for the tripod, and a third man readied an ammunition belt.

"Hit the bastards!" I yelled.

Will Boswell was up on one knee firing well before I finished my sentence. He shot the three men closest to having their machine gun operational. Our other riflemen cut loose with a vengeance. The phony German medics staggered under the impact of our lead. The enemy platoon dissolved. Surviving Germans evaporated, leaving their dead and wounded on the slope below our little hummock.

Again and again, I checked behind us. No messenger darted forward to tell me we had reinforcements. No reinforcing platoon moved through the trees to our position.

The intensity of combat must have dulled my senses. It finally came to me: Our commanders hadn't believed we'd made it three miles behind enemy lines. If artillery support was difficult, reinforcements were impossible. We were holding this ridge for nothing.

I didn't have any fear of dying myself. It seemed, at this point, that the loss of my life would leave no great hole in the world. But I was more afraid for my men and our chances of doing any meaningful damage to the Germans.

My soldiers crouched along the perimeter and stared at me. I can still see their faces—I see them every day, in my mind. Danny Belk was no longer crisp; his creases and cheeks sagged. His normally ebullient face was pancaked with dirt and dried blood. Twigs and bark hung from the netting on his helmet.

The other men radiated hopelessness and exhaustion. Even with our scavenged ammunition we were down to one or two clips each, too little to do anything—attack, stay put, or depart. I reluctantly called for our withdrawal.

My men moved out ahead of me. I lingered for a few moments to catch any Germans who might be waiting for this opportunity to renew their attack. I was not disappointed. Four enemy soldiers immediately appeared at the edge of the draw. I shot one in the chest, and the other three disappeared. They didn't come back.

Mortars started again as we hit the olive groves running. Another one of my men went down. I jerked the dog tags from his neck.

We pushed on. Sniper rounds pinged around our heads. One caught my last living medic.

"Keep moving!" I shouted.

Thomas went crazy. He rolled behind a tree, brought his BAR around, and started shooting in the direction of the sniper. A German rifle clattered downslope toward us. Thomas had killed him in the time it took me to free my medic's dog tags.

I kept my men hustling back to Hill X. Until we heard the machine-gun fire. Unbelievable as it seemed, we had missed a pair of machine-gun nests on the trek up. Now they spewed five hundred rounds a minute, making sure no one moved up or down the hill. For the moment, fortunately, they were focused toward Hill X and not in our direction. Still, we couldn't get around them.

Without deliberation, Thomas shouldered his BAR as lightly as I would have lifted a balsa-wood replica and set it chattering. I hit the ground cradling my M1 in my elbows. I started wiggling like a snake toward the backside of the machine-gun nest. Thomas's bullets barely whistled over my head, and I began wondering about the possibilities of him accidentally running round my rump. The crowning end to a disastrous day.

I made it to the waist-high hole of the nest, likely the access port for the gunners. I ripped a grenade from my jacket, yanked the pin, and lobbed the grenade inside without ever rising off the ground. Then I sucked the

M1 to my chest and rolled away from the machine-gun nest. A geyser of dirt split through the timbers and branches on top of the bunker. A dull *unnhh* followed—perhaps the last reaction of a surprised soldier.

Thomas moved to where he could cover my journey to the other machine-gun nest. I kept up my crawl, came in close, and repeated the grenade toss. It was all reflex. Serious contemplation would have been paralyzing. When the *whump* sounded at the end of the second nest, I lay for a few seconds to catch my breath. A very few.

I stayed at the rear of our column to continue the watch for a German attack. When we reached the last tip of Hill X, I heard the *whump* of two more grenades. I ran to catch my men and found another German surprise we had missed: a tank dug into the hillside, to the point where only the turret poked out, like a huge mosquito stinger. Before I reached it, my men had pulled open the hatch and popped grenades inside. We kept running.

From the tank, we plunged straight down the face of Hill X instead of dealing with the switchbacks of the path. Brush crackled under our charge for hundreds of yards, until we emerged amid our own chaos. Highway One was dizzy with tanks, jeeps, and wounded men hobbling around with the help of others.

"You men who are hurt, go find an aid station," I ordered the moment we reached the road. "The rest of you, hit the command post and report in."

I turned, lowered myself to the side of the road, hung my head between my knees, and heaved my guts out.

APRIL 5, 1945, LATE AFTERNOON, NEAR HILL X
Oblivious to the world around me, I shuddered and heaved, shuddered and heaved. Seeing the men you live with, eat with, and fight beside blown to pieces, hour after hour, seizes your soul and finds the place where anguish lives, no matter how artfully you hide it. Here, I was no match for my emotions. It was unnerving, after so many months of combat, to be so affected, to lose control. Violent death wasn't new to me. Something about this day was beyond overwhelming.

Too preoccupied to notice my misery, the men and machines of war moved along the highway, beside me. I wasn't the first soldier to lose it after a battle, so I hardly was a spectacle. I was grateful for this anonymity.

I was too exhausted to get up after my stomach settled. I sat in the boiling sun, even though the smell between my boots was vile. Once I thought to finally check my watch again, the first time since Runyon and I had sat on the edge of the ravine, I discovered it was well past 5:00 p.m. I regained my feet and started for the command post to report my return.

A sergeant, just transferred to the company, saluted me and reached for the telephone to report my presence. He hung up and turned to me with bad news.

"Sir, Colonel Murphy at Battalion wants to see you right away. Jeep and driver?"

I nodded, gathered my rifle, and asked for a drink of water to rinse the taste of bile from my tongue. The sergeant gave me a canteen cup and I tossed it down. It didn't relieve the bad taste, but cut a little of the dust in my throat.

Lieutenant Colonel Murphy had been in charge of the First Battalion for six months, and I'd had only three or four conversations with him. I didn't give much thought to his wanting to see me. I just rode along, thankful to be sitting down, wishing the din of the day's shelling would leave my ears.

We pulled up to Murphy's headquarters within minutes. Inside, Murphy's aide pointed upstairs.

"Go to the first door, straight across from the top step, knock, and announce yourself," he instructed. "The colonel is expecting you."

Fatigue tore at my legs as I climbed the steps. I made it to the top slowly, crossed the hallway, and rapped on the massive door.

"Lieutenant Baker?" the voice inside shouted.

"Aye, sir," I said.

"Let yourself in."

Murphy was covered in soapsuds and parked in a tin washtub in the center of the room. I brought myself to attention with a weary salute.

"Sit down, Bake; forget the formalities," Murphy said. He was the only white officer who had the warmth to use my nickname. And it was a credit to Murphy that he'd bothered to learn it.

"Hear you had a pretty rough day up there," Murphy said. He pointed in the general direction of Castle Aghinolfi with the soap clenched in his hand. "Runyon was here," he added.

This was a kindness—to forewarn me that my company commander had already delivered an assessment. What Murphy didn't share was more significant: Runyon had told him not to worry about the men left behind, that we were wasted. I didn't learn this until the war was over. Another reason why there hadn't been reinforcements.

I nodded. "Rough. Yes, sir. But we did it. We got within a few hundred yards of the castle. With more men we'd have taken it."

"Tell me about it," Murphy said.

I recounted the basics, including all the information, but choosing not to explain my feelings toward Runyon, the lack of reinforcements, or our trouble getting artillery support.

Murphy scrubbed, soaked, listened, and said little. "How many came back with you?" he asked.

"Six besides myself, sir. Lost my last medic to a sniper as we pulled back."

Murphy grunted sympathetically. "Tough. Damn tough."

He asked a dozen more questions: How many enemy mortar batteries did I estimate? Were the Germans firing 88mm cannons at us, or something bigger? How many enemy soldiers did I think held the castle? He covered every significant strategic angle.

"Okay, Bake. Appreciate you coming over," Murphy finally said. "You've got to be dammed tired. Better go back to your company and see if you can get a little rest."

I pulled myself up and walked to the door.

"Bake?"

"Sir?"

"Damn fine work today with those machine-gun nests and the bunkers," Murphy said. "And snagging those telephone wires was smart soldiering. Tell your boys I appreciate it."

"Yes, sir. Thank you."

He waved good-bye with his bar of soap.

I slipped my hand in the pocket of my Eisenhower jacket as I descended the stairs. My hand encountered the rounded metal corners of dog tags. Damn. Another chore. I wanted to get rid of the dead men's tags before I tried to sleep. I asked the driver to take me to Regimental Headquarters.

I fingered the dog tags as we drove to a three-story villa. The villa was perfect for regimental commanders because it had both the comfort the commanders believed they should be afforded and because it was connected to an underground tunnel they could use during shellings.

The dog tags felt oddly warm, as if they breathed the life their owners had lost. I started to pull the handful of metal out with the purpose of inspecting the lettering in the fading twilight, to memorize each name, to remember who among the members of the new recruits and members of my old rifle platoon had died, and to make peace with those nineteen faces.

My arm refused to move, my hand similarly paralyzed in a half grip around the pile of metal in my pocket. In my mind I heard a sniper's rifle crack, and my medic pitched forward. A succession of mortar rounds exploded, and the chest of one of my riflemen, who hadn't heard the scream to move, was too stunned by earlier poundings to react, erupted in a pinkish fog. Everything I saw, everything I heard in battle, rang in my mind.

On January 13, 1997, fifty-two years after Baker's World War II military service, President Bill Clinton presented him with the Medal of Honor.

FROM THE CITATION

For extraordinary heroism in action on 5 and 6 April 1945, near Viareggio, Italy. Then Second Lieutenant Baker demonstrated outstanding courage and leadership in destroying enemy installations, personnel, and equipment during his company's attack against a strongly entrenched enemy in mountainous terrain. When his company was stopped by the concentration of fire from several machine-gun emplacements, he crawled to one position and destroyed it, killing three Germans. Continuing forward, he attacked an enemy observation post and killed two occupants. With the aid of one of his men, Lieutenant Baker attacked two more machine-gun nests, killing or wounding the four enemy soldiers occupying these positions. He then covered the evacuation of the wounded personnel of his company by occupying an exposed position and drawing the enemy's fire. On the following night Lieutenant Baker voluntarily led a battalion advance through enemy minefields and heavy fire toward the division objective. Second Lieutenant Baker's fighting spirit and daring leadership were an inspiration to his men and exemplify the highest traditions of the Armed Forces.

CHAPTER SEVEN

Taking Suribachi: Marines on Iwo Jima

Colonel Joseph H. Alexander

EDITOR'S NOTE: TWENTY-SEVEN MEN RECEIVED THE CONGRESSIONAL Medal of Honor for conspicuous gallantry during the battle of Iwo Jima: twenty-two marines, four navy corpsmen, and one navy landing craft commander. Half were posthumous. The awards for Iwo Jima represented more than one-fourth of the eighty Medals of Honor presented to US Marines during World War II.

D-DAY

Weather conditions around Iwo Jima on D-day morning, February 19, 1945, were almost ideal. At 0645 Admiral Turner signaled: "Land the landing force!"

Shore bombardment ships did not hesitate to engage the enemy island at near-point-blank range. Battleships and cruisers steamed as close as two thousand yards to level their guns against island targets. Many of the "Old Battleships" had performed this dangerous mission in all theaters of the war. Marines came to recognize and appreciate their contributions. It seemed fitting that the old *Nevada*, raised from the muck and ruin of Pearl Harbor, should lead the bombardment force close ashore. Marines also admired the battleship *Arkansas*, built in 1912, and recently returned from the Atlantic where she had battered German positions at Pointe du Hoc at Normandy during the epic Allied landing on June 6, 1944.

Lieutenant colonels Donald M. Weller and William W. "Bucky" Buchanan, both artillery officers, had devised a modified form of the "rolling barrage" for use by the bombarding gunships against beachfront targets just before H-hour. This concentration of naval gunfire would advance progressively as the troops landed, always remaining four hundred yards to their front. Air spotters would help regulate the pace. Such an innovation appealed to the three division commanders, each having served in France during World War I. In those days, a good rolling barrage was often the only way to break a stalemate.

The shelling was terrific. Admiral Hill would later boast that "there were no proper targets for shore bombardment remaining on Dog-Day morning." This proved to be an overstatement, yet no one could deny the unprecedented intensity of firepower Hill delivered against the areas surrounding the landing beaches. As General Kuribayashi would ruefully admit in an assessment report to Imperial General Headquarters, "we need to reconsider the power of bombardment from ships; the violence of the enemy's bombardments is far beyond description."

The amphibious task force appeared from over the horizon, the rails of the troopships crowded with combat-equipped marines watching the spectacular fireworks. The Guadalcanal veterans among them realized a grim satisfaction watching American battleships leisurely pounding the island from just offshore. The war had come full cycle from the dark days of October 1942 when the 1st Marine Division and the Cactus Air Force endured similar shelling from Japanese battleships.

The marines and sailors were anxious to get their first glimpse of the objective. Correspondent John P. Marquand, the Pulitzer Prize–winning writer, recorded his own first impressions of Iwo: "Its silhouette was like a sea monster, with the little dead volcano for the head, and the beach area for the neck, and all the rest of it, with its scrubby brown cliffs for the body." Lieutenant David N. Susskind, USNR, wrote down his initial thoughts from the bridge of the troopship *Mellette*: "Iwo Jima was a rude, ugly sight.... Only a geologist could look at it and not be repelled." As described in a subsequent letter home by US Navy lieutenant Michael F. Keleher, a surgeon in the 25th Marines:

The naval bombardment had already begun, and I could see the orange-yellow flashes as the battleships, cruisers, and destroyers blasted away at the island broadside. Yes, there was Iwo—surprisingly close, just like the pictures and models we had been studying for six weeks. The volcano was to our left, then the long, flat black beaches where we were going to land, and the rough rocky plateau to our right.

The commanders of the 4th and 5th Marine Divisions, Major Generals Clifton B. Cates and Keller E. Rockey, respectively, studied the island through binoculars from their respective ships. Each division would land two reinforced regiments abreast. From left to right, the beaches were designated Green, Red, Yellow, and Blue. The 5th Division would land the 28th Marines on the left flank, over Green Beach, the 27th Marines over Red. The 4th Division would land the 23rd Marines over Yellow Beach and the 25th Marines over Blue Beach on the right flank. General Schmidt reviewed the latest intelligence reports with growing uneasiness and requested a reassignment of reserve forces with General Smith. The 3rd Marine Division's 21st Marines would replace the 26th Marines as corps reserve, thus releasing the latter regiment to the 5th Division. Schmidt's landing plan envisioned the 28th Marines cutting the island in half, then returning to capture Suribachi, while the 25th Marines would scale the Rock Quarry and then serve as the hinge for the entire corps to swing around to the north. The 23rd Marines and 27th Marines would capture the first airfield and pivot north within their assigned zones.

General Cates was already concerned about the right flank. Blue Beach Two lay directly under the observation and fire of suspected Japanese positions in the Rock Quarry, whose steep cliffs overshadowed the right flank like Suribachi dominated the left. The 4th Marine Division figured that the 25th Marines would have the hardest objective to take on D-day. Said Cates, "If I knew the name of the man on the extreme right of the right-hand squad, I'd recommend him for a medal before we go in."

The choreography of the landing continued to develop. Iwo Jima would represent the pinnacle of forcible amphibious assault against a heavily fortified shore, a complex art mastered painstakingly by the Fifth Fleet over many campaigns. Seventh Air Force Martin B-24 Liberator bombers flew in from the Marianas to strike the smoking island. Rocket ships moved in to saturate nearshore targets. Then it was time for the fighter and attack squadrons from Mitscher's Task Force 58 to contribute. The navy pilots showed their skills at bombing and strafing, but the troops naturally cheered the most at the appearance of F4U Corsairs flown by Marine Fighter Squadrons 124 and 213, led by Lt. Col. William A. Millington from the fleet carrier *Essex*. Col. Vernon E. Megee, in his shipboard capacity as air officer for General Smith's Expeditionary Troops staff, had urged Millington to put on a special show for the troops in the assault waves. "Drag your bellies on the beach," he told Millington. The marine fighters made an impressive approach parallel to the island, then virtually did Megee's bidding, streaking low over the beaches, strafing furiously. The geography of the Pacific War since Bougainville had kept many of the ground marines separated from their own air support, which had been operating in areas other than where they had been fighting, most notably the Central Pacific. "It was the first time a lot of them had ever seen a marine fighter plane," said Megee. The troops were not disappointed.

The planes had barely disappeared when naval gunfire resumed, carpeting the beach areas with a building crescendo of high-explosive shells. The ship-to-shore movement was well under way, an easy thirty-minute run for the tracked landing vehicles (LVTs). This time there were enough LVTs to do the job: 68 LVT(A)4 armored amtracs mounting snub-nosed 75mm cannon leading the way, followed by 380 troop-laden LVT 4s and LVT 2s.

The waves crossed the line of departure on time and chugged confidently toward the smoking beaches, all the while under the climactic bombardment from the ships. Here there was no coral reef, no killer neap tides to be concerned with. The navy and marine frogmen had reported the approaches free of mines or tetrahedrons. There was no premature cessation of fire. The "rolling barrage" plan took effect. Hardly a vehicle was lost to the desultory enemy fire.

The massive assault waves hit the beach within two minutes of H-hour. A Japanese observer watching the drama unfold from a cave on the slopes of Suribachi reported, "At nine o'clock in the morning several hundred landing craft with amphibious tanks in the lead rushed ashore like an enormous tidal wave." Lt. Col. Robert H. Williams, executive officer of the 28th Marines, recalled that "the landing was a magnificent sight to see—two divisions landing abreast; you could see the whole show from the deck of a ship." Up to this point, so far, so good.

The first obstacle came not from the Japanese but from the beach and the parallel terraces. Iwo Jima was an emerging volcano; its steep beaches dropped off sharply, producing a narrow but violent surf zone. The soft black sand immobilized all wheeled vehicles and caused some of the tracked amphibians to belly down. The boat waves that closely followed the LVTs had more trouble. Ramps would drop, a truck or jeep would attempt to drive out, only to get stuck. In short order a succession of plunging waves hit the stalled craft before they could completely unload, filling their sterns with water and sand, broaching them broadside. The beach quickly resembled a salvage yard.

The infantry, heavily laden, found its own "foot-mobility" severely restricted. In the words of Corp. Edward Hartman, a rifleman with the 4th Marine Division: "The sand was so soft it was like trying to run in loose coffee grounds." From the 28th Marines came this early, laconic report: "Resistance moderate, terrain awful."

The rolling barrage and carefully executed landing produced the desired effect, suppressing direct enemy fire, providing enough shock and distraction to enable the first assault waves to clear the beach and begin advancing inward. Within minutes six thousand Marines were ashore. Many became thwarted by increasing fire over the terraces or down from the highlands, but hundreds leapt forward to maintain assault momentum. The 28th Marines on the left flank had rehearsed on similar volcanic terrain on the island of Hawaii. Now, despite increasing casualties among their company commanders and the usual disorganization of landing, elements of the regiment used their initiative to strike across the narrow neck of the peninsula. The going became progressively costly as more and more Japanese strongpoints along the base of Suribachi seemed to spring to life. Within ninety minutes of the landing, however, elements of the 1st Battalion, 28th Marines, had reached the western shore, seven hundred yards across from Green Beach. Iwo Jima had been severed—"like cutting off a snake's head," in the words of one marine. It would represent the deepest penetration of what was becoming a very long and costly day.

The other three regiments experienced difficulty leaving the black sand terraces and wheeling across toward the first airfield. The terrain was an open bowl, a shooting gallery in full view from Suribachi on the left and the rising tableland to the right. Any thoughts of a "cakewalk" quickly vanished as well-directed machine-gun fire whistled across the open ground and mortar rounds began dropping along the terraces. Despite these difficulties, the 27th Marines made good initial gains, reaching the southern and western edges of the first airfield before noon.

The 23rd Marines landed over Yellow Beach and sustained the brunt of the first round of Japanese combined arms fire. These troops crossed the second terrace only to be confronted by two huge concrete pillboxes, still lethal despite all the pounding. Overcoming these positions proved costly in casualties and time. More fortified positions appeared in the broken ground beyond. Col. Walter W. Wensinger's call for tank support could not be immediately honored because of congestion problems on the beach. The regiment clawed its way several hundred yards toward the eastern edge of the airstrip.

No assault units found it easy going to move inland, but the 25th Marines almost immediately ran into a buzz saw trying to move across Blue Beach. General Cates had been right in his appraisal. "That right flank was a bitch if there ever was one," he would later say. Lt. Col. Hollis W. Mustain's 1st Battalion, 25th Marines, managed to scratch forward three hundred yards under heavy fire in the first half-hour, but Lieutenant Colonel Chambers's 3rd Battalion, 25th Marines, took the heaviest beating of the day on the extreme right, trying to scale the cliffs leading to the Rock Quarry. Chambers landed fifteen minutes after H-hour. "Crossing that second terrace," he recalled, "the fire from automatic weapons was coming from all over. You could've held up a cigarette and lit it on the stuff going by. I knew immediately we were in for one hell of a time."

This was simply the beginning. While the assault forces tried to overcome the infantry weapons of the local defenders, they were naturally blind to an almost imperceptible stirring taking place among the rocks and crevices of the interior highlands. With grim anticipation, General

Kuribayashi's gunners began unmasking the big guns—the heavy artillery, giant mortars, rockets, and antitank weapons held under tightest discipline for this precise moment. Kuribayashi had patiently waited until the beaches were clogged with troops and material. Gun crews knew the range and deflection to each landing beach by heart; all weapons had been preregistered on these targets long ago. At Kuribayashi's signal, these hundreds of weapons began to open fire. It was shortly after 10:00 a.m.

The ensuing bombardment was as deadly and terrifying as any the marines had ever experienced. There was hardly any cover. Japanese artillery and mortar rounds blanketed every corner of the 3,000-yard-wide beach. Large-caliber coast defense guns and dual-purpose antiaircraft guns firing horizontally added a deadly scissors of direct fire from the high ground on both flanks. Marines stumbling over the terraces to escape the rain of projectiles encountered the same disciplined machine-gun fire and minefields which had slowed the initial advance. Casualties mounted appallingly.

Two marine combat veterans observing this expressed a grudging admiration for the Japanese gunners. "It was one of the worst blood-lettings of the war," said Major Karch of the 14th Marines. "They rolled those artillery barrages up and down the beach—I just didn't see how anybody could live through such heavy fire barrages." Said Lt. Col. Joseph L. Stewart, "The Japanese were superb artillerymen.... Somebody was getting hit every time they fired." At sea, Lieutenant Colonel Weller tried desperately to deliver naval gunfire against the Japanese gun positions shooting down at 3rd Battalion, 25th Marines, from the Rock Quarry. It would take longer to coordinate this fire: The first Japanese barrages had wiped out the 3rd Battalion, 25th Marines' entire shore fire control party.

As the Japanese firing reached a general crescendo, the four assault regiments issued dire reports to the flagship. Within a ten-minute period, these messages crackled over the command net:

1036: (From 25th Marines) "Catching all hell from the quarry. Heavy mortar and machine-gun fire!"
1039: (From 23d Marines) "Taking heavy casualties and can't move for the moment. Mortars killing us."

1042: (From 27th Marines) "All units pinned down by artillery and mortars. Casualties heavy. Need tank support fast to move anywhere."
1046: (From 28th Marines) "Taking heavy fire and forward movement stopped. Machine-gun and artillery fire heaviest ever seen."

The landing force suffered and bled but did not panic. The profusion of combat veterans throughout the rank and file of each regiment helped the rookies focus on the objective. Communications remained effective. Keen-eyed aerial observers spotted some of the now-exposed gun positions and directed naval gunfire effectively. Carrier planes screeched in low to drop napalm canisters. The heavy Japanese fire would continue to take an awful toll throughout the first day and night, but it would never again be so murderous as that first unholy hour.

Marine Sherman tanks played hell getting into action on D-day. Later in the battle these combat vehicles would be the most valuable weapons on the battlefield for the marines; this day was a nightmare. The assault divisions embarked many of their tanks on board medium landing ships (LSMs), sturdy little craft that could deliver five Shermans at a time. But it was tough disembarking them on Iwo's steep beaches. The stern anchors could not hold in the loose sand; bow cables run forward to "deadmen" LVTs parted under the strain. On one occasion the lead tank stalled at the top of the ramp, blocking the other vehicles and leaving the LSM at the mercy of the rising surf. Other tanks bogged down or threw tracks in the loose sand. Many of those that made it over the terraces were destroyed by huge horned mines or disabled by deadly accurate 47mm antitank fire from Suribachi. Other tankers kept coming. Their relative mobility, armored protection, and 75mm gunfire were most welcome to the infantry scattered among Iwo's lunar-looking, shell-pocked landscape.

Both division commanders committed their reserves early. General Rockey called in the 26th Marines shortly after noon. General Cates ordered two battalions of the 24th Marines to land at 14:00; the 3rd Battalion, 24th Marines, followed several hours later. Many of the reserve battalions suffered heavier casualties crossing the beach than the assault units, a result of Kuribayashi's punishing bombardment from all points on the island.

Mindful of the likely Japanese counterattack in the night to come—and despite the fire and confusion along the beaches—both divisions also ordered their artillery regiments ashore. This process, frustrating and costly, took much of the afternoon. The wind and surf began to pick up as the day wore on, causing more than one low-riding DUKW to swamp with its precious 105mm howitzer cargo. Getting the guns ashore was one thing; getting them up off the sand was quite another. The 75mm pack howitzers fared better than the heavier 105s. Enough marines could readily hustle them up over the terraces, albeit at great risk. The 105s seemed to have a mind of their own in the black sand. The effort to get each single weapon off the beach was a saga in its own right.

Somehow, despite the fire and unforgiving terrain, both Col. Louis G. DeHaven, commanding the 14th Marines, and Col. James D. Waller, commanding the 13th Marines, managed to get batteries in place, registered, and rendering close fire support well before dark, a singular accomplishment.

Japanese fire and the plunging surf continued to make a shambles out of the beachhead. Late in the afternoon, Lt. Michael F. Keleher, USNR, the battalion surgeon, was ordered ashore to take over the 3rd Battalion, 25th Marines, aid station from its gravely wounded surgeon. Keleher, a veteran of three previous assault landings, was appalled by the carnage on Blue Beach as he approached: "Such a sight on that beach! Wrecked boats, bogged-down jeeps, tractors and tanks; burning vehicles; casualties scattered all over."

On the left center of the action, leading his machine-gun platoon in the 1st Battalion, 27th Marines' attack against the southern portion of the airfield, the legendary "Manila John" Basilone fell mortally wounded by a Japanese mortar shell, a loss keenly felt by all marines on the island. Farther east, Lt. Col. Robert Galer, the other Guadalcanal Medal of Honor marine (and one of the Pacific War's earliest fighter aces), survived the afternoon's fusillade along the beaches and began reassembling his scattered radar unit in a deep shell hole near the base of Suribachi.

Late in the afternoon, Lt. Col. Donn J. Robertson led his 3rd Battalion, 27th Marines, ashore over Blue Beach, disturbed at the intensity of fire still being directed on the reserve forces this late on D-day. "They were really ready for us," he recalled. He watched with pride and won-derment as his marines landed under fire, took casualties, and stumbled forward to clear the beach. "What impels a young guy landing on a beach in the face of fire?" he asked himself. Then it was Robertson's turn. His boat hit the beach too hard; the ramp wouldn't drop. Robertson and his command group had to roll over the gunwales into the churning surf and crawl ashore, an inauspicious start.

The bitter battle to capture the Rock Quarry cliffs on the right flank raged all day. The beachhead remained completely vulnerable to enemy direct-fire weapons from these heights; the marines had to storm them before many more troops or supplies could be landed. In the end, it was the strength of character of Capt. James Headley and Lt. Col. "Jumping Joe" Chambers who led the survivors of the 3rd Battalion, 25th Marines, onto the top of the cliffs. The battalion paid an exorbitant price for this achievement, losing twenty-two officers and five hundred troops by nightfall.

The two assistant division commanders, brigadier generals Franklin A. Hart and Leo D. Hermle, of the 4th and 5th Marine Divisions, respec-tively, spent much of D-day on board the control vessels, marking both ends of the Line of Departure, four thousand yards offshore. This reflected yet another lesson in amphibious techniques learned from Tarawa: Hav-ing senior officers that close to the ship-to-shore movement provided landing force decision-making from the most forward vantage point.

By dusk Gen. Leo D. Hermle opted to come ashore. At Tarawa he had spent the night of D-day essentially out of contact at the fire-swept pier-head. This time he intended to be on the ground. Hermle had the larger operational picture in mind, knowing the corps commander's desire to force the reserves and artillery units onshore despite the carnage in order to build credible combat power. Hermle knew that whatever the night might bring, the Americans now had more troops on the island than Kuribayashi could ever muster. His presence helped his division to forget about the day's disasters and focus on preparations for the expected counterattacks.

Japanese artillery and mortar fire continued to rake the beachhead. The enormous spigot mortar shells (called "flying ashcans" by the troops) and rocket-boosted aerial bombs were particularly scary—loud, whis-tling projectiles, tumbling end over end. Many sailed completely over the island; those that hit along the beaches or the south runways invariably caused dozens of casualties with each impact. Few marines could dig a proper foxhole in the granular sand ("like trying to dig a hole in a barrel of wheat"). Among urgent calls to the control ship for plasma, stretchers, and mortar shells came repeated cries for sandbags.

Veteran marine combat correspondent Lt. Cyril P. Zurlinden, soon to become a casualty himself, described that first night ashore:

> *At Tarawa, Saipan, and Tinian, I saw Marines killed and wounded in a shocking manner, but I saw nothing like the ghastliness that hung over the Iwo beachhead. Nothing any of us had ever known could compare with the utter anguish, frustration, and constant inner battle to maintain some semblance of sanity.*

Personnel accounting was a nightmare under those conditions, but the assault divisions eventually reported the combined loss of 2,420 men to General Schmidt (501 killed, 1,755 wounded, 47 dead of wounds, 18 missing, and 99, combat fatigue). These were sobering statistics, but Schmidt now had 30,000 marines ashore. The casualty rate of 8 percent left the landing force in relatively better condition than at the first days at Tarawa or Saipan. The miracle was that the casualties had not been twice as high. General Kuribayashi had possibly waited a little too long to open up with his big guns.

The first night on Iwo was ghostly. Sulfuric mists spiraled out of the earth. The marines, used to the tropics, shivered in the cold, waiting for Kuribayashi's warriors to come screaming down from the hills. They would learn that this Japanese commander was different. There would be no wasteful, vainglorious *banzai* attacks, this night or any other. Instead, small teams of infiltrators, which Kuribayashi termed "Prowling Wolves," probed the lines, gathering intelligence. A barge full of Japanese special landing forces tried a small counter landing on the western beaches and died to the man under the alert guns of the 28th Marines and its support-ing LVT crews.

Otherwise, the night was one of continuing waves of indirect fire from the highlands. One high velocity round landed directly in the hole occupied by the 1st Battalion, 23rd Marines' commander, Lt. Col. Ralph Haas, killing him instantly. The marines took casualties throughout the night. But with the first streaks of dawn, the veteran landing force stirred. Five infantry regiments looked north; a sixth turned to the business at hand in the south: Mount Suribachi.

SURIBACHI

The Japanese called the dormant volcano Suribachi-yama; the marines dubbed it "Hotrocks." From the start the marines knew their drive north would never succeed without first seizing that hulking rock dominating the southern plain. "Suribachi seemed to take on a life of its own, to be watching these men, looming over them," recalled one observer, adding, "the mountain represented to these Marines a thing more evil than the Japanese."

Col. Kanehiko Atsuchi commanded the two thousand soldiers and sailors of the Suribachi garrison. The Japanese had honeycombed the mountain with gun positions, machine-gun nests, observation sites, and tunnels, but Atsuchi had lost many of his large-caliber guns in the direct naval bombardment of the preceding three days. General Kuribayashi considered Atsuchi's command to be semiautonomous, realizing the invaders would soon cut communications across the island's narrow southern tip. Kuribayashi nevertheless hoped Suribachi could hold out for ten days, maybe two weeks.

Some of Suribachi's stoutest defenses existed down low, around the rubble-strewn base. Here nearly seventy camouflaged concrete block-houses protected the approaches to the mountain; another fifty bulged from the slopes within the first hundred feet of elevation. Then came the caves, the first of hundreds the marines would face on Iwo Jima.

The 28th Marines had suffered nearly four hundred casualties in cutting across the neck of the island on D-day. On D+1, in a cold rain, they prepared to assault the mountain. Lt. Col. Chandler Johnson, commanding the 2nd Battalion, 28th Marines, set the tone for the morning as he deployed his tired troops forward: "It's going to be a hell of a day in a hell of a place to fight the damned war!" Some of the 105mm batteries of the 13th Marines opened up in support, firing directly overhead. Gun crews fired from positions hastily dug in the black sand directly next to the 28th Marines command post. Regimental executive officer Lt. Col. Robert H. Williams watched the cannoneers fire at Suribachi "eight hundred yards away over open sights."

As the marines would learn during their drive north, even 105mm howitzers would hardly shiver the concrete pillboxes of the enemy. As the prep fire lifted, the infantry leapt forward, only to run immediately into very heavy machine-gun and mortar fire. Col. Harry B. "Harry the Horse" Liversedge bellowed for his tanks. But the 5th Tank Battalion was already having a frustrating morning. The tankers sought a defilade spot in which to rearm and refuel for the day's assault. Such a location did not exist on Iwo Jima those first days. Every time the tanks congregated to service their vehicles they were hit hard by Japanese mortar and artillery fire from virtually the entire island. Getting sufficient vehicles serviced to join the assault took most of the morning. Hereafter the tankers would maintain and reequip their vehicles at night.

This day's slow start led to more setbacks for the tankers; Japanese antitank gunners hiding in the jumbled boulders knocked out the first approaching Shermans. Assault momentum slowed further. The 28th Marines overran forty strongpoints and gained roughly two hundred yards all day. They lost a marine for every yard gained. The tankers unknowingly redeemed themselves when one of their final 75mm rounds caught Colonel Atsuchi as he peered out of a cave entrance, killing him instantly.

Elsewhere, the morning light on D+1 revealed the discouraging sights of the chaos created along the beaches by the combination of Iwo Jima's wicked surf and Kuribayashi's unrelenting barrages. In the words of one dismayed observer:

> *The wreckage was indescribable. For two miles the debris was so thick that there were only a few places where landing craft could still get in. The wrecked hulls of scores of landing boats testified to one price we had to pay to put our troops ashore. Tanks and half-tracks lay crippled where they had bogged down in the coarse sand. Amphibian tractors,*

victims of mines and well-aimed shells, lay flopped on their backs.
Cranes, brought ashore to unload cargo, tilted at insane angles, and
bulldozers were smashed in their own roadways.

Bad weather set in, further compounding the problems of general unloading. Strong winds whipped sea swells into a nasty chop; the surf turned uglier. These were the conditions faced by Lt. Col. Carl A. Youngdale in trying to land the 105mm-howitzer batteries of his 4th Battalion, 14th Marines. All twelve of these guns were preloaded in DUKWs, one to a vehicle. Added to the amphibious trucks' problems of marginal seaworthiness with that payload was contaminated fuel. As Youngdale watched in horror, eight DUKWs suffered engine failures, swamped, and sank, with great loss of life. Two more DUKWs broached in the surf zone, spilling their invaluable guns into deep water. At length Youngdale managed to get his remaining two guns ashore and into firing position.

General Schmidt also committed one battery of 155mm howitzers of the corps artillery to the narrow beachhead on D+1. Somehow these weapons managed to reach the beach intact, but it then took hours to get tractors to drag the heavy guns up over the terraces. These, too, commenced firing before dark, their deep bark a welcome sound to the infantry.

Concern with the heavy casualties in the first twenty-four hours led Schmidt to commit the 21st Marines from corps reserve. The seas proved to be too rough. The troops had harrowing experiences trying to debark down cargo nets into the small boats bobbing violently alongside the transports; several fell into the water. The boating process took hours. Once afloat, the troops circled endlessly in their small Higgins boats, waiting for the call to land. Wiser heads prevailed. After six hours of awful seasickness, the 21st Marines returned to its ships for the night.

Even the larger landing craft, the LCTs and LSMs, had great difficulty beaching. Sea anchors needed to maintain the craft perpendicular to the breakers rarely held fast in the steep, soft bottom. "Dropping those stern anchors was like dropping a spoon in a bowl of mush," said Admiral Hill.

Hill contributed significantly to the development of amphibious expertise in the Pacific War. For Iwo Jima, he and his staff developed armored bulldozers to land in the assault waves. They also experimented with hinged Marston matting, used for expeditionary airfields, as a temporary roadway to get wheeled vehicles over soft sand. On the beach at Iwo, the bulldozers proved to be worth their weight in gold. The Marston matting was only partially successful—LVTs kept chewing it up in passage—but all hands could see its potential.

Admiral Hill also worked with the Naval Construction Battalion (NCB) personnel—Seabees, as they were called—in an attempt to bring supply-laden causeways and pontoon barges ashore. Again the surf prevailed, broaching the craft, spilling the cargo. In desperation, Hill's beach masters turned to round-the-clock use of DUKWs and LVTs to keep combat cargo flowing. Once the DUKWs got free of the crippling load of 105mm howitzers, they did fine. LVTs were probably better, because they could cross the soft beach without assistance and conduct resupply or medevac missions directly along the front lines. Both vehicles suffered from inexperienced LST crews in the transport area who too often would not lower their bow ramps to accommodate LVTs or DUKWs approaching after dark. In too many cases, vehicles loaded with wounded marines thus rejected became lost in the darkness, ran out of gas, and sank. The amphibian tractor battalions lost 148 LVTs at Iwo Jima. Unlike Tarawa, Japanese gunfire and mines accounted for less than 20 percent of this total. Thirty-four LVTs fell victim to Iwo's crushing surf; eighty-eight sank in deep water, mostly at night.

Once ashore and clear of the loose sand along the beaches, the tanks, half-tracks, and armored bulldozers of the landing force ran into the strongest minefield defenses yet encountered in the Pacific War. Under General Kuribayashi's direction, Japanese engineers had planted irregular rows of antitank mines and the now-familiar horned antiboat mines along all possible exits from both beaches. The Japanese supplemented these weapons by rigging enormous makeshift explosives from five-hundred-pound aerial bombs, depth charges, and torpedo heads, each triggered by an accompanying pressure mine. Worse, Iwo's loose soil retained enough metallic characteristics to render the standard mine detectors unreliable.

The marines were reduced to using their own engineers on their hands and knees out in front of the tanks, probing for mines with bayonets and wooden sticks.

While the 28th Marines fought to encircle Suribachi and the beach masters and shore party attempted to clear the wreckage from the beaches, the remaining assault units of the VAC resumed their collective assault against Airfield No. 1. In the 5th Marine Division's zone, the relatively fresh troops of the 1st Battalion, 26th Marines, and the 3rd Battalion, 27th Marines, quickly became bloodied in forcing their way across the western runways, taking heavy casualties from time-fuzed air bursts fired by Japanese dual-purpose antiaircraft guns zeroed along the exposed ground. In the adjacent 4th Division zone, the 23rd Marines completed the capture of the airstrip, advancing eight hundred yards, but sustaining high losses.

Some of the bitterest fighting in the initial phase of the landing continued to occur along the high ground above the Rock Quarry on the right flank. Here the 25th Marines, reinforced by the 1st Battalion, 24th Marines, engaged in literally the fight of its life. The marines found the landscape, and the Japanese embedded in it, unreal.

The second day of the battle had proven unsatisfactory on virtually every front. To cap off the frustration, when the 1st Battalion, 24th Marines, finally managed a breakthrough along the cliffs late in the day, their only reward was two back-to-back cases of "friendly fire." An American air strike inflicted eleven casualties; misguided salvos from an unidentified gunfire support ship took down ninety more. Nothing seemed to be going right.

The morning of the third day, D+2, seemed to promise more of the same frustrations. Marines shivered in the cold wind and rain; Admiral Hill twice had to close the beach due to high surf and dangerous undertows. But during one of the grace periods, the 3rd Division's 21st Marines managed to come ashore, all of it extremely glad to be free of the heaving small boats. General Schmidt assigned it to the 4th Marine Division at first.

The 28th Marines resumed its assault on the base of Suribachi—more slow, bloody fighting, seemingly boulder by boulder. On the west coast, the 1st Battalion, 28th Marines, made the most of field artillery and naval gunfire support to reach the shoulder of the mountain. Elsewhere, murderous Japanese fire restricted any progress to a matter of yards. Enemy mortar fire from all over the volcano rained down on the 2nd Battalion, 28th Marines, trying to advance along the eastern shore. Recalled rifleman Richard Wheeler of the experience, "It was terrible, the worst I can remember us taking."

That night the amphibious task force experienced the only significant air attack of the battle. Fifty kamikaze pilots from the 22nd Mitate special attack unit left Katori Airbase near Yokosuka and flung themselves against the ships on the outer perimeter of Iwo Jima. In a desperate action that would serve as a prelude to Okinawa's fiery engagements, the kamikazes sank the escort carrier *Bismarck Sea* with heavy loss of life and damaged several other ships, including the veteran *Saratoga*, finally knocked out of the war. All fifty Japanese planes were expended.

It rained even harder on the fourth morning, D+3. Marines scampering forward under fire would hit the deck, roll, attempt to return fire—only to discover that the loose volcanic grit had combined with the rain to jam their weapons. The 21st Marines, as the vanguard of the 3rd Marine Division, hoped for good fortune in its initial commitment after relieving the 23rd Marines. The regiment instead ran headlong into an intricate series of Japanese emplacements which marked the southeastern end of the main Japanese defenses. The newcomers fought hard all day to scratch and claw an advance of two hundred net yards. Casualties were disproportionate.

On the right flank, Lieutenant Colonel Chambers continued to rally the 3rd Battalion, 25th Marines, through the rough pinnacles above the Rock Quarry. As he strode about directing the advance of his decimated companies that afternoon, a Japanese gunner shot him through the chest. Chambers went down hard, thinking it was all over: "I started fading in and out. I don't remember too much about it except the frothy blood gushing out of my mouth. . . . Then somebody started kicking the hell out of my feet. It was [Captain James] Headley, saying, "Get up; you were hurt worse on Tulagi!"

Captain Headley knew Chambers's sucking chest wound portended a grave injury. He sought to reduce his commander's shock until they could get him out of the line of fire. This took doing. Lt. Michael F. Keleher, USNR, now the battalion surgeon, crawled forward with one of his corpsmen. Willing hands lifted Chambers on a stretcher. Keleher and several others, bent double against the fire, carried him down the cliffs to the aid station, and eventually on board a DUKW, making the evening's last run out to the hospital ships.

All three battalion commanders in the 25th Marines had now become casualties. Chambers would survive to receive the Medal of Honor; Captain Headley would command the shot-up 3rd Battalion, 25th Marines, for the duration of the battle. By contrast, the 28th Marines on D+3 made commendable progress against Suribachi, reaching the shoulder at all points. Late in the day, combat patrols from the 1st Battalion, 28th Marines, and the 2nd Battalion, 28th Marines, linked up at Tobiishi Point at the southern tip of the island. Recon patrols returned to tell Lieutenant Colonel Johnson that they found few signs of live Japanese along the mountain's upper slopes on the north side.

At sundown Admiral Spruance authorized Task Force 58 to strike Honshu and Okinawa, then retire to Ulithi to prepare for the Ryukyuan campaign. All eight Marine Corps fighter squadrons thus left the Iwo Jima area for good. Navy pilots flying off the ten remaining escort carriers would pick up the slack. Without slighting the skill and valor of these pilots, the quality of close air support to the troops fighting ashore dropped off after this date. The escort carriers, for one thing, had too many competing missions, namely combat air patrols, antisubmarine sweeps, searches for downed aviators, and harassing strikes against neighboring Chichi Jima. Marines on Iwo Jima complained of slow response time to air-support requests, light payloads (rarely greater than one-hundred-pound bombs), and high delivery altitudes (rarely below 1,500 feet). The navy pilots did deliver a number of napalm bombs. Many of these failed to detonate, although this was not the fault of the aviators; the early napalm "bombs" were simply old wing-tanks filled with the mixture, activated by unreliable detonators. The marines also grew concerned about these notoriously inaccurate area weapons being dropped from high altitudes.

By Friday, February 23 (D+4), the 28th Marines stood poised to complete the capture of Mount Suribachi. The honor went to the 3rd Platoon (reinforced), Company E, 2nd Battalion, 28th Marines, under the command of 1st Lt. Harold G. Schrier, the company executive officer. Lieutenant Colonel Johnson ordered Schrier to scale the summit, secure the crater, and raise a fifty-four-by-twenty-eight-inch American flag for all to see. Schrier led his forty-man patrol forward at 0800. The regiment had done its job, blasting the dozens of pillboxes with flame and demolitions, rooting out snipers, knocking out the masked batteries. The combined-arms pounding by planes, field pieces, and naval guns the past week had likewise taken its toll on the defenders. Those who remained popped out of holes and caves to resist Schrier's advance, only to be cut down. The Marines worked warily up the steep northern slope, sometimes resorting to crawling on hands and knees.

Part of the enduring drama of the Suribachi flag-raising was the fact that it was observed by so many people. Marines all over the island could track the progress of the tiny column of troops during its ascent ("Those guys oughta be getting flight pay," said one wag). Likewise, hundreds of binoculars from the ships offshore watched Schrier's marines climbing ever upward. Finally they reached the top and momentarily disappeared from view. Those closest to the volcano could hear distant gunfire. Then, at 1020, there was movement on the summit; suddenly the Stars and Stripes fluttered bravely.

Lusty cheers rang out from all over the southern end of the island. The ships sounded their sirens and whistles. Wounded men propped themselves up on their litters to glimpse the sight. Strong men wept unashamedly. Navy Secretary Forrestal, thrilled by the sight, turned to Holland Smith and said, "The raising of that flag means a Marine Corps for another five hundred years."

Three hours later an even larger flag went up to more cheers. Few would know that Associated Press photographer Joe Rosenthal had just captured the embodiment of the American warfighting spirit on film. *Leatherneck* magazine photographer SSgt. Lou Lowery had taken a picture of the first flag-raising and almost immediately got in a firefight with a couple of enraged Japanese. His photograph would become a valued collector's item. But Rosenthal's would enthrall the free world.

Capt. Thomas M. Fields, commanding officer of Company D, 2nd Battalion, 26th Marines, heard his men yell "Look up there!" and turned in time to see the first flag go. His first thought dealt with the battle still at hand: "Thank God the Japs won't be shooting us down from behind anymore."

The 28th Marines took Suribachi in three days at the cost of more than five hundred troops (added to its D-day losses of four hundred men). Colonel Liversedge began to reorient his regiment for operations in the opposite direction, northward. Unknown to all, the battle still had another month to run its bloody course.

CHAPTER EIGHT

Mustering the Dead: Clinton Romesha

Clinton Romesha

IF YOU WANTED TO SELECT THE MOST LIKELY PLACE FOR AN AMERICAN soldier to get picked off by an enemy gunner from the ridges surrounding Keating, it would be hard to come up with a better spot than the thirty-yard stretch of bare dirt and loosely scattered pebbles that lay just beyond the south side of the Shura Building. Inside this zone the ground was open, the terrain sloped uphill, and the entire space was exposed to direct fire from virtually every sector. Nobody in his right mind would voluntarily step into that killing ground. Yet that's exactly what was required of the men who would spearhead the push to recover our dead and rescue our team at the mortar pit.

Our right flank would be formed by Stanley and Dulaney, with Dulaney and his SAW [a light machine gun] on the far end, because I wanted the weapon that could inflict the heaviest casualties to shield us, as much as possible, from the Taliban gunners who would be trying to take us down from across the river in Urmul and far up in the Switchbacks. Larson and Raz would take the left flank, while I'd be directly in the center. From there I could serve as command and control, directing our movements while simultaneously communicating with Bundermann back in the command post.

"Redcon One," I radioed to Bundermann, a code that signaled we were ready to launch.

"Roger that," replied Bundermann, who waited until Hill confirmed the same. Then Bundermann called the launch.

"Red—move," he ordered.

"*Go!*" I yelled. And with that, the five of us burst through the west door of the Shura Building and moved out into the killing ground.

The moment the Taliban realized what we were doing, their gunners opened up and we began taking heavy fire, the first shots coming in from Urmul and the Waterfall area. Then all of a sudden, the Switchbacks and the Putting Green kicked in, followed finally by the North Face. Hundreds of bullets ripped up the dirt around our feet while multiple RPGs snaked in, pulling their trails of white smoke behind them and exploding on all sides of us.

The incoming fire was dense and intimidating—but we had the jump on them, and before the enemy gunners could get a solid bead on any of us, we'd sprinted across the open ground and were stacked in a line against the first available cover. Directly to my left was Raz, and beyond him was Larson, who was crouched behind Truck 2 at the far left of our line. Stanley was to my immediate right, and beyond him, Dulaney was butted against the wall of Hescos that made up Keating's outer perimeter. From there, Dulaney was unleashing wicked-sounding bursts from his SAW toward the Switchbacks. Each of us was spaced fifteen meters apart to ensure that an RPG could take out only one of us at a time.

From my position in the center, where I was huddled on the south side of the laundry trailer, I glanced to both sides to confirm that all four of my guys had secured solid cover before keying my radio.

"*Set!*" I yelled—alerting everyone on the combat net that we were in position and that Hill's team now had a green light to start their move.

Then I glanced directly behind us and spotted something that left me disoriented and confused.

Thirty yards to our rear, Hill was standing in the west door of the Shura Building.

I spun and looked to my left, where a line of six men should have been charging uphill toward the chow hall.

They were nowhere to be seen.

Hill wasn't even remotely close to where he was supposed to be, while the assault that he should have been leading seemed to have disappeared. *What in God's name did he think he was doing?*

The moment I raised that question in my mind, I understood that the answer, whatever it might be, simply didn't matter. Perhaps Hill had failed to grasp how this maneuver was supposed to work. Maybe he thought he was doing some good by shooting directly over our heads rather than providing crossfire support, which was what we needed in order to keep moving forward. Or perhaps he was reluctant to order his men into the teeth of the same murderous barrage we had just run through and risk losing all of them now that the Taliban gunners were wise to what we were trying to pull off.

Regardless, it made no difference. The only thing that mattered was that me and my team were on our own with no supporting fire whatsoever, and highly exposed to the enemy's guns from virtually every quadrant.

Right then, the prudent move—indeed, the only option that qualified as a smart play—would have been for us to withdraw. But if we pulled back to the Shura Building, it was unlikely that we could launch out a second time after having telegraphed our move so clearly. Having lost both momentum and surprise, we would have squandered our best chance of retrieving our dead. And that was a price I wasn't willing to pay.

"Hey, we're already committed," I yelled out to the guys on either side of me, while deliberately avoiding any mention of the fact that we had no flank support on our left. "We can't sit here, so we're gonna do this in teams."

Every man knew what this meant: We would split in half and execute the same maneuver that we'd been planning to conduct in tandem with Hill's team, but within a narrower area, and without nearly as much protection.

"We gotta push now," I barked, turning back for one last glance at the Shura Building to confirm that Hill and his team weren't moving—and it was then that something caught my eye.

It was the body of an American soldier, tucked underneath the east side of the laundry trailer.

We'd found our mechanic, Vernon Martin.

Ducking under the trailer, I could see that Martin was lying on his stomach with his feet facing me. There was no sign of his weapon.

Reaching out with both hands, I grabbed the handle of his body armor, just below the back of his neck, pulled him out, and gave him a once-over. He'd been hit in the leg—probably shrapnel from the RPG that had exploded inside the turret of Gallegos's gun truck—and he had placed a tourniquet over the wound with a strip of olive-colored cloth. That had slowed him down enough to prevent him from covering the final patch of open ground between the laundry trailer and the Shura Building, so he'd crawled underneath the trailer in the hopes of staying hidden. Once there, he'd had nowhere else to go as he succumbed to his wound, dying isolated and alone.

Glancing downhill toward the Shura Building, I keyed my radio, called up Avalos, and told him that he needed to launch out with his body-recovery team to collect Martin.

The job that we'd given Avalos and his helpers, Grissette and Kahn, was both dangerous and exceptionally unpleasant. Thanks to the massive effort that's required to carry a dead body over uneven terrain, they would be forced to leave their weapons behind. What's more, in order to move as fast as possible and hopefully avoid being shot, they also would not be bringing a stretcher with them.

Avalos and Kahn were the first to make the dash up to the laundry trailer. When they arrived, they took hold of Martin and immediately started running downhill as fast as they could, dragging his body through the dirt and rocks. It was an appalling way to treat anyone who had died, much less a person they both had known. But they had no choice—the Taliban gunners fired at them the entire way in the hopes of taking one or both men out.

As they reached the entrance to the Shura Building, they were met by Grissette, who was horrified by what he had just witnessed. As two of the few African Americans at Keating, Grissette and Martin had been close friends; they'd leaned on each other for support, and they'd confided in each other when they needed advice or a sympathetic ear. Now Grissette's buddy was being yanked through the dirt like a tin can tied to the bumper of a car.

"*Man*," he cried out to Avalos in anguish and disgust, "not my *boy!*"

Little did Avalos know that within the next few minutes, he would be treated to the very same horror with a fallen soldier whose friendship and support *he* had known.

While all of this was unfolding, I was yelling, "*Go!*" and my five-man squad was making our next push, which would take us uphill another forty yards from the laundry trailer to the latrines, where we would once again have some cover.

Larson and Raz went first, racing madly, and followed by Stanley, Dulaney, and me.

When I arrived, Raz was moving toward the door to the latrines while pulling a grenade from his vest pouch.

"Raz," I barked, "please don't frag the shitter!"

He turned around and shot me a look of pure confusion.

"If you throw that grenade in there," I explained, "the explosion's gonna blast through the open space at the bottom of the building and probably kill us all."

"Oh ... roger that," he said.

"Plus, we're all gonna get covered in shit," I added. "So just enter and clear, okay?"

"Thank God I'm not the one in charge here," he muttered as he stepped up, yanked open the door with his weapon raised—and found himself staring down the barrel and directly into the face of an Afghan man.

It was Ron Jeremy, the interpreter (or "terp," as we called him) who had tried to warn us, just before 6 a.m., that the Taliban were about to attack. Since then, he had been crouching inside one of the latrine stalls with his legs pulled up to his chest, which is why he could now barely walk.

One way of gauging the intensity of combat—a crude but revealing index of the psychic hold that it can take on those who are swept into its dark energy—is to consider what was going through Raz's head in that instant. A part of his mind, of course, fully recognized Ron: a man whom we all knew and liked, and who had done his best to prevent us from being obliterated. But another part of his mind, the part that was connected to the hand that Raz now had wrapped around the trigger housing of his rifle, registered only one thing: the figure of a man from Afghanistan. And the main thing that Raz wanted to do right then—the *only* thing he wanted to do—was to shoot this fucker in the face and wallpaper the inside of the latrines with his brains.

Part of what made Raz such a superb soldier was that he maintained his violence of action during a firefight by refusing to pause or hesitate. That sort of momentum and focus is essential because sometimes it's the only thing that can propel a man through a set of obstacles and bring him out on the other side. But for reasons that even Raz didn't fully fathom— something that would later leave him puzzled and curious—he *did* hesitate just long enough to allow a mildly disturbing question to break the surface of his thoughts:

This dude standing in front of me is a terp, not a Taliban, so if I shoot him in the head . . . will I get in trouble for that?

Better to ask for permission first.

"Can I shoot him?" he begged me, still glaring down the barrel of the rifle at Ron.

"No, Raz!" I yelled.

"Well, I had to ask." Raz sighed as he lowered his weapon, seized Ron by the shirt, and yanked him outside. "I really, really wanted to."

"We're not allowed to shoot the terp—at least not till we figure out what side he's on," I said, turning to face Ron.

"Where the *fuck* have you come from?!" I demanded.

"I was needing to take a shit at 6 a.m.," he explained, "and since that time I am hiding inside!"

I paused, thought about that for a second or two, then looked downhill across the open ground toward the Shura Building.

"Well, if you survived this long, I'm pretty sure you can make it back on your own," I told him. "You can't stay here, and you can't come with us. So you know what, Ron? You better start running, and you better *run like hell.*"

Ron was short and fat and covered with hair. As he took off at a furious waddle, he looked pretty much exactly like a hedgehog trying to run on its hind legs—a spectacle that caused all of us to start laughing.

We were still cackling, and Ron was still running, when I glanced around me on both sides and realized that we were missing somebody.

"Where the hell's Larson?" I asked.

Everybody shot me a blank look and shook their heads.

"Red Dragon, come in!" I said, keying my radio. "Red Dragon—where are you at?"

No response.

Oh no, I thought to myself, *we just lost our first guy on the assault.*

Furiously scanning the ground around us, I suddenly caught sight of a figure in an American army uniform crumpled in a ditch about twenty yards away on the south side of the latrines. He was lying facedown, and was clearly dead.

"Get your team up here—we've got another body to bring down," I radioed to Avalos. Then I resumed screaming for Larson.

My closest friend was still missing. But we'd found Gallegos.

Back at the Shura Building, Grissette was still distraught over the savage manner in which Martin's body had been treated. Seeing how upset he was, Avalos didn't think that Grissette was in the right frame of mind to run back through the gunfire and subject Gallegos's body to the same treatment.

"It's just gonna be us," Avalos said, turning to Kahn. "On the count of three, we go. One—two—"

This time, they faced an even longer sprint.

Within the first few yards, Avalos had left Kahn, who was somewhat overweight and out of shape, far behind. By the time Avalos made it to the corner of the latrines, where I pointed him toward Gallegos, he was on his own. (Kahn had been forced to pause and take cover on the north side of the latrines.)

When Avalos reached the body, he realized that Gallegos could not have picked a worse spot to die. Without any assistance, it would be virtually impossible for Avalos to heft the biggest man at Keating to the lip of the ditch. Complicating things still further, one of Gallegos's legs had become wedged between some rocks at the base of the ditch in a manner that would make it even harder to extract him. Finally, the Taliban gunners in the Waterfall area and in the Switchbacks had now caught sight of Avalos and were directing a significant portion of their fire toward him.

Initially, Avalos was so shocked to see Gallegos dead that he barely noted the RPGs and the machine-gun fire because, just like Grissette and Martin, Gallegos and Avalos had some history between them that made this loss personal. As two of the only Hispanic guys at Keating, they shared a powerful bond at the ethnic and cultural level. But their connection went even deeper than that.

Back at Fort Carson when they were first getting to know each other, Gallegos had sort of taken Avalos under his wing in the way that an older brother or a cousin might. In the process, Avalos had seen a different side of the harsh and belligerent badass from Tucson, a side that the rest of us were barely aware of.

The November before we'd deployed to Afghanistan, Gallegos got word that Avalos, who was single, couldn't afford to fly home to California to be with his family during Thanksgiving. So Gallegos had insisted that Avalos join him, his wife, Amanda, and their small son, Mac, at their home in Colorado Springs.

Toward the end of that evening, the family had showed Avalos a Christmas stocking that they'd made for him and were planning to hang above their fireplace. In Avalos's mind, the unspoken message from Gallegos was: *Hey, you don't have to be here for Christmas—but if you don't have anywhere else to go, there's a place for you here, and you will be welcome.*

Since then, they'd been tight enough that Gallegos had shared his feelings about some hard turns that his life had taken, which included a divorce from Amanda and being passed over for a promotion. Avalos had been there to listen, and the trust between the two men had grown even stronger. In fact, only about a week earlier when they were sitting in one of the gun trucks in the middle of the night, pulling guard duty, they'd had a conversation about what might happen if Keating was overrun and one of them didn't survive.

For reasons that seemed strange at the time, but that now made Avalos wonder if his friend might not have had some sort of weird premonition about what was about to go down, Gallegos had tried to make a joke about how, if he was killed, he'd make absolutely certain that he died in the most difficult place for the rest of the platoon to get to him as a kind of final gesture of defiance. Upon hearing that, Avalos had decided that he didn't find the joke very funny, and he'd resolved to make his friend a promise.

"No matter what happens, I'm gonna be there for you," he pledged. "If I'm alive, regardless of where you're at, I'm going to come get you, and I'm gonna bring you back."

Now, as Avalos recalled those words, he realized that in order to keep his promise, he was first going to have to survive by hunkering down and riding things out until the Taliban gunners turned to other targets. Which meant that he was going to have to call upon Gallegos for one last favor—something that neither of them could have anticipated.

Scrunching down on the ground next to his friend, Avalos hoisted Gallegos's body and draped it over himself as a makeshift shield to protect him from the bullets and the jagged pieces of shrapnel that were now caroming off the rocks and drilling into the sides of ditch. It was an ugly thing to do, using your dead friend as body armor—but it was the only option he could think of to stay alive and complete his job.

Several minutes passed before the gunfire seemed to shift away from the ditch. When it did, Avalos shuffled out from beneath Gallegos and cautiously poked his head over the top of the ditch.

About twenty yards to his north he spotted Kahn, and motioned for him to lend a hand. Kahn raced over and jumped into the ditch, and together they were able to hoist Gallegos out. Then both men began dragging Gallegos down toward the Shura Building.

As they disappeared downhill, I was still crouched on the north side of the latrines and continuing, without success, to call out for Larson on the radio.

Unbeknownst to me, Larson's final bound had taken him to a point that was just a few yards below the mechanics' bay, where he'd sought cover by ducking inside a connex that we had been planning to use to back-haul equipment to Bostick. As I called for him on my radio, I moved around to the east side of the latrines, which brought this connex into my field of vision and enabled me to look through its doors.

He was crouched inside with his gun in one hand and his radio in the other. From the earnest manner in which he was scanning the North Face while trying to talk on the radio, it was clear that he hadn't considered the possibility that by placing himself inside a steel-sided structure like a connex, he'd cut himself off from all electronic communications.

"Get your ass over here!" I screamed, motioning furiously with my arm.

"What's up?" he asked in confusion when he arrived, still oblivious to fact that his move inside the shipping container had left me convinced that he'd gone off and gotten himself smoked.

"What the *fuck* were you doing over there?" I demanded.

"I was trying to make our linkup with Blue Platoon," he exclaimed. "Where the hell are those guys?"

"Don't worry about them," I replied. "We're kind of on our own right now."

By this point, me, Larson, Raz, Stanley, and Dulaney were tucked behind the north side of the latrines. For the moment, this offered some cover and we felt reasonably secure. But without any support by fire from Blue, we would be horribly exposed—and dangerously far from any assistance—as we tried to cover the final fifty yards of ground leading up to the mortar pit while simultaneously scanning for Hardt. Moreover, if we did find Hardt, it would be impossible for us to provide effective suppressing fire to protect Avalos and his recovery team as they made their way up from the Shura Building for a third time, and then attempted to drag Hardt back.

Knowing that we were stretched too thin and poised on the threshold of overcommitting ourselves, I keyed my radio and called up the mortar pit.

Just before we launched this assault, I'd spoken to Sergeant Breeding for the first time since the attack had kicked off. For the past eight hours, he and his crew had been hunkered down inside their concrete hooch, unable to reach their guns in the pit or even extract the body of Thomson, their slain comrade. During much of that time, they had also been cut off from all communication, until Breeding had managed to jury-rig an antenna and reestablish a working radio link. When he and I spoke, I'd urged Breeding to hang on because we were on our way, and I'd assured him that when we reached the mortar pit we'd get him, his men, and Thomson's body back down to the center of camp.

Now it was time to have another talk with Big John.

"Look, I got some bad news," I told him. "I'm sorry, brother, but we don't have the manpower to complete this final push. We're not gonna make it to you."

Breeding didn't miss a beat.

"Don't worry about it; you did what you could," he replied evenly. "You do what you gotta do to take care of your team down there, and we'll take care of ourselves up here. We can hang on a bit longer, and if they come for us, we're gonna take a bunch of them out."

Before we signed off, I reminded Breeding that the QRF was already on its way down from Fritsche and that their first stop upon reaching Keating's outer perimeter would be the mortar pit. I also told him that as soon as we got back to the Shura Building, my squad would break a hole in the southwest wall of the building and set up a machine gun to look directly over the top of the pit so that we could waste anyone who even thought about trying to come at him or his guys.

I don't know whether he appreciated those assurances. But as I heard the words coming out of my mouth, I could barely contain my disgust and shame. Earlier that morning, I'd failed to uphold a pledge to a fellow soldier when I'd been forced to retreat from the generator without giving Gallegos the cover fire that I'd promised him. That man's corpse had just been used as a human shield, dragged the length of a football field, and was now lying on the floor of the Shura Building while I fumbled to explain to yet another soldier who needed my help why I was breaking my word.

The whole point of this mission—the thing that had justified the risks we'd taken—was that we were supposed to grab *everybody* and bring them *all* back. Instead, we'd managed to snatch only two bodies while leaving behind a trio of surviving soldiers, plus a third body. On top of that, we still didn't have a clue where the fourth and last body might be.

I suppose I could have laid some of the blame for this on the shoulders of Sergeant Hill. But as I signed off with Breeding and ordered my team to begin displacing back to the Shura Building, the person I was most enraged at was myself.

In war, you play for keeps—and because of that, there are no second chances and no do-overs. The calculus of combat, at its most brutal essence, is binary: You either overcome the hurdles that are flung in front of you and figure out a way to make things happen, or you don't. It's a zero-sum, win-or-lose game with no middle ground—and no points for trying hard.

The bottom line was that I'd failed. And when me and my team completed our withdrawal and stepped through the Shura Building, the knowledge of that failure added another layer of bitterness to the taste and smell of blood and gunpowder and death that clung to the air within that building.

Once we were back inside the Shura Building, the first order of business was to break open a portal in the southwest wall and set up a SAW to keep watch over the mortar pit. As soon as that was taken care of, I radioed Breeding to let him know that the gun was in place. Then I made another dash back to the command post to let Bundermann know where things stood.

At this point, my main concern was the lingering question of what had happened to Hardt. After filling in Bundermann on where we'd searched and how much terrain we'd covered before falling back, I laid out what I thought we should do next.

"My guess is that there's an 80 percent probability that his body is no longer on station, but we need to be sure," I said. "I want to put together one more recon push."

"No way," he replied, shaking his head. "We've pushed our luck out a little bit too far already."

With that, Bundermann ordered me to get back to the Shura Building, make sure that the front gate was fully reinforced with concertina wire, and sit tight until the rescue team arrived from Fritsche. When they got down the mountain, he said, we could resume the search for Hardt.

It was a solid decision, and probably the right one. But when I returned to the Shura Building, I wasn't able to shake the feeling that there was something terribly wrong about the fact that we still didn't have everyone accounted for. It was right about then that Larson buttonholed me with a request. He wanted to conduct a solo reconnaissance run to look for Hardt one last time, and he needed me to give the nod.

My first reaction was that this was a lousy idea. I was okay with sending out a squad of men who could support one another. But one guy all by himself? That sounded ludicrous.

Larson, however, had no interest in taking no for an answer. Hardt, he pointed out, was not only one of our own platoon—a compelling reason by itself—but he'd been lost while trying to rescue fellow members of Red, including Larson himself. Plus, there was the fact that Larson had been training up Hardt in the same way that I had once trained up Larson: by taking him under his wing and teaching him not only how to perform, but also how to think. Which meant that Larson had some insight into what was probably going through Hardt's mind during his final moments: where he was trying to get to, how he intended to do that—and therefore, where he might now be.

On and on Larson went, relentlessly trotting out one point after another until finally (and ironically), he'd worn me down in much the same way that Hardt had done a few hours earlier when I'd reluctantly green-lighted the rescue mission that had cost him his life—and thereby set up the argument that Larson and me were having right now.

"All right, you can go," I conceded. "But you need to make sure you get light—and you need to *hustle*."

With that, he started stripping off all of his gear: weapons, ammo, rack, body armor, anything that might slow him down. When he was down to his T-shirt, pants, and boots, he stepped to the side of the door, waited a few seconds for the fire to abate, and broke west.

This wasn't a dash-and-pause sort of venture but a full-on, all-out, heels-on-fire sprint in a massive loop that would take him all the way from the front gate to the laundry trailer, the latrines, and Gallegos's gun truck before he cut east toward the mechanics' bay, then headed back past the shower trailers and the piss tubes to finish off by darting through the east door of the Shura Building.

The assumption behind this planned route was that when Hardt had fled his immobilized gun truck, he was almost certainly headed toward the toolshed and the chow hall. If that was the case—and if Hardt's body hadn't yet been snatched away by the enemy—he was now probably somewhere west of the mechanics' bay.

Larson started taking the fire the second he hit the ground. But just like in those football games back in Iraq and at Fort Carson, he was unbelievably fast. So fast that the gunners who were trying to hit him never got him locked in their sights and thus never even came close to anticipating the way he cut and swerved and dodged.

He was lost from our sight the moment he passed the shower trailer, and from there we had no idea how he was faring. But three minutes later, he appeared around the defunct Afghan Army mortar pit and whipped back to us as bullets lamely kicked up dust several yards behind him.

When he came through the door, he fell to his knees, gasping for breath, and shook his head in answer to the unspoken question of whether he'd caught sight of Hardt.

Nothing.

Staring out toward the front gate and the river beyond, I shook my head in frustration. It was as if Hardt had vanished into thin air. Or, much more likely, the Taliban had swooped in, scooped him up, and were now spiriting his body into the hills. That prospect was horrifying enough that once he caught his breath, Larson started campaigning for permission to conduct a *second* run and do the whole thing all over again, but cutting an even wider circuit—and exposing himself to even more danger—on the slim chance that maybe Hardt was still out there somewhere.

"No way," I said, and this time there would be no arguing.

Among the many low points we experienced that day, this was surely one of the lowest. After all the effort we'd expended and the risks we'd taken, Hardt was still missing, and Breeding and his team were still trapped at the mortar pit.

Meanwhile, one hundred yards to the east of the Shura Building, a separate struggle was still being fought as Keating's medics desperately battled to save the life of a gravely wounded Stephan Mace before the wildfire that had already consumed the entire eastern half of the outpost spread to the aid station itself, and burned the thing to the ground.

From the Citation

Staff Sergeant Clinton L. Romesha distinguished himself by acts of gallantry and intrepidity at the risk of his life above and beyond the call of duty while serving as a Section Leader with Bravo Troop, 3rd Squadron, 61st Cavalry Regiment, 4th Brigade Combat Team, 4th Infantry Division, during combat operations against an armed enemy at Combat Outpost Keating, Kamdesh District, Nuristan Province, Afghanistan, on 3 October 2009. On that morning, Staff Sergeant Romesha and his comrades awakened to an attack by an estimated 300 enemy fighters occupying the high ground on all four sides of the complex, employing concentrated fire from recoilless rifles, rocket-propelled grenades, antiaircraft machine guns, mortars, and small-arms fire. Staff Sergeant Romesha moved uncovered under intense enemy fire to conduct a reconnaissance of the battlefield and seek reinforcements from the barracks before returning to action with the support of an assistant gunner. Staff Sergeant Romesha took out an enemy machine-gun team and, while engaging a second, the generator he was using for cover was struck by a rocket-propelled grenade, inflicting him with shrapnel wounds. Undeterred by his injuries, Staff Sergeant Romesha continued to fight, and upon the arrival of another soldier to aid him and the assistant gunner, he again rushed through the exposed avenue to assemble additional soldiers. Staff Sergeant Romesha then mobilized a five-man team and returned to the fight equipped with a sniper rifle. Staff Sergeant Romesha's discipline and extraordinary heroism above and beyond the call of duty reflect great credit upon himself, Bravo Troop, 3rd Squadron, 61st Cavalry Regiment, 4th Brigade Combat Team, 4th Infantry Division, and the United States Army.

CHAPTER NINE

The Warrior: Roy P. Benavidez

Roy Benavidez, with John R. Craig

WHILE THE MEN WERE FACING HOT COMBAT, I WAS AT A CHURCH SER-
vice. The chaplain was using the hood of a jeep as the altar. The first I
knew that anyone was in trouble, I heard the clattering of weapons over
the radio and a voice begging for help.

I ran for the airstrip, knowing they would need all the help they could
get. Everyone was gathered around the radio, listening for news. We
learned that one of the choppers, piloted by Warrant Officer Curry, had
gone down, but that a second pilot had stopped to pick up the crew, and
they were headed back.

One chopper returned. It was badly shot up, but no one seemed to
be injured. The second chopper to come in, though, was a whole different
story. The pilots flew in, landing as fast as they could with their beat-up
chopper. For a moment I stood there, staring at the chopper. I didn't see
how it could still fly.

That's when I saw Michael Craig, the door gunner for that chopper. He had taken a couple of hits, and I knew that he was going to die.
He was only nineteen years old. We had celebrated his birthday just two
months earlier.

I helped them take Michael out of the helicopter, then I sat with him
on the ground. I put my arms around him and called for help. His pilot
was Roger Waggie, and he joined me. Michael was still conscious and in
great pain, gasping for breath.

Michael was like our son, or little brother. We all loved him, but he had been a real favorite of Waggie's, for whom the experience of losing him was pure hell. Michael had always been so eager to serve. Full of life and happiness, Michael couldn't do enough to please other people, and in spite of his youth, he was known as the best crew chief in the 240th. I wish that I could hear him say again as a mission began, "Let's go get them now."

"Oh my God, my mother and father . . . ," he said as I held him. Then he died, right there in my arms, his parents' only child.

I lowered Craig's body and turned to the copilot of the chopper.

"Who's in trouble down there?"

Waggie told me it was Wright's team, and I felt my heart sink. Those were my brothers. There wasn't much anyone could do to help them. My mind seemed to explode.

No one was giving up. After changing out a few parts, one of the pilots, Larry McKibben, announced he was going back in. While they were working on the chopper, members of the different crews compared notes about what they had seen. One of them claimed there were more NVA down there than the man before him had.

I had to go with McKibben. When I heard his chopper start, I jumped in and buckled up.

"You're going to need a belly man," I told him. "I'm it."

Midway there, I wondered what I was doing. I hadn't really thought my actions through before I got on the chopper. But once I could hear the cracking of guns below me, I began to think. I needed a plan.

"I don't think I can get down there," McKibben said. "It's just too hot."

That's when I really made up my mind: I couldn't leave them down there. We had to do something. Everyone had been trying hard, of course, but there had to be a way. I just couldn't sit there and listen to my buddies die on the radio.

"I'll get down there," I promised McKibben. "Just get me as close as you can."

My fear was gone. I can't explain what happened inside me. The best way to express my action is that it seemed all I had been taught in my entire lifetime just kicked in, and my body went on autopilot.

McKibben flew straight into the gunfire, zigzagging and making every attempt to dodge the bullets that were being fired at the aircraft. I crossed myself one last time, threw a bag of medical supplies out of the doorway, and rolled out with nothing but my buddies on my mind.

Gunships above us were diving and firing in a desperate attempt to draw enemy fire away from us.

I managed to get safely to a tree line, but I hadn't been on the ground more than a few seconds when the first bullet hit my leg. To be honest, I thought it was a thorn until I took a good look at it. That's how pumped up I was.

The gunships overhead were now out of ammo and were almost out of fuel. They headed back to Loc Ninh to rearm and refuel.

I found Mousseau first, and even though I knew the team was in trouble, I was shocked by what I saw. Mousseau had taken a round in the eye and in the shoulder. His right eye had been blown out of its socket, and his eyeball was hanging down on his cheek. He had dragged himself to a tree and propped himself up against it, running out of energy. But he was a good soldier, and he could still fire his weapon. He was determined to keep going. The CIDGs (Civilian Irregular Defense Group) were in what seemed to be a pool of blood, but everyone seemed to be patched up as well as could be expected.

I used Mousseau's radio to call McKibben.

"You better come get us fast," I said. "We're in real bad shape."

The firing had died down some. I couldn't see any of the enemy, and I figured that the gunship strikes might have slowed them down. But I did see O'Connor, and he indicated that two of them were still alive.

I told O'Connor that we were going to get out. "We're going to live. We don't have permission to die yet. Not here."

He and the other survivor, his interpreter, half dragged themselves toward us, but suddenly the firing started up again, and I motioned them back.

That's when I took another round, in my thigh. I wondered how I was going to be able to walk back to the chopper, but I sent green smoke up to signal McKibben anyway, and yelled for everyone to run for the chopper.

Everyone who could make it got in. The crew chief inside dragged the men into the chopper, but O'Connor and the interpreter were still out there. I ran along the tree line, spraying it with an AK-47 until I reached O'Connor. McKibben and the chopper were right behind me.

"What does Wright still have on him?" I asked O'Connor.

He told me Wright had been carrying the Standard Operating Instructions (SOI), some maps, and the intelligence-gathering device. I knew the documents were classified, and if I left them on his body, they would fall into enemy hands. I would have to get them. There was no choice.

I tried to get the interpreter to his feet, but he couldn't make it. He begged me not to leave him, and I promised I wouldn't. I told him to crawl toward O'Connor, and for both of them to get to the chopper. Then I went looking for the SOI.

I needed the documents, but I also needed Wright. I had no intention of leaving him there like that. But as I was crying and dragging him toward the chopper, a third shot caught me square in the back. I dropped my friend's body and fell forward.

I guess I was knocked unconscious. When I woke up, I rolled onto my stomach and got to my knees. I had a hard time breathing and I was soaked in blood. I knew I was going to have to leave Wright. I didn't have the strength to carry him.

But when I turned to run to the chopper, I saw it was nothing more than a smoking mess. It had crashed to the ground just before I had passed out. McKibben was dead, that much I knew. The copilot, Fernan, ran out from around the nose of the chopper. He had a blood-covered tree branch sticking out of his ear. He was waving a gun, dazed and in pain.

O'Connor and the interpreter were lying about ten feet from the crash. They hadn't made it all the way there. A CIDG who seemed to be only mildly wounded also lay on the ground. I sent him to get O'Connor's radio, certain he was dead. I was mistaken. He called out that he was okay.

Five men, including Mousseau, survived the crash. They were hanging out of the chopper's tail, returning enemy fire. I knew that I had to get them out of there. The NVA could have easily blown up the whole chopper with them inside. When we got the men out, I shot out the radio so it could no longer transmit.

We tried to set up a perimeter around a small clump of trees. We divided into two groups, and I followed Mousseau's team. I called for heavy air support, and when it came, I dispensed morphine shots. One of the CIDGs who was badly wounded pleaded with me to kill him. The poor guy's guts were hanging out, and with the sun and the wind, they were drying up. Man, that's a tough thing to take.

Our air force forward air controller was Lt. Robin Tornow, who was now overhead. He had located two F-100s in the area, with ordnance on board, being flown by captains Howard "Howie" Hansen and Robert Knopoka. He was calling them as the ground battle kept getting worse.

Tornow called out, "This is a Daniel Boone tactical emergency. I say again, this is a Daniel Boone tactical emergency."

Captains Hanson and Knopoka had taken off from Phan Rang Air Base, Republic of South Vietnam, on a preplanned mission targeting somewhere north of Saigon. Their call signs were "Bobcat" followed by two numerical digits. Their mission had been uneventful, until they were about to drop their ordnance on the preplanned target.

Just before they received clearance to drop, they heard Tornow on the UHF "guard channel" requesting immediate assistance for "US troops in heavy contact." That was the highest-priority request, and always brought US fighters to those in contact.

Howie Hanson, as flight lead, contacted the forward air controller and was told to vector north into an area where they were generally not permitted to fly.

That area was Cambodia.

With FAC clearance they screamed across the border from South Vietnam into Cambodia and were the first fighters on the scene. Tornow, at great personal risk, hung tight and vectored the F-100s to the target. Both planes were loaded with two napalm canisters each, which they dropped first, followed by two CBU-29s each. These were delayed-fuse cluster bomblets in clamshell containers, and were dropped from approximately three thousand feet aboveground. The CBU containers opened at a prescheduled height and scattered the bomblets over the entire area.

Each baseball-sized bomblet (of which there were about 250 in each canister—times two canisters carried by each plane) had several hundred ball bearings in it. When the bomblet fuse detonated, it sprayed the ball bearings in all directions.

Tornow was excitedly transmitting a message to the F-100s about how much the ordnance was helping. Bomblets were going off like popcorn, which was giving us some immediate relief.

The following minutes belonged to TAC AIR and the gunship strike—after strike, after strike. They were pouring it on the PZ, and came back into the woodlines and clearing in front of us that intersected with the small road. Branches, slivers of wood, metal, dirt, and body parts were stinging us from the percussion caused by the bombing. We could feel the tremendous heat of the afterburners of the F-100s—that's how low they were flying.

Gunships were diving and diving between the passes of the jets. Air support was like a swarm of killer bees attacking us. It later reminded me of that passage of scripture from the Book of Revelations, about the sky turning black with locusts.

Through the middle of this moment of hell came a lone slick that touched down about twenty to thirty meters away. We knew that this was our last hope to leave alive. We loaded the last of our ammunition.

This was it. Now or never.

I learned later that the fighters had run their fuel down to a level which would not allow them to return to Phan Rang, and they diverted to Ben Hoa near Saigon, where they refueled and flew back to Phan Rang.

I got to O'Connor and gave him his third shot of morphine. I also took another shot in the leg. We were under heavy fire again. I wasn't sure what was going to happen to us. I tried to reassure O'Connor. He must have thought I was losing it, because I don't think any of us really thought we were going to get out of there. We were surrounded. There was no way we could fire back at the NVA, because it was impossible to tell where their shots were coming from. They seemed to be coming from everywhere. He had no way of knowing until later that our LZ was surrounded by over 350 NVA and 30 crew-served machine guns.

The air attack managed to stop the assault for a few moments, long enough for that single chopper to lower right in front of us, and a Special Forces medic, Sergeant Sammons, ran to us from the aircraft. Roger Waggie and his newly recruited volunteers—Warrant Officer Bill Darling as crew chief, and Warrant Officer Smith as door gunner—came to our rescue. What I saw was the American fighting man at his best.

Two of us carried or dragged as many of the men as we could. But the NVA were firing directly at the chopper, shooting the men as they were lifted aboard. Two of the men were shot in the back as they tried to crawl to safety inside the chopper. I could barely see through the matted blood in my eyes due to the shrapnel wounds on my face and head.

Waggie's chopper was badly shot up. He and his copilot were shooting through their front windshield with their .38 pistols, while Darling and the door gunner and Smith were firing their M60s at separate groups of NVA charging from the sides. Darling and Smith had volunteered to man a gun because they knew they were running out of men, and as officers, they didn't have to volunteer for this situation. All I know is that because they did, soldiers would live.

I made another trip to find Mousseau. He was lying in the grass. I tried to carry him to the chopper. I didn't even notice when one of the NVA soldiers, lying on the ground, got to his feet. I also didn't notice when he slammed his rifle butt into the back of my head. I turned to look at him. Both of us were surprised—me, because I hadn't seen him, and he, because I had turned around after he had delivered the blow. But he reacted quickly and hit me again. I fell, my head swimming in pain.

I now had only one weapon with me: my Special Forces knife. I reached for it, and when I did he pointed his bayonet at the front of my belly. Fortunately, he hesitated, which gave me enough time to get to my feet. He sliced my left arm with the bayonet, and I shouted to O'Connor to shoot him. But he was too drugged to move, so I did the only thing I could: I stabbed him with every bit of strength I had left, and when he died, I left my Special Forces knife in him.

The last round in my stomach had exposed my intestines, and I was trying to hold them in with my hands. I could see Mousseau lying on the floor, staring at me with his one good eye. I reach down and clasped his hand and prayed that he would make it until we reached Saigon, where the medics could help him. Sadly, he would be among the approximately two hundred men who died on both sides during that battle.

I hoped that LeRoy was with us, that at least his body was going home to his family. I had loaded some bodies on the chopper, and I prayed that his was among them. The problem was that I couldn't always see what I was doing because I was bleeding profusely, and the blood had obscured my vision.

How Waggie flew the chopper is a miracle in itself. No instruments left, shot up, the cabin floor ankle-deep in blood, and we were headed in the wrong direction. Some air force jets showed up and turned us around for home.

Later, I realized that LeRoy did not make it out of the jungle. Sgt. Rodolfo "Bonzai" Montalvo led a platoon of Chinese Nung mercenaries into the area the next day on a body recovery mission, where they located LeRoy and the other dead CIDGs.

Bonsai told me that the NVA had been waiting for us that day. He said that he counted approximately thirty foxholes with crew-served machine guns around the LZ, and more dead NVAs than he had time to count. As they were attacked by NVAs and had to leave the area, he observed that the entire area was a carnage of dead bodies.

My next semiconscious memory was that of lying on the ground outside the chopper. I couldn't move or speak. I was in deep shock, but I knew that the medics were placing me in a body bag.

They thought I was dead and I couldn't respond. To this day I can still hear the sound of the snaps being closed on the green bag.

My eyes were blinded. My jaws were broken. I had over thirty-seven puncture wounds. My intestines were exposed.

Jerry Cottingham recognized my face in the body bag before it was closed. I remember Jerry screaming, "That's Benavidez. Get a doc!"

When the doctor placed his hand on my chest to feel for a heartbeat, I spat into his face. He quickly reversed my condition from dead to "He won't make it, but we'll try."

I was truly once again totally in God's hands.

It took many years for Roy Benavidez to be awarded the Medal of Honor. Decades after his heroics, a crucial witness, Brian O'Connor, was found living in Fiji. President Ronald Reagan presented the Medal of Honor to Mr. Benavidez at the Pentagon on February 24, 1981.

FROM THE CITATION

On the morning of 2 May 1968, a 12-man Special Forces Reconnaissance Team was inserted by helicopters in a dense jungle area west of Loc Ninh, Vietnam, to gather intelligence information about confirmed large-scale enemy activity. This area was controlled and routinely patrolled by the North Vietnamese Army. After a short period of time on the ground, the team met heavy enemy resistance, and requested emergency extraction. Three helicopters attempted extraction, but were unable to land due to intense enemy small-arms and anti-aircraft fire. Sergeant Benavidez was at the Forward Operating Base in Loc Ninh, monitoring the operation by radio, when these helicopters returned to offload wounded crew members and to assess aircraft damage. Sergeant Benavidez voluntarily boarded a returning aircraft to assist in another extraction attempt. Realizing that all the team members were either dead or wounded, and unable to move to the pickup zone, he directed the aircraft to a nearby clearing where he jumped from the hovering helicopter and ran approximately 75 meters under withering small-arms fire to the crippled team.

Prior to reaching the team's position, he was wounded in his right leg, face, and head. Despite these painful injuries, he took charge, repositioning the team members and directing their fire to facilitate the landing of an extraction aircraft, and the loading of wounded and dead team members. He then threw smoke canisters to direct the aircraft to the team's position. Despite his severe wounds, and under intense enemy fire, he carried or dragged half of the wounded team members to the awaiting aircraft. He then provided protective fire by running alongside the aircraft as it moved to pick up the remaining team members.

As the enemy's fire intensified, he hurried to recover the body of the dead team leader, along with classified documents. When he reached the leader's body, Sergeant Benavidez was severely wounded by small-arms fire in the abdomen and grenade fragments in his back. At nearly the same moment, the aircraft pilot was mortally wounded, and his helicopter crashed. Although in extremely critical condition due to his multiple wounds, Sergeant Benavidez secured the classified documents and made his way back to the wreckage, where he aided the wounded out of the overturned aircraft, and gathered the stunned survivors into a defensive perimeter.

Under increasing enemy automatic weapons and grenade fire, he moved around the perimeter, distributing water and ammunition to his weary men, reinstilling in them a will to live and fight.

CHAPTER TEN

"I Could Hardly Stand Up": Dr. Mary E. Walker

Mercedes Graf

IN MARCH 1864 MARY WALKER WAS FINALLY ASSIGNED TO DUTY WITH
a regiment. This slight progress cost two and a half years of hard work and
effort. The position of contract surgeon (the great majority were acting
assistant surgeons) was considered the fourth step of seven groupings for
a medical officer connected with the army. Such a contract brought small
recognition, no commission, no rank, little if any hope for promotion.
Furthermore, pay was equivalent to that of a first lieutenant, and the contract surgeon was frequently overworked, since the bulk of medical care
fell to this group, along with the regimental medical officers. Yet Walker
was satisfied for the moment because such a position, to her knowledge,
had never before been offered to a woman.

At the same time the civilian population badly needed medical services. In her free time, Walker was soon doing simple surgery and even
pulling teeth. In her notes she indicated that she took great pride in
performing such services. Furthermore, she was able to cement her relationship with Colonel McCook. While he seems to have given her great
latitude in traveling about the area, the young doctor learned that such
rides were also fraught with danger.

What follows is a partial account of her experiences.

GORDON'S MILLS, GEORGIA

General Dan McCook . . . had charge of the forces at that point, but while acting general, he was at the time but a colonel. A grand review was to be had a few miles north of that, and as he wanted to go early in the morning with other of his officers, [he] instructed me to take off my green sash and put on a red one and review the videttes [mounted sentries] in his absence. I did so, having the orderly ride by my side; and on his return he asked me if the guards had turned out for me. I replied that they did. This is the only instance in the war, far as I am aware, [that a] woman made a review.

Our headquarters were stationed in the house of the miller, and my sleeping room was in the kitchen, which was a large room where there were several beds, the miller and his wife and several of his children occupying the room. There was a hall between this room and another large room, and the headquarters were in this spacious hall, while the other room was the officers' sleeping room. I never rode without being in the company of the officers and orderlies.

As there was great distress outside of the Union lines, people not only suffering for food but for medical assistance, habitants [were] sent in, begging for a doctor. I was the only one immediately at headquarters and, while General McCook did not—and could not, by any authority—order me outside of the lines, I consented to go. I had cases in medicine and surgery obstetrics.

One of my cases was a young man about sixteen. He resided several miles outside of the lines, and was very ill with typhoid fever. His mother stated to me that he had gotten sick by exposure in the timber where he had hidden for a long time; that she and one of her girls had carried food out there for him and other boys that were in hiding; that they took a little bucket and put the food in, then carried it under their dress, holding on to the pail from the outside so that no Confederate officer could see what they were doing. She stated that the guard had been around and searched him, when he had become so tired out in the timber, what in the North we call woods, and that the guard finally took him, with others, and as he was unfit to go with them, had allowed him to remain until he was able to march.

I carried medicine with me and gave a prescription sufficient to last some little time, perhaps until his recovery. It was dangerous going out there, and the two officers and two orderlies that accompanied me were armed, and I had two revolvers in my saddle as well.

I had a nice orange in my bucket that had been given to me a short time before I started, and as our rations at that place were not first-class hotel menial, and as no orange had been seen for a long time by anyone, passed it around for the officers and those present to take the order from. I had been studying just what disposition to make [of] that orange, as dividing it into so many pieces as it could be divisible into would not make enough to go around, I had waited to conclude what I would do with it. When I saw this lovely young man in the condition in which he was, I did not have to wait long to decide, and gave it to him.

At another time I was called out to see a very sick child. It was in the afternoon, and the patient was several miles from our headquarters, and in a dangerous part of the country, as General McCook supposed, as he said that he did not dare to trust his officers and orderlies in such a place when we had so few at headquarters. As they begged so hard for a physician, I stated to General McCook that I would go alone and relieve that distress if he would not allow anyone to go with me; and here I will say that when I went alone, I always removed the revolvers from my saddle.

As General McCook was a man of great sympathy and large sense of justice, he said that if I so much desired, that he would allow two of the officers and two orderlies to go with me.

We had to pass through a wood where we had to manage not to have the branches get into the eyes of our horses, and when we arrived at the house, I said that the officers [should] wait, as had been provided before we started. And let me see if there was a necessity for my remaining with the patient longer than it would be safe for them to remain before it would be dark.

They kindly waited outside, and when I had examined the case I saw a beautiful child, and only one, [who] was affected with tetanus. I knew that there was but one chance in a very large number of its recovery, and when I thought of my remaining there alone so far from headquarters, where there was but one woman, and that, the young mother, the child being about between one and two years of age, and four or five men in the house, I felt a little afraid to stay, and especially as the mother looked up to me and answered me "Yes sir" and "No sir."

I accordingly gave as full directions as possible, telling the mother that I would try to see the child in the next day. I went out, [and] in [a] quiet tone told my escort that there were so many men in the house that I did not think I would stay. We went away very leisurely, and we had not proceeded but a short distance before we hastened as rapidly as possible toward our headquarters. As none of us knew anything about that part of the country, we returned the way we came; going through that wood, it began to be dark, so that we were obliged to hold up our arms and protect our eyes.

I felt the deepest of interest in that patient, and finally thought that my fears were groundless. On the next day I determined to keep my word and go to see the child again; but General McCook had carriers come in from near that part of the country, and he would not consent to any of his officers going in that direction again, neither would he allow me to go alone. I have often desired to know whether that child recovered or not, but have had no means of knowing.

At one time I was being called out to extract a tooth for the wife of Colonel Gordon, who was himself a long distance away in the Confederate Army. The house had a large aperture made through it, caused by a shell. Much to the relief of the suffering, I drew the wicked tooth away in triumph.

Another time I called in to see a woman who had a frog-felon [an abscess] on her hand. The whole hand was in a very much inflamed condition, and there were no medical officers within a great many miles on the Confederate side. I had several times been told that all of the physicians in that part of the country had been pressed into service. When I lanced the hand, and gave directions concerning the treatment of it, there was the greatest of gratitude expressed, since there was an immediate relief to pain.

The people, while they were grateful for the services rendered, were in the greatest of financial distress. In but one case did I take a fee, and then it was a five-dollar greenback that was so urged on me in an obstetrical case that I [accepted] it.

At another time, when I was out on my mission—and here let me state that I finally removed the revolvers from my saddle and went out alone without even an orderly. The people expressed so much gratitude that I lost all fear of anything being done to myself. When I was some three miles, I think, from headquarters, as I was passing an old barn that was enclosed on three sides by a high board fence, the boards so close together that one could not see through the cracks, I saw two men emerge therefrom and "Halt!" was cried out.

I stopped, and one of them came quite near me and said: "Where are you going?"

I replied that I was going several miles farther to tend to some patients.

He immediately recognized that I was from the Union Army by my dress and speech, and said for me to drive in there. I very coolly asked him what for, and then said that I was in a hurry to see the patient. He asked if I had any revolvers in my saddle; I told him that I had not, that I was going out in that direction to extract some teeth for a woman, and I would show him my surgical instruments.

I was about to change my bridle reins from my right hand to my left when he said, "Stop. I do not want to see your instruments." I think now that he supposed I was going to get a revolver, and that was the reason he stopped me. He hesitated a moment after that, and told me to wait there until he came back. He went toward the other man. Both then consulted with each other for a few minutes, then he came out and said I could go on.

I left and went to my patients, and when I returned to headquarters, I spoke with them of this little adventure, and they asked me, General McCook and the other staff officers, how the man looked, and when I gave a description of the man, in a second of time every officer arose quickly to his feet, then sat down. Then General McCook said: "I wonder if it can be [blank]." Then someone spoke up and said, "No, it cannot be him, for I do not think he can be in this part of the country." Another reason why they did not believe it was him was because it was well known that he had sworn that he would shoot every Yankee to death that came across his path.

A good many years afterward, I found a Dr. Hall, a watchman in the General Post Office Building of Washington, and he gave me a book of his memoirs. While I was looking it over, I saw a picture of that very man, which I recognized immediately, and I was so faint with the very thought of how narrowly I had escaped death that I could hardly stand up.

A POW AT CASTLE THUNDER

On April 10, 1864, while on an expedition, Walker took the wrong road, and encountered an enemy sentry. She threw up her hands and declared that she was unarmed. Taken into Confederate custody, only two months after her assignment to the 52nd Ohio, she found herself a prisoner of war.

In postwar years, her military exploits were among Walker's favorite lecture topics. Therefore, it seemed surprising that she never wrote about the prison experience that followed her capture. In a three-page hand-written memorandum that was placed with her *Notes,* she explained why this was the case.

While in prison she would write her parents: "I hope you are not grieving about me because I am a prisoner of war. I am living in a three-story brick 'castle' with plenty to eat, and a clean bed to sleep in. I have a roommate, a young lady about twenty years of age from near Corinth, Mississippi. The officers are gentlemanly and kind, and it will not be long before I am exchanged."

But Walker was not telling her parents the truth. Castle Thunder had not earned its name by accident. The prisoners themselves applied the officious title to the institution as a cynical reference to having evoked the Thunder of the Gods. The Castle had formerly been Glea-nor's Tobacco Factory, a large brick building on Cary Street in Richmond. Two smaller brick buildings, Palmer's Factory and Whitlock's Warehouse, had been added. The prisoners were segregated, with political prisoners going to the Gleanor's building, blacks and women confined to Whitlock's Warehouse, and deserters and federal POWs held in Palmer's Factory. The capacity for all three sites was 1,400 prisoners, but the estimated capacity was quickly reached and surpassed, as was the case with other prisons.

The prison rapidly acquired a reputation for unnecessary brutality, and by the spring of 1863, the Confederate House of Representatives ordered an investigation of the site. Captain Alexander was in charge, and it was said that he patrolled the prison "with his large, magnificent black dog, Nero, following at his heels." The dog had been taught to go for anybody wearing blue cloth.

Conditions in Castle Thunder, while not as abominable as other stockade prisons, were still deplorable. One historian noted, "If Castle Thunder was anything like the Confederate prison in Andersonville, Georgia, it was an overcrowded death camp in which exposure, starvation, and other sorts of 'savage and barbarous treatment' were common fare."

Walker found the prison to be dirty, and her mattress infested with vermin. There were also vermin of a larger species which raced along the floors, particularly in the hours before dawn, making sleep impossible.

In later years, the doctor sometimes talked about how uncomfortable she was in prison, and how grateful she was for the newspapers she used to cover the filthy furniture. She frequently gave her foul rations to the rats.

Within the prison, water was available with the guards' approval; outside exercise was eliminated; and air circulation was so poor that the odor emanating from the prisoners themselves was foul. Most of the captives slept on ragged blankets or piles of straw. A large whitewashed room with four barred windows, known as the "prison parlor," was the only place where civilian prisoners could stroll without interference. Those on sentry duty made nothing of watching for an excuse to pop off one of the Yanks at the windows.

Harassment from the guards was something the young doctor would never forget. Walker told of an incident that happened one day as she stood in the doorway to her cell. A guard fired, just missing her head. It was passed off as an accident, but such accidents happened frequently. Many years after the war, one of Walker's nieces said that there was also a "death line," which, if crossed, meant being shot. Such cruelty was most commonplace, and this kind of treatment contributed to the stress and suffering prisoners of war endured, especially after the formal exchange of prisoners was ceased.

No doubt Walker dealt with bouts of anxiety, loneliness, and depression related to her confinement. In addition, she had to come to terms with problems associated with heat and humidity, as well as her lack of liberty. Characteristically, she dealt with the temperature as only a real patriot could. A fellow prisoner, for example, remembered her sitting at an open window fanning herself with one hand and holding an American flag in the other.

In May 1864, Asa Isham, Henry Davidson, and Henry Furness, three young cavalrymen who had been captured as prisoners of war, marched into Richmond. They spied a nondescript shape upon the balcony of the jail. The shape "made us a salutation and, with some misgivings, we returned it. It was Dr. Mary Walker."

Despite her own problems, Walker offered to care for the wounded in Castle Thunder, regardless of their affiliation. She probably realized that one reason so many perished in prison was the lack of medical care. But her offer was refused because the authorities would not trust her.

At one point, Walker herself became very ill, possibly due to the effects of physical and emotional exhaustion. In her later years, during lectures, she said that having been served "with rations of a disgusting character," her system was reduced to such a condition that nothing but albumen could save her life. She found means through a commissary clerk, though it was against the rules, of procuring some fresh eggs; without them, she believed she would have died in prison. Walker's niece stated that as a rule, "there were very scanty rations once a day, rice being full of maggots and the bread moldy."

Walker was released from Castle Thunder on August 12, 1864, after four months of imprisonment. Along with several hundred other prisoners, she was placed aboard the *New York*, a flag-of-truce steamer which sailed to Fort Monroe at Hampton Roads inside Union lines. She was exchanged as a surgeon for a Southern officer with the rank of major. This was one of her greatest personal triumphs. Finally, the government was forced to become aware of her value; this was the first time a woman had been exchanged for an officer. The fact that the officer was six feet tall made her even more proud. She never forgot this event, or permitted others to forget it.

After the war, President Andrew Johnson awarded her the Congressional Medal of Honor. In 1917, when the criteria for awarding the Congressional Medal of Honor changed, Dr. Walker's award was rescinded, along with more than nine hundred others. She refused to return it, however, and wore it always. President Jimmy Carter restored the award to her in 1917.

From the Citation
Whereas it appears from official reports that Dr. Mary E. Walker, a graduate of medicine, "has rendered valuable service to the Government, and her efforts have been earnest and untiring in a variety of ways," and that she was assigned to duty and served as an assistant surgeon in charge of female prisoners at Louisville, Kentucky, upon the recommendation of Major Generals Sherman and Thomas, and faithfully served as contract surgeon in the service of the United States, and has devoted herself with much patriotic zeal to the sick and wounded soldiers, both in the field and hospitals, to the detriment of her own health, and has also endured hardships as a prisoner of war [for] four months in a Southern prison while acting as contract surgeon. In the opinion of the President, an honorable recognition of her services and sufferings should be made.

CHAPTER ELEVEN

Taking Prisoners: Alvin York

Sam K. Cowan

WHEN ALVIN WENT TO WAR HE CARRIED WITH HIM A SMALL, RED-cloth-covered memorandum book, which was to be his diary. He knew that beyond the mountains that encircled his home there was a world that would be new to him. He kept the little volume—now worn, and with a broken spine—constantly with him, and he wrote in it while in camp, on shipboard, and in the trenches in France. It was in his pocket while he fought the German machine-gun battalion in the Forest of Argonne.

This book was intended for no eyes but his own. Yet painstakingly, using ink, he had headed the volume: "A History of Places Where I Have Been." As a whole, the volume would be unintelligible to an average reader, for while it records the things he wished to remember of his camp-life, the trip through England, his stay in France, and tells in order the "places he had been," it is made up of swift-moving notes that enter into no explanatory details. But to him the notations could—even in the evening of his life—revive the chain of incidents in memory. His handling of his diary is typical of his mind and his methods.

To him details were essential, but when his duties were completed carefully and thoroughly and the events were over, thereafter he found them uninteresting. They were but the steps that had to be taken to walk a given distance. His mind instead dwelled upon the object of the journey.

When he left his home at Pall Mall he reported to the local recruiting station at Jamestown, the county seat. He was sent to Camp Gordon near Atlanta, Georgia, reaching his destination the night of November 16, 1917. His diary runs: "I was placed in the 21st training battalion. Then I was called the first morning of my army life to police up in the yard all the old cigarette butts, and I thought that was pretty hard as I didn't smoke. But I did it just the same."

His diary records his experience of months of training with the "awkward squad" and of his regimental assignment in one sentence: "I stayed there and done squads right and squads left until the first of February, 1918, and then I was sent to Company G, 328 Inf. 82nd Div." This was the "All America" Division, made up of selected men from every state in the Union. In its ranks were the descendants of men who had come from every nation that composed the Allies that were fighting Germany.

In his notes Alvin records temptations that came to him while at Camp Gordon: "Well, they gave me a gun and, oh my! that old gun was just full of grease, and I had to clean that old gun for inspection. So I had a hard time to get that old gun clean, and oh, those were trying hours for a boy like me, trying to live for God and do his blessed will. . . . Then the Lord would help me to bear my hard tasks. So there I was. I was the homesickest boy you ever seen."

When he entered the army Alvin York stood six feet in the clear. There were few in camp physically his equal. In any crowd of men he drew attention. The huge muscles of his body glided lithely over each other. He had been swinging with long, firm strides up the mountainsides. His arms and shoulders had developed by lifting hay-laden pitchforks in the fields and in the swing of the sledge in his father's blacksmith's shop. The military training coordinated these muscles, and he moved among the men as a commanding figure, whose quiet power seemed never fully called into action by the arduous duties of the soldier.

The strength of his mind, the mental ability he possessed, had yet to be recognized and tested. And even in the early days of his military training, with all the experiences he had and the advancement he made, that force had not yet been measured. It would be in the years to come that the real mission of Sergeant York would be told.

He came out of the mountains of Tennessee with an education equal to that of a child of eight or nine years of age, with no experience in the world beyond the primitive, wholesome life of his mountain community. He had little knowledge of the lives and customs, the ambitions and struggles of men who lived over the summit of the Blue Ridge and beyond the foothills of the Cumberlands.

But he was wise enough to know there were many things he did not know. He was brave enough to frankly admit them. When placed in a situation that was new to him, he would quietly try to think his way out of it; and through inheritance and training, he thought calmly. He had the mental power to stand at ease under any condition and await sufficient developments to justify whether to speak or act. Even German bullets could not hurry or disconcert him.

Alvin York was keenly observant of all that went on around him in the training camp. Few sounds or motions escaped him, though it was with a seemingly stoic mien that he contemplated the things that were new to him. In the presence of those whose knowledge or training he recognized as superior to his own, he calmly waited for them to act. So accurate were his observations that the officers of his regiment looked upon him as one by nature a soldier, and they said of him that he "always seemed instinctively to know the right thing to do."

Placed at his first banquet board—the guest of honor—with a row of silverware by his plate so different from the table service in his humble home, he did not misuse a piece from among them or select one in error. But throughout the courses he was not the first to pick up a needed piece.

His ability to think clearly and quickly, under conditions that tried both heart and brain, was shown in the fight in the Argonne. With eight men, not twenty yards away, charging him with bayonets, he calmly decided to shoot the last man first, and to continue this policy in selecting his mark, so that those remaining would "not see their comrades falling and in panic stop and fire a volley at him."

Military critics analyzing the tactics York used in this fight have been able to find no superior way for removing the menace of the German machine guns that were over the crest of the hill, and between him and his regiment, than to form the prisoners he had captured in a column, put the officers in front, and march directly to each machine-gun nest, compelling the German officers to order the gunners to surrender and to take their place in line.

Calm and self-controlled, with hair of copper-red and face and neck browned and furrowed by the sun and mountain winds, inured to hardships and ready for them, this young mountaineer moved among his new-found companions at Camp Gordon. Although he seemed reticent, his answer to an inquiry was direct, and his quiet blue eyes never shifted from the eyes of the man who addressed him. As friendships were formed, his moods were noted by his comrades. At times he was playful as a boy, using cautiously, even gently, the strength he possessed. Then again he would remain, in the midst of the sports, thoughtful, and as though he was troubled.

Back in the mountains he had had little opportunity to attend school, and his sentences were framed in the quaint construction of his people, and nearly all of them were ungrammatical. There were many who would have regarded him as ignorant. By the standards that hold up education as the enlightenment that comes from acquaintance with books, and wisdom as the knowledge of the ways of the world, he was. But he had a training that is rare, and advantages that come to too few.

From his father he inherited physical courage; from his mother, moral courage. And both of them spent their lives developing these qualities of manhood in their boy. His father hiked him through the mountains on hunts that would have stoutened the heart of any man to have kept the pace. And he never tolerated the least evidence of fear of man or beast. He taught his boy to live so that he owed apology or explanation to no man.

While I was at Pall Mall, one of his neighbors, speaking of Alvin, said: "Even as a boy he had his say and did his do, and never stopped to explain a statement or tell what prompted an act. Left those to stand for themselves."

And Alvin's mother, whose frail body was worn from hard work and wracked by the birth of eleven children, was the embodiment of gentleness, spirit, and faith. When he came from the hunt into the door of that cabin home and hung his gun above the mantel, or came in from the fields where the work was physical, he put from him all feeling of the possession of strength. When he was with her, he was as gentle as the mother herself. She, too, wanted her son to live in such a way that he would not fear any man. But she wanted his course through life to be along the path her Bible pointed out, so that he would not have the impulse to do those deeds that called for explanation or demanded apology.

From her he inherited those qualities of mind that gave him at all times the full possession of himself. Her simple, homemade philosophy was ever urging her boy to "think clear through" whatever proposition was before him, and when in a situation where those around him were excited, "to slow down on what he was doing, and think fast." I have heard her say: "There hain't no good in gitting excited; you can't do what you ought to do."

She had not seen a railroad train until she went to the capital of Tennessee to the presentation of the medal of honor that was given to her son by the people of the state. She came upon the platform of the Tabernacle at Nashville wearing the sunbonnet she wore to church in the "Valley of the Three Forks o' the Wolf." In greeting her, the governor lifted off her sunbonnet. His possession of it was momentary, for Mrs. York recaptured it in true York style. Her smiling face and nodding head revealed that the governor had capitulated. It was pantomime, for thousands were on their feet, waving to her and cheering her on. Calm and still smiling, she looked over the demonstration in the vast auditorium more as a spectator than as the cause of the outburst of applause. Later, during the reception at the governor's mansion, guests gathered around her, and she held a levee that crowded one of the big drawing-rooms. Those who sought to measure wit with her found her never at a loss for a reply, and woven through her responses were many similes drawn from her mountain life.

Under her proctorship the moral courage of her son had developed. In her code of manhood there was no tolerance for infirmity of purpose, and mental fear was as degrading and as disintegrating as physical cowardice. He had been a man of the world in the miniature world that the miles of mountains had enclosed around him. He had lived every phase of the life of his people, and lived them openly. When he renounced drinking and gambling, he was through with them for all time. When he joined the church, he made his religion the large part of the new plan of his life.

It was while at Camp Gordon that he reconciled his religious convictions with his patriotic duty to his country. The rugged manhood within him had made him refuse to ask for exemption from service and danger on the grounds that the doctrine of his church opposed war. But his conscience was troubled that he was deliberately on a mission to kill his fellow man. It was these thoughts that caused his companions to note his moody silences.

On behalf of his mother, who, with many mothers of the land, was bravely trying to still her heart with the thought that her son was on an errand of mercy, the pastor of the church in the valley made out the strongest case he could for Alvin's exemption, and sent it to the officers of his regiment.

Lt. Col. Edward Buxton Jr. and Maj. E. C. B. Danford, who was then the captain of York's company, sent for him. They explained the conditions under which it would be possible, if he chose, to secure exemption. They pointed out the ways he could remain in the service of his country and not be among the combat troops. York's sincerity and earnestness impressed the officers, and they had not one but a number of talks in which the Scriptures were quoted to show the Savior's teachings, "when man seeth the sword come upon the land." They brought out many facts about the war that the Tennessee mountaineer had not known.

York did not take the release that lay within his grasp. Instead, he thumbed his Bible in search of passages that justified the use of force.

One day, before the regiment sailed for France, when York's company was leaving the drill-field, Captain Danford sent for him. Together they went over many passages of the Bible which both had found, including "If my kingdom were of this world, then would my servants fight." They were together for several hours. At last York said: "All right; I'm satisfied." After that, there was no reference to religious objection. From the first he had seen the justice of the war; now he saw the righteousness of it.

York's abilities as a soldier were soon revealed. He quickly qualified as a sharpshooter, both as a skirmisher and from the top of the trench. In battalion contest formation, where the soldiers run and fall and fire, "shooting at moving targets," it was not difficult for him to score eight hits out of ten shots, even with a rifle that was new to him. This, too, over a range that began at six hundred yards and went down to one hundred yards, with the targets in the shape of the head and shoulders of a man. In these maneuvers he attracted the attention of his officers.

The impressive figure of this man with his ever-present evidence of reserve force, the strength of his personality, uneducated as he was, made him a natural leader of the men around him. Officers of the regiment have said that he would have received a promotion while in the training camp but for the policy of not placing in command a man who might be a conscientious objector.

The "All America" Division passed through England on its way to France, and the first real fighting they had was in the Saint-Mihiel Salient. From there they went to the Argonne Forest, where the division was on the front line of the battle for twenty-six days and nights without relief.

It was in the Saint-Mihiel Salient that York was made a corporal, and when he came out of the Argonne Forest, he was a sergeant. The armistice was signed a fortnight later.

The war made York even more deeply religious. The diary he kept passed from simple notations about "places he had been" to a record of his thoughts and feelings. In it are many quotations from the Bible; many texts of sermons he heard while on the battlefields of France. With the texts were brief notes that would recall the sermons to his memory. The book is really a history of his religious development.

When he would kneel by a dying soldier he would record in his diary the talk he'd had with his comrade, and would write the passages of Scripture that he or the dying man had spoken. It was upon this his interests centered. To others he left the task of telling of the battle's result.

He wrote in his diary this simple story of his fight with a battalion of German machine guns:

On the 7th day of October we lay in some little holes on the roadside all day. That night we went out and stayed a little while and came back to our holes, the shells bursting all around us. I saw men just blown up by the big German shells which were bursting all around us.

So the order came for us to take Hill 223 and 240 the 8th.

So the morning of the 8th just before daylight, we started for the hill at Chatel-Chéhéry. Before we got there it got light and the Germans sent over a heavy barrage and also gas, and we put on our gasmasks and just pressed right on through those shells and got to the top of Hill 223 to where we were to start over at 6:10 a.m.

They were to give us a barrage. The time came and no barrage, and we had to go without one. So we started over the top at 6:10 a.m. and the Germans were putting their machine guns to working all over the hill in front of us and on our left and right. I was in support and I could see my pals getting picked off, until it almost looked like there was none left.

So seventeen of us boys went around on the left flank to see if we couldn't put those guns out of action.

So when we went around and fell in behind those guns, we first saw two Germans with Red Cross bands on their arms. Some one of the boys shot at them and they ran back to our right. So we all ran after them, and when we jumped across a little stream of water that was there, there was about fifteen or twenty Germans jumped up and threw up their hands and said, "Comrade." The one in charge of us boys told us not to shoot; they were going to give up anyway.

By this time the Germans from on the hill was shooting at me. Well, I was giving them the best I had. The Germans had got their machine guns turned around. They killed six and wounded three. That just left eight, and then we got into it right. So we had a hard battle for a little while.

I got hold of a German major and he told me if I wouldn't kill any more of them he would make them quit firing. So I told him all right, if he would do it now. So he blew a little whistle and they quit shooting and came down and gave up. I had about eighty or ninety Germans there.

They disarmed and we had another line of Germans to go through to get out. So I called for my men and one answered me from behind a big oak tree and the other men were on my right in the brush. I said, "Let's get these Germans out of here." One of my men said, "It's impossible." So I said, "No, let's get them out of here."

My men said that this German major said, "How many have you got?" And I said, "I got a plenty," and pointed my pistol at him all the time. In this battle I was using a rifle or a .45 Colt automatic pistol. So I lined the Germans up in a line of twos and I got between the ones in front and I had the German major before me. So I marched them right straight into those other machine guns, and I got them. When I got back to my major's P.C., I had 132 prisoners.

So you can see here in this case of mine where God helped me out. I had been living for God and working in church work sometime before I came to the army. I am a witness to the fact that God did help me out of that hard battle, for the bushes were shot off all around me and I never got a scratch. So you can see that God will be with you if you will only trust Him, and I say He did save me.

By this time, the Germans from on the hill was shooting at me. Well, I was giving them the best I had.

That best was the courage to stand his ground and fight it out with them, regardless of their number, for they were the defilers of civilization, murderers of men, the enemies of fair play who had shown no quarter to his pals who were slain, unwarned, while in the act of granting mercy to men in their power.

That best was the morale of the soldier who believes that justice is on his side, and that the justness of God will shield him from harm.

And in physical qualities, it included a heart that was stout and a brain that was clear—a mind that did not weaken when all the hilltop above flashed in a hostile blaze, when the hillside rattled with the death drumbeat of machine-gun fire, and while the very air around him was filled with darting lead. As he fought, his mind visualized the tactics of the enemy in the moves they made, and whether the attack upon him was with rifle or machine gun, hand grenade or bayonet, he met it with an unfailing marksmanship that equalized the disparity in numbers.

Another passage in his direct and simple story shows the character of this man who came from a distant recess of the mountains with no code of ethics except a confidence in his fellow man. Those Americans who were not killed or wounded in the first machine-gun fire had saved themselves, as York had done. They had dived into the brush and lay flat upon the ground, behind trees, among the prisoners, protected by any obstruction they could find while the stream of bullets passed over them.

York was at the left, beyond the edge of the thicket. The others were shut off by the underbrush from a view of the German machine guns that were firing on them. York had the open of the slope of the hill, and it fell to him to fight the fight. He wrote in his diary when he could find time, and the story was written in foxholes in the Forest of Argonne, in the evenings after the American soldiers had dug in. Although his records were for no one but himself, he had no thought that raised his performance of duty above that of his comrades: "They killed six and wounded three. That just left eight, and we got into it right. So we had a hard battle for a little while."

Yet, in the height of the fight, not a shot was fired but by York.

In their admiration for him and his remarkable achievement, so that the honor should rest where it belonged, the members of the American patrol who were the survivors of the fight made affidavits that accounted for all of them who were not killed or wounded, and showed the part each had taken. These affidavits are among the records of Lieut. Col. G. Edward Buxton Jr., official historian of the Eighty-Second Division. At the time of the fight Sergeant York was still a corporal.

From the affidavit by Pvt. Patrick Donohue:

> *During the shooting, I was guarding the mass of Germans taken prisoner, and devoted my attention to watching them. When we first came in on the Germans, I fired a shot at them before they surrendered. Afterwards I was busy guarding the prisoners and did not shoot. I could only see Privates Wills, Sacina, and Sok. They were also guarding prisoners as I was doing.*

From the affidavit by Pvt. Michael A. Sacina:

> *I was guarding the prisoners with my rifle and bayonet on the right flank of the group of prisoners. I was so close to these prisoners that the machine gunners could not shoot at me without hitting their own men.*

This I think saved me from being hit. During the firing, I remained on guard, watching these prisoners, and unable to turn around and fire myself for this reason. I could not see any of the other men in my detachment. From this point I saw the German captain and had aimed my rifle at him when he blew his whistle for the Germans to stop firing. I saw Corporal York, who called out to us, and when we all joined him, I saw seven Americans beside myself. These were Corp. York, Privates Beardsley, Donohue, Wills, Sok, Johnson, and Konatski.

From the affidavit by Pvt. Percy Beardsley:

I was at first near Corp. York, but soon after thought it would be better to take to cover behind a large tree about fifteen paces in rear of Corp. York. Privates Dymowski and Waring were on each side of me and both were killed by machine-gun fire. I saw Corp. York fire his pistol repeatedly in front of me. I saw Germans who had been hit fall down. I saw the German prisoners who were still in a bunch together waving their hands at the machine gunners on the hill as if motioning for them to go back. Finally the fire stopped and Corp. York told me to have the prisoners fall in columns of two's and take my place in the rear.

From the affidavit by Pvt. George W. Wills:

When the heavy firing from the machine guns commenced, I was guarding some of the German prisoners. During this time I saw only Privates Donohue, Sacina, Beardsley, and Muzzi. Private Swanson was right near me when he was shot. I closed up very close to the Germans with my bayonet on my rifle and prevented some of them who tried to leave the bunch and get into the bushes from leaving. I knew my only chance was to keep them together and also keep them between me and the Germans who were shooting. I heard Corp. York several times shouting to the machine gunners on the hill to come down and surrender, but from where I stood, I could not see Corp. York. I saw him, however, when the firing stopped and he told us to get along sides of the column. I formed those near me in columns of two's.

The report which the officers of the Eighty-Second Division made to General Headquarters contained these statements:

> *The part which Corporal York individually played in this attack [the capture of the Decauville Railroad] is difficult to estimate. Practically unassisted, he captured 132 Germans [three of whom were officers], took about 35 machine guns, and killed no less than 25 of the enemy, later found by others on the scene of York's extraordinary exploit.*
>
> *The story has been carefully checked in every possible detail from Headquarters of this Division and is entirely substantiated.*
>
> *Although Corporal York's statement tends to underestimate the desperate odds which he overcame, it has been decided to forward to higher authority the account given in his own words.*
>
> *The success of this assault had a far-reaching effect in relieving the enemy pressure against American forces in the heart of the Argonne Forest.*

In decorating Sergeant York with the Croix de Guerre with Palm, Marshal Foch said to him: "What you did was the greatest thing accomplished by any private soldier of all of the armies of Europe."

When the officers of York's regiment were securing the facts for their report to General Headquarters and were recording the stories of the survivors, York was questioned on his efforts to escape the onslaught of the machine guns. He replied, "By this time, those of my men who were left had gotten behind trees, and the men sniped at the Boche. But there wasn't any tree for me, so I just sat in the mud and used my rifle, shooting at the machine gunners."

The officers recall his quaint and memorable answer to the inquiry on the tactics he used to defend himself against the Boche who were in the gun-pits, shooting at him from behind trees and crawling toward him through the brush. His method was simple and effective: "When I seed a German, I jes' tetched him off."

On the afternoon of October 8—York had brought in his prisoners by ten o'clock in the morning—the seventeenth hour of that day, the

Eighty-Second Division cut the Decauville Railroad and drove the Germans from it. The pressure against the American forces in the heart of the Argonne Forest was not only relieved, but the advance of the division had aided in the relief of the "Lost Battalion" under the command of the late Colonel Whittlesey, which had made its stand in another hollow of those hills only a short distance from the hillside where Sergeant York made his fight.

As the Eighty-Second Division swept up the three hills across the valley from Hill No. 223, the hill on the left—York's Hill—was found cleared of the enemy; there was only the wreckage of the battle that had been fought there.

York's fight occurred on the eighth day of the twenty-eight-day battle of the Eighty-Second Division in the Argonne. They were in the forest, fighting on, when the story spread around the world that an American soldier had fought and captured a battalion of German machine gunners.

Even military men doubted its possibility, until the "All America" Division came out of the forest with the records they had made upon the scene, and with the clear exposition of the tactics and the remarkable bravery and generalship that made Sergeant York's achievement possible.

Alvin York faced a new experience then; he found himself famous.

From the Citation

After his platoon had suffered heavy casualties and 3 other noncommissioned officers had become casualties, Corporal York assumed command. Fearlessly leading 7 men, he charged with great daring a machine-gun nest which was pouring deadly and incessant fire upon his platoon. In this heroic feat the machine-gun nest was taken, together with 4 officers and 128 men and several guns.

CHAPTER TWELVE

Stealing the Train: The First Ever Medals

Rev. William Pittenger

PREFACE

War has a secret as well as a public story. Marches and battles are open to the popular gaze; but enterprises of another class are in their very nature secret, and these are scarcely less important and often much more interesting than the former. The work of spies and scouts, the enterprises that reach beyond the lines of an army for the purpose of surprise, the councils of officers, the intrigues by means of which great results often flow from apparently insignificant causes, and all the experiences of hospitals and prisons—these usually fill but a small place on the historian's page, though they are often of romantic interest, and not infrequently decide the course and fate of armies.

The enterprise described in these pages possesses all the unity of a drama, from the first plunge of the actors into the heart of the enemy's country, through all their adventures and changing fortunes, until the few survivors stood once more under the old flag! No single story of the war combines so many of the hidden, underground elements of the contest against rebellion as this. Disguise and secrecy, the perils of a forlorn hope, the exultation of almost miraculous success, the sufferings of prisoners, and the gloom of despair are all mingled in a varied and instructive war-picture.

In telling the story all fictitious embellishments have been rejected. No pains have been spared to ascertain the exact truth, and the reader will find names, dates, and localities so fully given that it will be easy to verify the prominent features of the account.

In narrating those events which fell under his own eye, the writer has waived all scruples of delicacy, and used the first personal pronoun. This is far more simple and direct, while an opposite course would have savored of affectation.

This is not a revision or new edition of the little volume published by the present writer during the rebellion. *Daring and Suffering*, like a number of similar sketches published in newspapers, magazines, and pamphlets, was a hasty narrative of personal adventure, and made no pretense of completeness. *Capturing a Locomotive* is broader and more historic; a large amount of valuable material is now employed for the first time; and the story is approached in an entirely different manner. No paragraph of the old book is copied into the new.

—Woodbury, New Jersey, January 1882

The Capture

The greater number of us arranged to pass the night at a small hotel adjoining the Marietta depot. Before retiring we left orders with the hotel clerk to rouse us in time for the northward-bound train, due not long after daylight. Notwithstanding our novel situation, I never slept more soundly. Good health, extreme fatigue, and the feeling that the die was now cast and further thought useless, made me sink into slumber almost as soon as I touched the bed. Others equally brave and determined were affected in a different way. Alfred Wilson says:

> *No man knows what a day may bring forth, and the very uncertainty of what that day's sun would bring forth in our particular cases was the reason that some of us, myself at least of the number, did not sleep very much. Our doom might be fixed before the setting of another sun. We might be hanging to the limbs of some of the trees along the railroad, with an enraged populace jeering and shouting vengeance because we had no more lives to give up; or we might leave a trail of*

fire and destruction behind us, and come triumphantly rolling into Chattanooga and Huntsville, within the Federal lines, to receive the welcome plaudits of comrades left behind, and the thanks of our general, and the praises of a grateful people. Such thoughts as these passed in swift review, and were not calculated to make one sleep soundly.

As the hotel was much crowded, we obtained a few rooms in close proximity, and crowded them to their utmost capacity. Andrews noted our rooms before retiring, that he might, if necessary, seek any one of us out for consultation before we rose. Porter and Hawkins were unfortunately overlooked; they had arrived on an earlier train and obtained lodging at some distance from the depot. The clerk failed to have them called in time for the morning train, as they had ordered, and, greatly to their regret and chagrin, they were left behind. This was a serious loss, as they were both cool, brave men, and Hawkins was the most experienced railway engineer of our company. W. F. Brown, who took his place in this work, was, however, fully competent, though possibly somewhat less cautious.

Long before the train was due, Andrews, who had slept little, if at all, that night, glided from room to room silently as a ghost, the doors being purposely left unfastened, and aroused the slumberers. It seemed to some of us scarcely a moment from the time of retiring until he came thus to the bedside of each sleeper in turn, and cautiously wakening him, asked his name, to prevent the possibility of mistake, and then told each one exactly the part he was expected to take in the enterprise of the day. There was hasty dressing, and afterwards an informal meeting held in Andrews's room, at which nearly one-half of the whole number were present, and plans were more fully discussed.

Then Marion A. Ross, one of the most determined of the whole number, took the bold step of advising and even urging the abandonment, for the present, of the whole enterprise. He reasoned with great force that under present circumstances, with the Rebel vigilance fully aroused by Mitchel's rapid advance, with guards stationed around the train we were to capture, as we had learned would be the case at Big Shanty, and with the road itself obstructed by numerous trains, the enterprise was sure to fail, and would cost the life of every man engaged in it. Andrews very gently answered his arguments and strove to show that the objections urged really weighed in favor of the original plan. No such attempt as we purposed had ever been made, and consequently would not be guarded against; the presence of a line of sentinels and of so many troops at Big Shanty would only tend to relax vigilance still further; and the great amount of business done on the road, with the running of many unscheduled trains, would screen us from too close inquiry when we ran our train ahead of time.

This reasoning was not altogether satisfactory, and some of the others joined Ross in a respectful but firm protest against persisting in such a hopeless undertaking. But Andrews, speaking very low, as was his wont when thoroughly in earnest, declared that he had once before postponed the attempt, and returned to camp disgraced. "Now," he continued, "I will accomplish my purpose or leave my bones to bleach in Dixie. But I do not wish to control any one against his own judgment. If any of you think it too hazardous, you are perfectly at liberty to take the train in the opposite direction and work your way back to camp as you can."

This inflexible determination closed the discussion, and as no man was willing to desert his leader, we all assured him of our willingness to obey his orders to the death. I had taken no part in the discussion, as I was not in possession of sufficient facts to judge of the chance of success, and I wished the responsibility to rest upon the leader, where it properly belonged.

The train was now nearly due, and we proceeded to the station for the purchase of tickets. By the time they had been procured—not all for one place, as we wished to lessen the risk of suspicion—the train swept up to the platform. Hastily glancing at it in the early morning light, and seeing only that it was very long and apparently well filled, the twenty adventurers entered by different doors, but finally took their places in one car.

From Marietta to Big Shanty the railroad sweeps in a long bend of eight miles around the foot of Kennesaw Mountain, which lies directly between the two stations. This elevation is now scarred all over with Rebel entrenchments, and was the scene of one of the severest contests of the war. This, however, as well as the whole of the three months' struggle from Chattanooga to Atlanta, came a year and a half later. At this time the nearest Federal soldiers were more than two hundred miles away.

When the train moved on and the conductor came to take our tickets, we observed him carefully, as we knew not how closely his fate and ours might be linked together in the approaching struggle. The most vivid anticipation fell far short of the reality. Upon the qualities of that one man our success or failure hinged. He was quite young—not more than twenty-three or -four—and looked like a man of resolution and energy. We noticed that he was also scrutinizing us and the other passengers very closely, and naturally feared that he had in some manner been put on his guard. In fact, as we learned long afterwards, he had been warned that some of the new conscripts who were reluctant to fight for the Confederacy were contemplating an escape, and might try to get a ride on the cars. His orders were to watch for all such and arrest them at once. But he did not think that any of the men who got on at Marietta looked in the least like conscripts or deserters.

The train ran slowly, stopping at several intervening points, and did not reach Big Shanty until it was fully daylight. This station had been selected for the seizure, because the train breakfasted there, and it was probable that many of the employees and passengers would leave it for their meal, thus diminishing the opposition we might expect. Another most important reason for the selection was the absence of any telegraph office. But, on the other hand, Camp McDonald had been lately located here, and a large body of soldiers—some accounts said as many as ten thousand men—were already assembled. Their camp included the station within the guard-line. When Andrews and the first party had been at Atlanta, three weeks earlier, few troops had yet arrived at this point. The capture of a train in the midst of a camp of the enemy was not a part of the original plan, but subsequently became necessary. It was certainly a great additional element of danger, but it was not now possible to substitute any other point.

The decisive hour had arrived. It is scarcely boastful to say that the annals of history record few enterprises more bold and novel than that witnessed by the rising sun of Saturday morning, April 12, 1862. Here was a train, with several hundred passengers, with a full complement of hands, lying inside a line of sentinels, who were distinctly seen pacing back and forth in close proximity, to be seized by a mere score of men, and to be carried away before the track could be obstructed, or the intruding engineer shot down at his post. Only the most careful calculation and prompt execution, concentrating the power of the whole band into a single lightning-like stroke, could afford the slightest prospect of success.

In the bedroom conference every action was predetermined with the nicest accuracy. Our engineer and his assistant knew the signal at which to start; the brakesmen had their work assigned; the man who was to uncouple the cars knew just the place at which to make the separation; the remainder of the number constituted a guard, in two divisions, who were to stand with ready revolvers abreast of the cars to be seized, and shoot down without hesitation anyone who attempted to interfere with the work. Andrews was to command the whole, and do any part of the work not otherwise provided for. Should there be any unexpected hindrance, we were to fight until we either overcame all opposition and captured the train or perished in a body. If we failed to carry off our prize we were inevitably lost; if any man failed to be on board when the signal was given, his fate also was sealed. A delay of thirty seconds after our designs became clearly known would have resulted in the slaughter of the whole party.

When our train rolled up to the platform, the usual announcement was shouted: "Big Shanty; twenty minutes for breakfast!" Most fortunately for us, the conductor, engineer, firemen, and train-hands generally, with many of the passengers, poured out, and hurried to the long, low eating-room which gave its name to the station. The engine was utterly unguarded. This uncommon carelessness was the result of perfect security, and greatly favored our design. Yet it was a thrilling moment! Victory or death hung on the next minute! There was no chance for drawing back, and I do not think any of us had the disposition. A little while before, a sense of shrinking came over the writer like that preceding a plunge into ice-water; but with the next breath it passed away, and left me as calm and quiet as if no enemy had been within a hundred miles. Still, for a moment, we kept our seats. Andrews went forward to examine the track and see if there was any hindrance to a rapid rush ahead. Almost immediately he returned, and said, very quietly, "All right, boys; let us go now." There was nothing in this to attract special observation; but whether it did or not was now a matter of indifference. The time of concealment was past.

We rose, left the cars, and walked briskly to the head of the train. With the precision of machinery, every man took his appointed place. Three cars back from the tender the coupling-pin was drawn out, as the load of passenger-cars would only have been an encumbrance. Wilson W. Brown, who acted as engineer, William Knight as assistant, Alfred Wilson as fireman, together with Andrews, mounted the engine, Knight grasping the lever, and waiting for the word to start. The appointed brakesmen threw themselves flat on the top of the cars. At a signal from Andrews, the remainder of the band, who had kept watch, climbed with surprising quickness into a boxcar which stood open. All was well! Knight, at Andrews's orders, jerked open the steam-valve, and we were off! Before the camp-guards or the bystanders could do more than turn a curious eye upon our proceedings, the train was under way, and we were safe from interruption.

The writer was stationed in the boxcar, and as soon as all were in, we pulled the door shut to guard against any stray musket-balls. For a moment of most intense suspense after we were thus shut in, all was still. In that moment a thousand conflicting thoughts swept through our minds. Then came a pull, a jar, a clang, and we were flying away on our perilous journey. Those who were on the engine caught a glimpse of the excited crowd, soldiers and citizens, swarming and running about in the wildest confusion. It has been said that a number of shots were fired after us, but those in the boxcar knew nothing of it, and it is certain that no one was injured. A widely circulated picture represented us as waving our hats and shouting in triumph. Nothing so melodramatic took place. The moment was too deep and earnest, and we had too many perils still to encounter for any such childish demonstration.

Yet it was a grand triumph, and having nothing of a more practical character for the moment to do, I realized it to the fullest extent. There are times in life when whole years of enjoyment are condensed into a single experience. It was so with me then. I could comprehend the emotion of Columbus when he first beheld through the dim dawn the long-dreamed-of shores of America, or the less innocent but no less fervent joy of Cortez when he planted the Cross of Spain on the halls of Montezuma. My breast throbbed fast with emotions of joy and gladness that words labor in vain to express. A sense of ethereal lightness ran through my veins, and I seemed [to be] ascending higher, higher, with each pulsation of the engine. Remember, I was but twenty-two then, full of hope and ambition. Not a dream of failure shadowed my rapture. We had always been told that the greatest difficulty was to reach and take possession of the engine, after which success was certain. But for unforeseen contingencies it would have been.

Away we rushed, scouring past field and village and woodland. At each leap of the engine our hearts rose higher, and we talked merrily of the welcome that would greet us when we dashed into Huntsville a few hours later, our enterprise done, and the brightest laurels of the war eclipsed!

We found the railroad, however, to be of the roughest and most difficult character. The grades were very heavy and the curves numerous and sharp. We seemed to be running toward every point of the compass. The deep valleys and steep hills of this part of the country had rendered the building of the road difficult and costly. There were numerous high embankments where an accident would be of deadly character. The track was also uneven and in generally bad condition, for the war had rendered railroad iron scarce and high-priced, besides diverting all attention and resources into other channels. This unfavorable character of the road very greatly increased the difficulty experienced by an engineer unfamiliar with the route in making rapid time, or in avoiding the varied difficulties incident to our progress. But we trusted implicitly that the farsighted plans of Andrews, the skill of our engineers, and our own willing efforts would overcome all hindrances.

Our first run was short. There was a sudden checking of speed and a halt. When those of us who were in the boxcar pushed open our door and asked the reason for stopping so soon, we were told that the fire was low and the steam exhausted. This was startling intelligence, and caused a moment of consternation. If our "General"—the name of the locomotive we had captured—failed us at the beginning of the race, we too well knew what the end would be. For hundreds of miles on every side of us were desperate and daring foes. A hundred times our number on horse and on foot could be gathered against us in a few hours. The most timid bird pursued by hounds feels safe, for its wings can bear it above their jaws. But if those wings should be broken! This engine gave us wings; but if it should be disabled, no valor of ours could beat back the hosts about us, no skill elude their rage.

But we found a less threatening explanation of our premature halt. The schedule time of our train was very slow—only about sixteen miles an hour—and the fires had been allowed to run down because of the expected stop of twenty minutes for breakfast at Big Shanty—a stop that we had reduced to less than two minutes. Then the valve being thrown wide open, the little steam in the boiler was soon exhausted. But this difficulty was of short duration. A rest of three minutes, with plenty of wood thrown into the furnace, wrought a change, and we again glided rapidly forward.

But when viewed soberly, and in the light of all the facts since developed, what were the chances of success and escape possessed by the flying party? Was the whole attempt, as has been frequently asserted, rash and foolhardy? Or had it that character of practicability which is ever the stamp of true genius? Historical accuracy, as well as justice to the memory of a brave but unfortunate man, compels me to pronounce the scheme almost faultless. In this estimate I have the full concurrence of all who were engaged on the opposite side. It is hard to see how the plan could have been improved without allowing its projector to have had a knowledge of the precise condition of the enemy such as no commander at the beginning of an important enterprise ever has. No one of the plans by which Generals Grant and Sherman finally overthrew the Rebellion presented a clearer prospect of success.

These are the elements of the problem upon which Andrews based his hopes. Big Shanty is twenty-eight miles north of Atlanta and thirty-two south of Kingston. Short of these places he was convinced that no engine could be obtained for pursuit. He could obstruct the road so that no train would reach Big Shanty for hours. Pinch-bars and other instruments for lifting track might be found on the captured engine, or obtained from some station or working-party. His force of twenty men was counted ample to overcome resistance at any switch or passing train. One irregular train only was expected to be on the road, and that would soon be met—certainly at Kingston or before—after which it would be safe to run at the highest speed to the first bridge, burn it, and pass on to the next, which, with all other large bridges, could be served in the same manner. Each bridge burnt would be an insuperable barrier to pursuit by an engine beyond that point. Thus, every part of the scheme was fair and promising. Only those critics who are wise after the event can pronounce the attempt rash and hopeless. The destruction of the telegraph would also be necessary; but this was not difficult. It seemed as if every contingency was provided for, and then there was the additional fighting power of twenty chosen men to guard against any possible emergency. We were now embarked on this most perilous but hopeful voyage. Coolness, precision of work, and calm effort could scarcely fail to sever the chief military communications of the enemy before the setting of the sun, and convince him that no enterprise was too audacious for the Union arms.

After the fire had been made to burn briskly, Andrews jumped off the engine, ran back to the boxcar, about the door of which we were standing, and clasped our hands in an ecstasy of congratulation. He declared that all our really hard work was done and that our difficulties were nearly passed; that we had the enemy at such a disadvantage that he could not harm us; and exhibited every sign of joy. Said he, "Only one train to meet, and then we will put our engine to full speed, burn the bridges that I have marked out, dash through Chattanooga, and on to Mitchel at Huntsville. We've got the upper hand of the Rebels now, and they can't help themselves!" How glad we all were! When, three years later, the capture of Richmond set all the bells of the North ringing out peals of triumph, the sensation of joy was more diffused but less intense than we then experienced. Almost everything mankind values seemed within our grasp. Oh, if we had met but one unscheduled train!

This reference of Andrews to one train which he expected to meet before we began to burn bridges has been quoted in many public sketches, and has led to some misapprehension. He did expect to meet three trains before reaching Chattanooga; but two of these were regular trains, and being also farther up the road, were not supposed to present any serious difficulty. Their position at any given time could be definitely ascertained, and we could avoid collision with them, no matter how far we ran ahead of time. But so long as there were any irregular trains on the road before us, our only safety was in keeping the regular time of the captured train. This was, unfortunately, very slow; but if we exceeded it we lost the right-of-way, and were liable to a collision at any moment.

This risk was greatly increased by our inability to send ahead telegraphic notifications of our position. The order of southward-bound trains, according to the information we then had, was as follows: First, a way-freight, which was very uncertain as to time, but which we expected to meet early in the morning, and felt sure that it would be at Kingston or south of that point. This was the only real hindrance according to our program, and it was to this train that Andrews referred. Behind this were the regular freight train, and still farther north, the regular passenger train. As a matter of fact, we did meet these trains at Adairsville and Calhoun, the latter being somewhat behind time; but we might have met them farther north had it not been for unforeseen hindrances.

There is considerable discrepancy in the many published accounts of the following chase, which the writer has not in every case been able to perfectly reconcile. In the intense excitement and novel situations involved men were not likely to observe or remember every event accurately. But no pains have been spared to combine fullness and completeness in the following account. Using the best of my own recollections, consulting my comrades, reading carefully all published accounts, and especially going over the whole route years after, with Fuller and Murphy, two of the pursuing party, who kindly gave me all the information in their power, it is hoped that substantial accuracy has been obtained. Some of the incidents of the chase, such as the number of times the track was torn up, and whether we were fired upon by pursuing soldiers, allow some room for a conflict of memory. But the variations are not material.

Side by side with the road ran the telegraph-wires, which were able, by the flashing of a single lightning message ahead, to arrest our progress and dissipate our fondest hopes. There was no telegraph station where we had captured the train, but we knew not how soon our enemies might reach one, or whether they might not have a portable battery at command. Therefore we ran but a short distance, after replenishing the furnace, before again stopping to cut the wire.

John Scott, an active young man of the Twenty-first Ohio, scrambled up the pole with the agility of a cat, and tried to break the wire by swinging upon it; but failing in this, he knocked off the insulating box at the top of the pole and swung with it down to the ground. Fortunately, a small saw was found on the engine, with which the wire was severed in two places, and the included portion, many yards in length, was taken away with us, in order that the ends might not be readily joined.

While one or two of the party were thus engaged, others worked with equal diligence in taking up a rail from the track. No good track-raising instruments had been found on the train, and we had not yet procured them from any other source. A smooth iron bar, about four feet long, was the only instrument yet found, and with this some of the spikes were slowly and painfully battered out. After a few had thus been extracted, a lever was got under the rail and the remainder were pried loose. This occupied much more time than cutting the wire, and it required no prophet to foretell that if we did not procure better tools, rail-lifting would have to be used very sparingly in our program. In the present instance, however, the loss of time was no misfortune, as we were ahead of the schedule time, which we still felt bound to observe.

After another rapid but brief run, we paused long enough to chop down a telegraph-pole, cut the wire again, and place the pole, with many other obstructions, on the track. We did not here try to lift a rail; indeed, we had little serious fear of any pursuit at this time, and merely threw on these obstructions because of having spare time to employ.

We thus continued—running a little ahead of time, then stopping to obstruct the track and cut the wire—until Cass Station was reached, where we took on a good supply of wood and water. At this place we also obtained a complete time schedule of the road. Andrews told the tank-tender that we were running a powder-train through to the army of General Beauregard at Corinth, which was almost out of ammunition, and that the greatest haste was necessary. He further claimed to be a Confederate officer of high rank, and said that he had impressed this train for the purpose in hand, and that Fuller, with the regular passenger train, would be along shortly. The whole story was none too plausible, as General Mitchel was now interposed between our present position and Beauregard, and we would never have been able to get a train to the army of the latter on this route; but the tender was not critical and gave us his schedule, adding that he would willingly send his shirt to Beauregard if that general needed it. When this man was afterwards asked if he did not suspect the character of the enemy he thus aided, he answered that he would as soon have suspected the President of the Confederacy himself as one who talked so coolly and confidently as Andrews did!

Keeping exactly on regular time, we proceeded without any striking adventures until Kingston was reached. This place—thirty-two miles from Big Shanty—we regarded as marking the first stage of our journey. Two hours had elapsed since the capture of the train, and hitherto we had been fairly prosperous. No track-lifting instruments had yet been obtained, notwithstanding inquiries for them at several stations. We had secured no inflammable materials for more readily firing the bridges, and the road was not yet clear before us. But, on the other hand, no serious hindrance had yet occurred, and we believed ourselves far ahead of any possible pursuit.

But at Kingston we had some grounds for apprehending difficulty. This little town is at the junction with the road to Rome, Georgia. Cars and engines were standing on the side track. Here we fully expected to meet our first train, and it would be necessary for us to get the switches properly adjusted before we could pass it to go on our way. When we drew up at the station there was handed to Andrews our first and last communication from the management of the road, in the shape of a telegram, ordering Fuller's train—now ours—to wait at Kingston for the local freight, which was considerably behind time. The order was not very welcome, but we drew out on the side track, and watched eagerly for the train. Many persons gathered around Andrews, who here, as always, personated the conductor of our train, and showered upon him many curious and somewhat suspicious questions. Ours was an irregular train, but the engine was recognized as Fuller's. The best answers possible were given. A red flag had been placed on our engine, and the announcement was made that Fuller, with another engine, was but a short way behind. The powder story was emphasized, and every means employed to avoid suspicion. Andrews only, and the usual complement of train-hands, were visible, the remainder of the party being tightly shut up in the car, which was designated as containing Beauregard's ammunition. The striking personal appearance of Andrews greatly aided him in carrying through his deception, which was never more difficult than at this station. His commanding presence, and firm but graceful address, marked him as a Southern gentleman—a member of the class from which a great proportion of the Rebel officers were drawn. His declarations and orders were therefore received with the greater respect on this account. But all these resources were here strained to the utmost.

At length the anxiously expected local freight train arrived, and took its place on another side track. We were about to start on our way, with the glad consciousness that our greatest obstacle was safely passed, when a red flag was noticed on the hindmost freight-car. This elicited immediate inquiry, and we were informed that another very long freight train was just behind, and that we would be obliged to wait its arrival also. This was most unfortunate, as we had been already detained at Kingston much longer than was pleasant.

There were many disagreeable elements in the situation. A crowd of persons was rapidly assembling. The train from Rome was also nearly due, and though it only came to the station and returned on its own branch, yet it was not agreeable to notice the constant increase of force that our enemies were gaining. If any word from the southward arrived, or if our true character was revealed in any other way, the peril would be imminent. But we trusted that this second delay would be brief. Slowly the minutes passed by. To us, who were shut up in the boxcar, it appeared as if they would never be gone. Our soldier comrades on the outside kept in the background as much as possible, remaining at their posts on the engine and the cars, while Andrews occupied attention by complaining of the delay, and declaring that the road ought to be kept clear of freight trains when so much was needed for the transportation of army supplies, and when the fate of the whole army of the West might depend upon the celerity with which it received its ammunition.

There was plausibility enough in his words to lull suspicion in all minds except that of the old switch-tender of the place, who grumbled out his conviction "that something was wrong with that stylish-looking fellow, who ordered everybody around as if the whole road belonged to him." But no one paid any attention to this man's complaints, and not many minutes after a distant whistle sounded from the northward, and we felt that the crisis had passed. As there was no more room on the side track, Andrews ordered the switch-tender to let this train run by on the main track. That worthy was still grumbling, but he reluctantly obeyed, and the long succession of cars soon glided by us.

This meant release from a suspense more intolerable than the most perilous action. To calmly wait where we could do nothing, while our destiny was being wrought out by forces operating in the darkness, was a terrible trial of nerve. But it was well borne. Brown, Knight, and Wilson, who were exposed to view, exhibited no more impatience than was to be expected of men in their assumed situation. Those of us in the boxcar talked in whispers only, and examined the priming of our pistols. We understood that we were waiting for a delayed train, and well knew the fearful possibilities of an obstructed track, with the speedy detection, and fight against overwhelming odds that would follow, if the train for which we waited did not arrive sooner than pursuers from Big Shanty. When we recognized the whistle of the coming train it was almost as welcome as the boom of Mitchel's cannon, which we expected to hear that evening after all our work was done. As it rumbled by us we fully expected an instant start, a swift run of a few miles, and then the hard work but pleasant excitement of bridge-burning. Alas!

Swift and frequent are the mutations of war. Success can never be assured to any enterprise in advance. The train for which we had waited with so much anxiety had no sooner stopped than we beheld on it an emblem more terrible than any comet that ever frightened a superstitious continent. Another red flag! Another train close behind! This was terrible, but what could be done?

With admirable presence of mind Andrews moderated his impatience, and asked the conductor of the newly arrived train the meaning of such an unusual obstruction of the road. His tone was commanding, and without reserve the conductor gave the full explanation. To Andrews it had a thrilling interest. The commander at Chattanooga had received information that the Yankee general Mitchel was coming by forced marches and in full strength against that town; therefore all the rolling-stock of the road had been ordered to Atlanta. This train was the first installment, but another and still longer section was behind. It was to start a few minutes after he did, and would probably not be more than ten or fifteen minutes behind.

In turn, the conductor asked Andrews who he was, and received the information that he was an agent of General Beauregard, and that he had impressed a train into military service in Atlanta, which he was running through with powder, of which Beauregard was in extreme need. Under such circumstances he greatly regretted this unfortunate detention. The conductor did not suspect the falsity of these pretenses, but told Andrews that it was very doubtful if he could get to Beauregard at Corinth by going through Chattanooga, as it was certain that Mitchel had captured Huntsville, directly on the line between them.

Andrews replied that this made no difference, as he had his orders, and should press on until they were countermanded, adding that Mitchel was probably only paying a flying visit to Huntsville, and would have to be gone soon, or find Beauregard upon him. Andrews also ordered the conductor to run far enough down the main track to allow the next train to draw in behind him, and for both trains there to wait the coming of Fuller with the regular mail. His orders were implicitly obeyed; and then to our party recommenced the awful trial of quiet waiting. One of the men outside was directed to give notice to those in the boxcar of the nature of the detention, and warn them to be ready for any emergency. Either Brown or Knight, I think, executed this commission. Leaning against our car, but without turning his eyes toward it, and speaking in a low voice, he said, "We are waiting for one of the trains the Rebels are running off from Mitchel. If we are detected before it comes, we will have to fight. Be ready." We *were* ready; and so intolerable is suspense that most of us would have felt as a welcome relief the command to throw open our door and spring into deadly conflict.

Slowly the leaden moments dragged themselves away. It seems scarcely creditable, but it is literally true, that for twenty-five minutes more we lay on that side track and waited—waited with minds absorbed, pulses leaping, and ears strained for the faintest sound which might give a hint as to our destiny. One precious hour had we wasted at Kingston—time enough to have burned every bridge between that place and Dalton! The whole margin of time on which we had allowed ourselves to count was two hours; now half of that was thrown away at one station, and nothing accomplished. We dared wait no longer. Andrews decided to rush ahead with the intention of meeting this extra train wherever it might be found, and forcing it to back before him to the next siding, where he could pass it. The resolution was in every way dangerous, but the danger would at least be of an active character. Just at this moment the long-expected whistle was heard, and soon the train came into plain view, bringing with it an almost interminable string of cars. The weight and length of its train had caused the long delay. Obedient to direction, it followed the first extra down the main track, and its locomotive was a long way removed from the depot when the last car cleared the upper end of the side track on which we lay. At length it had got far enough down, and it was possible for us to push on. Andrews instantly ordered the switch-tender to arrange the track so as to let us out.

But here a new difficulty presented itself. This man had been in an ill humor from the first, and was now fully convinced that something was wrong. Possibly the tone in which he was addressed irritated him still more. He therefore responded to Andrews's order by a surly refusal, and hung up the keys in the station-house. When we in the boxcar overheard his denial, we were sure that the time for fighting had come. There was no more reason for dreading the issue of a conflict at this station than at any other point, and we waited the signal with the confident expectation of victory.

But even a victory at that moment would have been most undesirable. We had no wish to shed blood unnecessarily. A telegraph office was at hand, and it was possible that before the wire could be cut a message might be flashed ahead. There were also engines in readiness for prompt pursuit, and while we might have overcome immediate opposition by the use of our firearms, our triumph would have been the signal for a close and terrible chase.

The daring coolness of Andrews removed all embarrassments. While men are hesitating and in doubt, boldness and promptness on the part of an opponent are almost sure to carry the day. Ceasing to address the switch-tender, Andrews walked hurriedly into the station, and with the truthful remark that he had no more time to waste, took down the key and began to unlock the switch. The tender cursed him terribly, and called for someone to arrest him. The crowd around also disliked the action, and began to hoot and yell; but before anyone had decided as to what ought to be done Andrews had unlocked and changed the switch, and waved his hand for the engineer to come on. It was an inexpressible relief when the cars moved forward and the sounds of strife died out. As soon as the loco-motive passed to the main track, Andrews tossed the keys to the ruffled owner of them, saying, in his blandest manner, "Pardon me, sir, for being in such a hurry, but the Confederacy can't wait for every man's notions. You'll find it is all right," and stepped on board his engine. The excitement gradually ceased, and no thought of pursuit was entertained until startling intelligence was received a few moments later from Big Shanty.

Before describing the terrible struggle above Kingston, it will be well to narrate the operations of the persons whose train had been so uncer-emoniously snatched from them at Big Shanty. From printed accounts published contemporaneously by several of those engaged in the pursuit, as well as from personal responses to inquiries made regarding the most material points, the writer is confident that he can tell the strange story without essential error. It is a striking commentary on the promptness of the seizure, that the bystanders generally reported that only eight men, instead of twenty, had been observed to mount the train.

William A. Fuller, conductor, Anthony Murphy, manager of the State railroad shops at Atlanta, and Jefferson Cain, engineer, stepped off their locomotive, leaving it unguarded save by the surrounding sentinels, and in perfect confidence took their seats at the breakfast-table at Big Shanty. But before they had tasted a morsel of food, the quick ear of Murphy, who was seated with his back toward the window, caught the sound of escap-ing steam, and he exclaimed, "Fuller, who's moving your train?" Almost simultaneously the latter, who was somewhat of a ladies' man, and was bestowing polite attentions upon two or three fair passengers, saw the same movement, and sprang up, shouting, "Somebody's running off with our train!" No breakfast was eaten then. Everybody rushed through the door to the platform. The train was then fully under way, just sweeping out of sight around the first curve. With quick decision Fuller shouted to Murphy and Cain, "Come on!" and started at a full run after the flying train! This attempt to run down and catch a locomotive by a foot-race seemed so absurd that as the three, at the top of their speed, passed around the same curve, they were greeted with loud laughter and ironical cheers by the excited multitude. To all appearances it was a foolish and hopeless chase.

Yet, paradoxical as the statement may seem, this chase on foot was the wisest course possible for Fuller and his companions. What else could they do? Had they remained quietly in camp, with no show of zeal, they would have been reproached with negligence in not guarding their train more carefully, even if they were not accused with being in league with its captors. As they ran, Fuller explained the situation and his purposes to his companions. They had neither electric battery nor engine. Had they obtained horses, they would necessarily have followed the common road, instead of the railroad, and if they thought of that expedient at all, it would be as distasteful to railroad men as abandoning their ship to sailors, and they preferred leaving that course for others. It would have been wise for those who could think of nothing else to do to ride as mounted couriers to the stations ahead; but whether this was done or not I have never learned. Certainly it was not done so promptly as to influence the fortunes of the day.

But the truth is that Fuller and Murphy were at first completely deceived as to the nature of the event which had taken place. They had been warned to guard against the escape of conscript deserters from that very camp; and although they would never have suspected an attempt on the part of the conscripts to escape by capturing their engine, yet when it was seen to dash off, the thought of this warning was naturally uppermost. Even then Fuller conjectured that they would use his engine only to get a mile or two beyond the guard-line, and then abandon it. He was therefore anxious to follow closely in order to find the engine and return for his passengers at the earliest moment possible. Little did he anticipate the full magnitude of the work and the danger before him. That any Federal soldiers were within a hundred miles of Big Shanty never entered his mind or that of any other person.

For a mile or two the three footmen ran at the top of their speed, straining their eyes forward for any trace of the lost engine which they expected to see halted and abandoned at almost any point on the road. But they were soon partially undeceived as to the character of their enemies. About two miles from the place of starting they found the telegraph wire severed and a portion of it carried away. The fugitives were also reported as quietly oiling and inspecting their engine. No mere deserters would be likely to think of this. The two actions combined clearly indicated the intention of making a long run, but who the men were still remained a mystery. A few hundred yards from this place a party of workmen with a handcar was found, and these most welcome reinforcements were at once pressed into service.

Fuller's plans now became more definite and determined. He had a good handcar and abundance of willing muscle to work it. By desperate exertions, by running behind the car and pushing it up the steep grades, and then mounting and driving it furiously downhill and on the levels, it was possible to make seven or eight miles an hour; at the same time, Fuller knew that the captive engine, if held back to run on schedule time, as the reports of the workmen indicated, would make but sixteen miles per hour. Fuller bent all his thoughts and energies toward Kingston, thirty miles distant. He had been informed of the extra trains to be met at that point, and was justified in supposing that the adventurers would be greatly perplexed and hindered by them, even if they were not totally stopped. Had the seizure taken place on the preceding day, as originally planned, he might well have despaired, for then the road would have been clear. Yet he had one other resource, as will appear in due time, of which his enemies knew nothing.

Fuller did not pause to consider how he should defeat the fugitives when he had overtaken them, and he might have paid dearly for this rashness. But he could rely on help at any station, and when he had obtained the means of conveyance, as he would be sure to do at Kingston, he could easily find an overwhelming force to take with him. This Saturday was appointed as a general muster of volunteers, State militia, and conscripts, and armed soldiers were abundant in every village. But Fuller's dominant thought was that his property—the property with which he had been entrusted—was wrested from his grasp, and it was his duty to recover it, at whatever personal hazard. That any serious harm was intended to the railroad itself he probably did not yet suspect.

Talking and wearying themselves with idle conjectures, but never ceasing to work, Fuller and his party pressed swiftly on. But suddenly there was a crash, a sense of falling, and when the shock allowed them to realize what had happened, they found themselves floundering in a ditch half filled with water, and their handcar embedded in the mud beside them! They had reached the place where the first rail had been torn from the track, and had suffered accordingly. But the bank was, fortunately for them, not very high at that spot, and a few bruises were all the damage they sustained. Their handcar, which was also uninjured, was lifted on the track and driven on again. This incident increased both their caution and their respect for the men before them.

Without further mishap they reached Etowah Station, on the northern bank of the river of the same name. Here was a large bridge, which the Andrews party might have burned without loss of time had they foreseen the long detention at Kingston; but its destruction was not a part of their plan, and it was suffered to stand. The mind of Fuller grew very anxious as he approached this station. What he should find there depended, in all probability, on his power to overtake the fugitives, whose intentions seemed more formidable with each report he received of their actions. Andrews had firmly believed that no engine for pursuit could be found south of Kingston; but Fuller had a different expectation.

Extensive iron-furnaces were located on the Etowah River, about five miles above the station. These works were connected with the railroad by a private track, which was the property of Major Cooper, as well as the works themselves. Murphy knew that Major Cooper had also bought an engine called the "Yonah." It had been built in the shop over which Murphy presided, and was one of the best locomotives in the State. "But where," Fuller and Murphy asked themselves, "is this engine now?" If it was in view of the adventurers as they passed, they had doubtless destroyed it, run it off the track, or carried it away with them. They could not afford to neglect such an element in the terrible game they were play-ing. But if it was now at the upper end of the branch at the mines, as was most probable, it would take the pursuers five miles out of their way to go for it, and even then it might not be ready to start. This diversion could not be afforded. Fuller and Murphy had come nineteen miles, and had already consumed two hours and three-quarters. The adventurers were reported as passing each station on time, and if this continued they must have reached Kingston forty-five minutes before Fuller and his compan-ions arrived at Etowah, thirteen miles behind them. One hour and a half more to Kingston—this was the very best that could be done with the handcar. It was clear that if the "Yonah" did not come to their assistance, they were as effectually out of the race as if on the other side of the ocean. Everything now hinged on the position of that one engine.

Here we may pause to note how all coincidences, we might almost say providences, seemed to work against the bridge-burning enterprise. We were at Kingston three-quarters of an hour before our pursuers reached Etowah, thirteen miles distant. If there had been no extra trains, or if they had been sharply on time, so that we could have passed the three with a delay not exceeding fifteen or twenty minutes, which ought to have been an abundant allowance, every bridge above Kingston would have been in ashes before sundown! Or if the delay had been as great as it actually was, even then, if the locomotive "Yonah" had occupied any position excepting one, the same result would have followed.

But Fuller, Murphy, and Cain, with the several armed men they had picked up at the stations passed, could not repress shouts of exultation when they saw the old "Yonah" standing on the main track, already fired up, and headed toward Kingston. It had just arrived from the mines, and in a short time would have returned again. Thus a new element of tre-mendous importance, which had been ignored in all our calculations, was introduced into the contest.

The pursuers seized their inestimable prize, called for all the volun-teers who could snatch guns at a moment's notice, and were soon swiftly but cautiously rushing with the power of steam toward Kingston. The speed of nearly a mile a minute was in refreshing contrast to the slow and laborious progress of the handcar, and they were naturally jubilant. But what lay before them at Kingston? The frequent obstructions of the track, the continued cutting of the telegraph, and especially the cool assumption of the leader of the adventurers in calling himself a Confederate officer of high rank in charge of an impressed powder train, all conspired to deepen their conviction that some desperate scheme was on foot.

But they did not pause long to listen to reports. Their eyes and their thoughts were bent toward Kingston. Had the adventurers been stopped there, or had they surprised and destroyed the trains met? The pursuers could scarcely form a conjecture as to what was before them; but the speed with which they were flying past station after station would soon end their suspense. Even the number of men on the flying train was a matter of uncertainty. At the stations passed observers reported that only four or five were seen; but the track-layers and others who had observed them at work were confident of a much larger number—twenty-five or thirty at the least.

Besides, it was by no means sure that they had not confederates in large numbers to cooperate with them at the various stations along the road. Fuller knew about how many persons had entered the train at Marietta; but it was not sure that these were all. A hundred more might be scattered along the way, at various points, ready to join in whatever strange plan was now being worked out. No conjecture of this kind that could be formed was a particle more improbable than the startling events that had already taken place. The cool courage of these pursuers, who determined to press forward and do their own duty at whatever risk, cannot be too highly rated. If they arrived at Kingston in time to unmask the pretension of the mysterious "Confederate officer," there would doubtless be a desperate fight; but the pursuers could count on assistance there, and all along the line.

Fuller reached Kingston at least an hour earlier than would have been possible with the handcar, and a single glance showed that the adventurers were gone, and his hopes of arresting them at that point were ended. They were, however, barely out of sight, and all their start had been reduced to minutes. But here again the pursuit was checked. The foresight of Andrews had blockaded the road as much as possible with the trains which had so long hindered his own movements. Two large and heavy trains stood on the main road; one of the two side tracks was occupied by the third freight, and the other by the engine of the Rome branch. There was no ready means for the passage of the "Yonah." Some precious time was employed in giving and receiving information, in telling of the seizure at Big Shanty, and hearing of the deportment of Andrews and his men at Kingston.

Then a dispute arose as to the best means of continuing the pursuit, which threatened to disunite Fuller and Murphy. The latter wished to continue the chase with the "Yonah," which was a fine engine, with large wheels; but Fuller would not wait to get the freights out of the way, and, jumping on the Rome engine, he called on all who were willing to assist him to come on. A large, enthusiastic, and well-armed company instantly volunteered; the new engine, the "Shorter," pulled out, and Murphy had only time to save himself from the disgrace of being left behind by jumping on the hindmost car as it swept past. With all the time lost in making this transfer, and in mutual explanations, the pursuers left Kingston just twenty minutes behind the Federals.

What Fuller and his friends learned at Kingston left no doubt in their minds that some deliberate and far-reaching military movement was on foot. While its precise nature was yet concealed, the probability that the road itself, and possibly Confederate towns and stores, were to be destroyed, was freely conceded. All agreed that the one thing to be done was to follow their enemies closely, and thus compel them to turn and fight or abandon their enterprise. A large force—one or two hundred well-armed men—was taken on board, and instructions left that as soon as the track could be cleared, another armed train was to follow for the purpose of rendering any needed assistance.

Note: William Pittenger was one of the first men to be awarded the Medal of Honor. Nineteen of the raiders were eventual recipients, but J. J. Andrews and William Campbell were ineligible, since they were civilians.

FROM THE CITATION

One of the 19 of 22 men who penetrated nearly 200 miles south into enemy territory and captured a railroad train at Big Shanty, Georgia, in an attempt to destroy the bridges and tract between Chattanooga and Atlanta.

Sources

"The Ridge: Michael Murphy," from *Lone Survivor*. Marcus Luttrell. New York: Little, Brown and Company, Hachette Book Group, 2007.

"San Juan Hill: Teddy Roosevelt," from *The Rough Riders*. Theodore Roosevelt. New York: Charles Scribner's Sons, 1899.

"Single-Handed," from *Single-Handed: The Inspiring True Story of Tibor "Teddy" Rubin*. Daniel M. Cohen. New York: Berkeley Caliber, Penguin Random House, 2015.

"The Siege of Fort Wagner: William Harvey Carney," from *History of the Fifty-fourth Regiment of Massachusetts Volunteer Infantry*. Luis F. Emilio. Boston: Boston Book Co., 1894.

"Above and Beyond: Frank Luke Jr.," from *Above and Beyond: The Incredible Story of Frank Luke Jr*. Keith Warren Lloyd. Middletown, DE: 2015.

"Lasting Valor: Vernon J. Baker," from *Lasting Valor*. Vernon J. Baker, with Ken Olsen. Columbus, MS: Genesis Press, 1997; Bantam Mass Market Edition (New York), 1999.

"Taking Suribachi: Marines on Iwo Jima," *from Closing In: Marines in the Seizure of Iwo Jima*. Joseph H. Alexander. Marines in World War II Commemorative Series. Washington, DC: US Marine Corps Historical Center, 1994.

"Mustering the Dead: Clinton Romesha," from *Red Platoon: A True Story of American Valor*. Clinton Romesha. New York: Dutton, An Imprint of Penguin Random House, 2016.

"The Warrior: Roy P. Benavidez," from *Medal of Honor: A Vietnam Warrior's Story*. Roy P. Benavidez, with John R. Craig. Washington, DC: Brassey's, 1995.

" 'I Could Hardly Stand Up'": Dr. Mary E. Walker," from *A Woman of Honor and the Civil War*. Mercedes Graf. Gettysburg, PA: Thomas Publications, 2001.

"Taking Prisoners: Alvin York," from *Sergeant York and His People*. Sam K. Cowan. New York: Grosset & Dunlap, 1922.

"Stealing the Train: The First Ever Medals," from *Capturing a Locomotive: A History of Secret Service in the Late War*. William Pittenger. Washington, DC: The National Tribune, 1885.